Student Friendly Statistics

Thomas Sanocki

University of South Florida
Tampa, Florida

Prentice
Hall

Upper Saddle River, New Jersey 07458

To Madeline and the innovators who will define their own future

Library of Congress Cataloging-in-Publication Data

Sanocki, Thomas.
  Student-friendly statistics / author, Thomas Sanocki.
    p. cm.
  Includes bibliographical references and index.
  ISBN 0-13-026521-7
  1. Statistics.   I. Title.

QA276.12.S27 2000
519.5–dc21   00-061158

VP, Editorial Director: Laura Pearson
Acquisitions Editor: Jayme Heffler
Editorial Assistant: April Dawn Klemm
Managing Editor: Mary Rottino
Production Liaison: Fran Russello
Project Manager: Kelly Ricci, The PRD Group
Prepress and Manufacturing Buyer: Tricia Kenny
Art Director: Jayne Conte
Cover Designer: Karen Sanatar
Marketing Manager: Sharon Cosgrove

This book was set in 9.5/10.5 Baskerville by The PRD Group
and was printed and bound by R. R. Donnelley, Harrisonburg.
The cover was printed by Phoenix Color.

©2001 by Prentice-Hall, Inc.
A Division of Pearson Education
Upper Saddle River, New Jersey 07458

Printed in the United States of America

10 9 8 7 6 5 4 3 2 1

ISBN 0-13-026521-7

Prentice-Hall International (UK) Limited, *London*
Prentice-Hall of Australia Pty. Limited, *Sydney*
Prentice-Hall Canada Inc., *Toronto*
Prentice-Hall Hispanoamericana, S.A., *Mexico*
Prentice-Hall of India Private Limited, *New Delhi*
Prentice-Hall of Japan, Inc., *Tokyo*
Pearson Education Asia Pte. Ltd., *Singapore*
Editora Prentice-Hall do Brasil, Ltda., *Rio de Janeiro*

Contents

Chapter 9   Using More Than Two Groups   115

Chapter 10   Using More Than One Independent Variable   127

Chapter 11   Relations Between Variables: Linear Regression and Correlation   148

Chapter 12   Analyzing Categorical Data   176

Chapter 13   Perspective: Looking Back at Your Journey   187

Appendix   Coping with Math and Test Anxiety   193

Index   195

PREFACE TO THE INSTRUCTOR

The purpose of this text is to make the major statistics accessible to all students while revealing the depth of the statistics and their meaning within research design. The statistics are explained completely, with simple terms and an interactive style. The main statistics concepts treated are the logic of statistical inference, the t-test, single-factor and multifactor analysis of variance (including interaction), linear regression and correlation, and chi-square. Because the tools of ANOVA, interaction, and correlation/regression are extremely important, I provide a foundation for them in the first parts of the book that is solid yet brief enough to allow major coverage of these advanced statistics in a semester course. Relations to experimental design are covered in order to increase the meaningfulness of statistics.

Any instructor knows that consistent effort is needed to learn statistics and to individuate them from each other. To get this idea across, I have developed the mountain-climbing journey metaphor illustrated. Each statistic is pictured as a mountain that can be unpacked into more basic concepts. The hikers represent student progress along the journey. A pair of hikers indicates the student's position as each chapter begins, and the spacing between hikers corresponds to chapter length. Initial chapters are short and easy for a gradual warm-up, followed by longer chapters as the material becomes more advanced. The journey metaphor also helps students learn to individuate statistics, an issue that is emphasized in the last chapter, as students look back at their path and the differences between statistics.

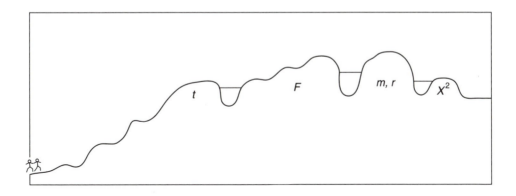

The exposition of the statistics is motivated by the psychologies of perception, cognition, and learning. The goal is to help students establish a core understanding that will be maintained in memory. All statistics are taught in the context of tables that break the computations into meaningful pieces. Page layouts are designed to group related ideas and figures, and to facilitate student interaction. Definitional formulas are used because they are meaningful; opaque computational formulas are eschewed because they are unnecessary in this age of computers. Major ideas common to most statistics are reinforced throughout the book.

Because context aids learning, the statistics are presented within meaningful research contexts. To simplify exposition, the most prototypical forms of statistics are emphasized. Other important distinctions are covered, but after the main exposition.

Active learning is encouraged throughout. You are invited to have students copy activity pages and hand them in for checking. Encourage students to copy formulas and

Preface to the Instructor

tables on their own paper (the tight spacing of this text was dictated by economics). Overheads can be found at the Internet address that follows.

This book is designed to be covered sequentially. However, it is possible to omit any of the more advanced chapters without loss of continuity. (These are Chapters 9 and 10 on multilevel and multifactor ANOVA, respectively, Chapter 11 on regression and correlation, and Chapter 12 on chi-square).

I thank the many students who have found statistics rewarding to learn. And I am happy to acknowledge the helpful comments and advice on this text from Madeline Altabe, Judy Bourgeois-Smith, Jacquelyn Fresenius, Jennifer Kisamore, Evelyn Mott, and Doug Rohrer. I am deeply indebted to Tracy Krueger and Jennifer Perone for writing the Exercises. And I thank Allison Westlake for finding a great cover, and Anne Mattson and the PRD Group for being so helpful in the production of this book. I am sure students will find that I've made some small errors, but (hopefully!) no large ones. I invite reports of errors and will post corrections as well as thanks, at *http://chuma.cas.usf.educ/~sanocki/SFS corrections.html.* Also, look for overheads, larger versions of the statistics worksheets, and step-by-step instructions at *http://chuma.cas. usf.edu/~sanocki/SFS readable.html.*

Thomas Sanocki
E-mail: Sanocki@chuma.cas.usf.edu

PREFACE TO THE STUDENT

Learning statistics is a journey that will require steady effort, but that will reward you and sometimes even surprise you pleasantly. This prefactory chapter provides a brief introduction to your journey, including tips for making the journey more pleasant. Statistics does not have to be a scary subject, as you will learn.

To help you maintain perspective along your journey, a "trail map" will be provided at the start of each chapter. It provides important landmarks. For example, the first large goal—the t-test—is represented by "Mount t." It is built on smaller concepts that we will take one step at a time. The placement of the hikers at the far left indicates that you are just beginning your journey.

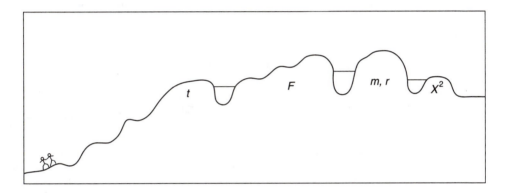

WHY DO STATISTICS SEEM DIFFICULT?

It helps to know what you are up against. Contrary to popular belief, behavioral statistics are not difficult because of the mathematics. Good teachers reduce mathematics for students of behavioral science. In this text, the math has been minimized. All concepts are taught in terms of their meaning first, and only simple arithmetic will be required. The real problem with statistics, in my view, is that statistics are very abstract and unlike anything you have met or even thought about previously. They are strange for your brain! This means that they are difficult to learn and very easy to forget.

How do you get to know a strange, different thing? The best way to get to know anything is to spend time with it, interact with it, and even play with it. Gradually, it can become familiar, even friendly. In the case of statistics, doing the statistics—doing the step-by-step calculation procedures—is an excellent way to get to know them. At the same time, remember that statistics are also meaningful, even deeply meaningful. While doing calculations, think about their meaning and act on their meaning. Write their meanings in your own words in spaces in the book or on your own paper. All of the procedures you will do in this book are designed to make their meaning apparent.

THINGS TO LOOK FOR

Your trail is well marked with signs. Look for them:

Important Definitions

These will be highlighted in boxes.

⋀ **CONCEPTUALIZATION AHEAD**

Especially important idea units are set off by markings like this.

CONCEPT DONE! ⋀

Other concepts will be designated by a simple boldface title or italics. These often are important linking concepts. You will also see white spaces; these are great places to summarize your thinking in your own words.

- **Important terms are listed at the end of each chapter.** Learn by actively summarizing their meaning.
- **Exercises are also provided.** No better way to learn!

THE MOST IMPORTANT FEATURE OF THIS BOOK

All of the features of this book pale in comparison to the most important feature—you! You will produce learning by interacting with this book. A substantial body of research on learning and memory indicates that self-relatedness adds greatly to memory. This is vitally important when you are learning something strange like statistics. The more you make the concepts meaningful to yourself, the better you will remember statistics. That means writing in this book, and on your own paper, using your own words to rephrase definitions, and doing calculations while thinking about what they mean.

The content of this book has been formatted to make it easier for you to integrate concepts. As much as possible, related text, figures, and tables have been grouped together on the same pages. This allows you to focus on meaning rather than looking for figures. What is critical is that you are creating a memory image, or an episodic trace (a record of your experience), that will become part of your memory. If the memory is meaningful and well integrated, it will last longer and be easier to recall later. Careful, active study of the concepts will be rewarded with better recall at testing time and in the future when you need to refer back to this book. Note that even advanced statisticians often return to their old textbooks. Their memory needs refreshing too. What a good course and text on statistics should do is make it easy for you to return to your text years later and, after some review, to remember what you had learned.

A PREVIEW OF WHAT IS AHEAD

Your journey will begin with a steady "climb" involving smaller concepts that build on each other. They climax at your first major statistic, the *t*-test (Mount *t*). The *t*-test was quite an intellectual feat when it was created, and your comprehension of it will also be worthy of praise. Once you understand the *t*-test, you will gain a new perspective on statistics. On the next part of your journey, you will cross a convenient bridge to an important series of statistics called analysis of variance (ANOVA). The most outstanding of these allows you to examine the multidimensional (multicausal) nature of behavior—multifactor ANOVA.

Next will be statistics that allow you to examine relations between variables, including complex relations involving multiple variables (correlation, regression, and multiple regression). The last statistic, chi-square, allows you to examine categories of behavior. Your introduction to statistics will be complete in the last chapter, when you will look back and gain perspective. This chapter compares statistics and begins to handle the question "How do I choose a statistic?"

THE STEP-BY-STEP PROCEDURES

Each statistic taught can be calculated with a step-by-step procedure. You can find these procedures on the following pages:

Standard Deviation   p. 28
t-test   p. 72
Analysis of Variance (one factor)   p. 108
Analysis of Variance (multi-factor)   p. 138
Correlation/Regression   p. 170
Chi-Square   p. 178

GET PROVISIONS FIRST

My last advice is to prepare yourself each time you travel on this journey. Your brain will learn much more efficiently if it is relaxed and well nourished. If statistics or test taking makes you anxious, the Appendix provides helpful tips. If this book's type seems small, try an inexpensive pair of reading lenses from a local drugstore—they can make interactions with this book more pleasant. Successful interactions will also generate good feelings, and there are plenty of those ahead.

You will need two provisions: a simple calculator and a pencil. Happy trails!

Chapter 1

THE RESEARCHER'S QUESTION

Statistics are marvelous tools that make behavioral research possible. A good way to become acquainted with tools is to learn why the tools are necessary. The first goal of this chapter, then, is to illustrate the need for statistics. Also, to make statistics more real, an example is introduced that will be used throughout this book. Get ready, you are starting your journey!

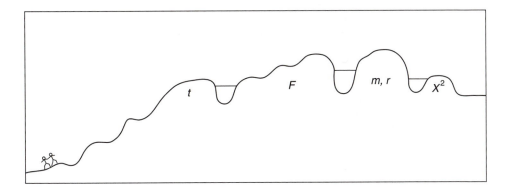

THE RESEARCHER'S QUESTION

Researchers become very interested in their research and often work for months and even years to collect data in an experiment that interests them. After the data have been collected, a big question arises:

Researcher's Question
"Did my experiment work?"

When this question is really understood, it is quite deep. We will be developing an understanding of the question throughout this book.

One way to learn about the meaning of the question is to rephrase it. Let us first rephrase it in terms of the **independent variable** (the variable that the researcher manipulates) and the **dependent variable** (the variable the researcher measures). In the simplest type of experiment, the independent variable is varied between two groups of participants. The dependent variable is measured for each group. We can rephrase the question as follows:

Researcher's Question Rephrased

"Did the independent variable cause a difference in the dependent variable—did it cause one group of participants to behave differently than the other group of participants?"

This question is answered by comparing the results for the two groups. To illustrate, let's consider two examples.

EXAMPLE 1: ISEN, CLARK, AND SCHWARTZ (1976)

The first example—from Isen, Clark, and Schwartz (1976)—was quite new when I first read it as part of an undergraduate research project. It is an interesting instance of research, and I've found that it provides a nice starting point.[1]

Isen, Clark, and Schwartz (1976) examined the relation between good mood and willingness to help. Their hypothesis was that good mood leads to an increased willingness to help other people. The participants in their field study were ordinary people who were in their homes during the day. The independent variable was mood. The experimenter's assistant ("confederate") came to the door, and either gave a sample packet of stationary to the participant (experimental group) or simply demonstrated the stationary (control group). Isen and her colleagues assumed that the free stationary put the experimental group in a good mood, and that the control group was unaffected. (Note that this study was conducted before the age of telemarketing, so interruptions in the home were less bothersome than today.) How did mood influence desire to help?

We will consider one condition from their experiments. Five minutes after the confederate came to the door, each participant received a phone call from a stranger who asked for help. ("I spent my last coin calling this number and it was the wrong one; could you look up a number and call it for me?") The dependent variable was whether or not the participant helped. The researchers found that participants in a good mood were more likely to help. Table 1.1 shows the results for each of the 11 control and 12 experimental participants in the relevant condition. Examine these results. Now, let me ask you, "Based on these data, did the experimental group behave differently than the control group?" Did the experiment "work"?

If your answer is "Yes!," then we are in agreement. The results are very strong. In the control group, only 1 participant helped, whereas in the experimental group 10 participants helped. (Also, note that Isen *et al.* did a good job of considering and testing alternative explanations of the effects, such as obligations that might be assumed because of the free gift; see Isen *et al.*, 1976.) Isen *et al.*'s effect is very likely to be a real effect, and we don't really need statistics to tell us that. However, this is an unusually effective experiment. In most other cases, we do need statistics because it is not obvious if an experimental effect is real, or if the effect could have occurred because of something called chance variation.

[1] Here is the reference, as well as some more recent references:

Isen, A. M., Clark, M., & Schwartz, M. F. (1976). Duration of the effect of good mood on helping: "Footprints on the sands of time." *Journal of Personality & Social Psychology, 34,* 385–393.

Isen, A. M. (1987). Positive affect, cognitive processes, and social behavior. In L. Berkowitz *et al.* (Eds.), *Advances in experimental social psychology* (Vol. 20, pp. 203–253). San Diego: Academic Press.

Ashby, A. F., Isen, A. M., & Turken, A. U. (1999). A neuropsychological theory of positive affect and its influence on cognition. *Psychological Review, 106,* 529–550.

TABLE 1.1.   Each Participant's Response to the Request for Help

CONTROL GROUP		EXPERIMENTAL GROUP	
1.	Did not	1.	Helped
2.	Did not	2.	Helped
3.	Did not	3.	Helped
4.	Did not	4.	Helped
5.	Helped	5.	Did not
6.	Did not	6.	Helped
7.	Did not	7.	Helped
8.	Did not	8.	Helped
9.	Did not	9.	Helped
10.	Did not	10.	Helped
11.	Did not	11.	Did not
		12.	Helped

Source: From Isen *et al.* (1976), Experiment 2.

EXAMPLE 2: A LASTING FRIENDSHIP

Let us now consider a hypothetical example. It is designed to be useful for teaching statistics, and we will use it throughout the book. Therefore, it is a good idea to make friends with it!

Let us assume that the researchers continued their research on mood and helping, but used a more continuous dependent variable (i.e., one with many possible values, rather than the two values of helped/did not). Assume that the experimenters used a confederate who asked the participant to help her do a task. The experimental group was put into a good mood before the request but the control group was not. The dependent variable was how long the participants helped, measured in minutes and seconds.

Some possible results for a total of 12 participants are shown in Table 1.2. The results have been rounded to the nearest minute for simplicity. In this table, I've given each participant a unique number, and I've calculated the mean (average) for each group. (We will cover means in Chapter 3.) Look at the results carefully and tell me, "Did the experimental group behave differently than the control group?"

I hope your answer is something like "Although the experimental group did help more overall, it is difficult to tell for sure if there is a real difference. Some experimental participants helped a lot (e.g., number 10), but so did some control participants

TABLE 1.2.   Amount of Time in Minutes That Each of 12 Hypothetical Participants Helped Another Person

CONTROL GROUP		EXPERIMENTAL GROUP	
1.	8	7.	10
2.	9	8.	16
3.	12	9.	12
4.	7	10.	14
5.	13	11.	11
6.	11	12.	15
Mean (average)	10	Mean (average)	13

(e.g., numbers 3 and 5)." In fact, these results are very close to an important statistical borderline that you will learn about. The overall difference between the groups could have been produced by chance variation. This example is similar to many experiments. Because it is often difficult to tell if there is a real difference in behavior, statistics are necessary. Statistics allow us to reach a principled conclusion about whether there is a real difference or if the difference can be attributed to chance. Among other things, statistics works by defining what "chance" means.

OTHER EXAMPLES OF STATISTICS

We will return to the helping experiment throughout this book. However, because this is an introductory chapter, I want to briefly mention two other interesting uses of statistics. These examples also help to develop some fundamental concepts to which we will return later.

INTERNATIONAL BANKING

A colleague of mine was employed by a large multinational bank to answer a critical question for them. The bank was developing Internet interfaces that would allow people from various countries to access the bank from their home computers. The bank's question was "Should we use the same program (the same type of interface) for all countries, or are cultures different enough that we should use different programs for different countries?" A correct answer to this question could be worth billions of dollars.

Statistics are needed to provide a sound answer to the question. In fact, the question can be answered by making a comparison that is fundamental to statistics. The comparison involves *variation*. In this case, the variation is differences in the way people think about banking. The critical comparison is in variation *between groups* on one hand, and between individuals *within groups* on the other hand. Specifically, the comparison is of variation between cultural groups (e.g., Are Americans as a whole different from Japanese as a whole?), and variation within groups (e.g., How different are Americans from each other and Japanese from each other?). This idea is illustrated in Figure 1.1. The central arrow refers to comparisons between groups (circles or countries), whereas the arrows within each country refer to comparisons within groups.

FIGURE 1.1.   An illustration of variation between groups (the central arrow) and within groups (within each circle).

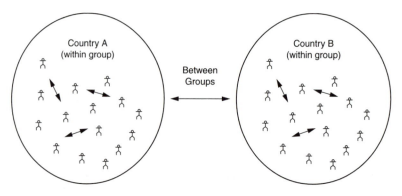

If the differences between cultures were greater than the differences within cultures, it would be reasonable to give differing cultures different interfaces—most people within each culture would want a different interface. On the other hand, if differences between cultures were *less* than differences within cultures, it would not help to give each culture a different interface—within each culture, many people might be unhappy. (It might be wisest to work out a system in which a choice of interfaces is available within each culture.)

Statistics provides a principled method for making this comparison. Fundamental to statistics is the comparison of variation between groups and variation within groups.

What Makes a Person Hardy?

"Hardiness" refers to the ability to retain one's happiness and sanity through somewhat prolonged, stressful situations. Obviously, it can be helpful to understand the factors that contribute to hardiness. However, ethical considerations prohibit researchers from creating prolonged stress in peoples' lives. So how can hardiness be studied?

One approach used a sample of people who were subjected to a 6-week-long, stressful experience—military training required of all young people in a war-torn Middle Eastern country.[2] The researchers measured a large number of personality characteristics, as well as mental health, before and after the experience. The authors then looked at the relations between personality factors and changes in mental health during training, using methods that you will find later in this book (regression and correlation in Chapter 11). The authors were able to use these methods to determine which factors predicted the ability to endure the stress and come out mentally healthy. Interestingly, some factors that were previously thought to be important had no effect. Furthermore, there was no evidence that hardiness was a fixed genetic trait that could not be altered. Instead, they found that the ability to successfully endure was best predicted by the people's coping strategies—their ability to face the stresses in an active, constructive, problem-solving manner. Such strategies are something that anyone can learn.

This example provides several lessons. First, we can gain information relevant to people in general (a *population*) by examining data for a subset of the population (a *sample*). The idea of using a sample to make conclusions about a population is again fundamental to statistics, and the idea will be expanded on in subsequent chapters. Second, we can examine potentially complex relations between large numbers of variables, as you will see in Chapter 11. The third lesson is personally relevant: Active problem strategies are very helpful for overcoming challenges, including statistics. The problem-solving strategies relevant here include working out problems, interacting with the book, and asking questions when you get stuck. However, don't expect statistics to be as stressful as military training! I've made every attempt to ensure that your journey will be safe and pleasant.

A BIT ABOUT TOOLS: SCALES OF MEASUREMENT

Before you go any further, you need to know something about the tools you will be using. Whenever a behavior is measured, the measurements form a "scale." Whether you measure minutes helping, banking attitudes, feelings of stress, or even distance in inches, your measurements form an implicit scale. Often, but not always, this scale is

---

[2] Florian, V., Mikulincer, M., & Taubman, O. (1995). Does hardiness contribute to mental health during a stressful real-life situation? *Journal of Personality and Social Psychology, 68,* 687–695.

quantitative in form, meaning that some items are larger or "more" than other items. Critically, your choice of a statistic depends on properties of the scale you are using. Therefore, we cover scales of measurement briefly here.

Thinking about scales of measurement is something like buying a stereo at the store: You can choose from models that have many or few features. In the present case, the features are quantitative features. Scales differ in the level of measurement, from the most quantitative to the least. We will start with the "deluxe" model, having the greatest number of quantitative features.

The best quantitative scale is the *ratio scale*. The number of minutes spent helping was measured on a ratio scale. To begin with, it has the basic feature of quantitative variation—the values (numbers of minutes) vary in how large they are. A second basic feature of this scale is that it has equal intervals. *Intervals* are distances between number pairs like 1 and 2 or 11 and 12. The term *equal intervals* means that the true difference between any equally-sized intervals is always the same. In our case of minutes, there are 60 seconds between each minute, for example. This is an obvious feature of time and also a feature of the ratio scale of length, as on a ruler. However, it is not obvious for all scales (see below).

The third feature, which is unique to ratio scales, is the *zero point*. For example, "no time" (zero minutes) is meaningful, as is no length. Furthermore, when there is a zero point and equal intervals, you can make ratio comparisons such as "2 minutes is twice as long as 1 minute." Other types of scales do not permit ratio comparisons. The features of each scale are summarized in Table 1.3.

The second best scale is the *interval scale*. It has equal intervals but no true zero point. Temperature is a good example of an interval scale because intervals between numbers are equal in size but the zero point is not meaningful—differing temperature scales (e.g., Fahrenheit versus Celsius) have different zero points! Interval scales do not permit ratio comparisons; it is not strictly true that "40 degrees is twice as hot as 20 degrees."

Ordinal scales lack equal intervals, but they do preserve the *order of numbers*. For example, in a race we typically focus on who was first, second, and third—we preserve order—but the distance between the finishers is not as important. There might be a large difference between first and second place, but little between second and third place. Thus, order of finishing is an ordinal scale.

The boundaries between scale types are fuzzy. Some scales fall between interval and ordinal. For example, if we had people rate their mood on a scale from 1 ("very bad") to 5 ("very good"), we would expect that a "4" would represent a better mood than "3." However, we cannot be sure that the true psychological difference between 1 and 2 is exactly the same amount as the distance between 3 and 4, for example. Because of this, rating scales may only approximate an interval scale.

The last type of scale is the *nominal scale*. It has no quantitative variation, not even order. Each value on the scale is a category, or even just a label or name (thus, "nominal"). For example, color is often experienced as a nominal scale (e.g, "red" and "blue"); for most perceivers, "blue" is not more or less than "red," for example. The categories cannot be compared with each other in a quantitative way.

TABLE 1.3. Features of the Four Scales of Measurement

SCALE NAME AND EXAMPLE	QUANTITATIVE VARIATION?	EQUAL INTERVALS?	ZERO POINT?	RATIO COMPARISONS?
Ratio (e.g., time, length)	Yes	Yes	Yes	Yes
Interval (e.g., temperature)	Yes	Yes	No	No
Ordinal (e.g., order in race)	Yes	No	No	No
Nominal (e.g., colors)	No	No	No	No

In this book we begin by focusing on statistics used with interval or ratio scales. These scales are typical of much behavioral research. The statistics used with such scales are called *parametric* statistics. The analysis of nominal scales is treated in Chapter 12.

THE TRAIL AHEAD

We are now ready to continue on our journey. We next focus on the simple case of a two-group experiment in which the dependent variable is measured on a ratio or interval scale. We will be doing two big things:

1. We will conceptualize the influences on behavior that affect each score. That is, what kinds of things make the numbers larger or smaller? The influences can be divided into between-group and within-group influences. This will be explained in the next chapter.
2. We will use a "theory of pure chance" (probability theory) to understand the relations between these influences in a precise way. We will compare differences between groups and within groups, and we will use samples to make conclusions about populations. These ideas will be developed in a step-by-step manner throughout the rest of this book.

REVIEW

What is the experimenter's question? Phrase your answer in meaningful ways.

Provide a definition of between-group and within-group variation.

Distinguish between samples and populations.

Recall the features of scales of measurement. Be ready to apply them in the exercises.

EXERCISES

1.1. The _____ _____ is the variable that the researcher manipulates and the _____ _____ is the variable that the researcher measures.
1.2. It is believed that classical music can help people to concentrate better and study more efficiently, whereas it is believed that heavy metal music is less conducive to helping people to concentrate and study. When we manipulate the type of music played during study times, we are manipulating the _____ _____ .
1.3. In the study of helping by Isen, Shalker and Karp (1976) where good mood was the independent variable, whether or not the participant helped the stranger who called was the _____ _____ .
1.4. Research has shown that when people are in an angry state their cortisol blood levels rise to varying degrees. In a study of the difference in cortisol levels between people from the eastern United States versus people from the western United States when those people are placed in a situation that may cause angry states, people from the eastern United States have significantly higher cortisol levels in their blood versus people from the western United States. This comparison of these two groups reflects a _____ group comparison. In contrast, differences caused by variations between individuals in the group would be considered a _____ group comparison.
1.5. The best quantitative scale is the _____ scale because it contains quantitative variation, equal intervals, zero point, and ratio comparisons.

1.6.   The scale used for measuring temperatures is called the _____ scale. It has equal intervals but no true zero point.

1.7.   The scale that has no quantitative variation or order and is only used to name value is called the _____ scale

1.8.   The scale that lacks equal intervals but preserves the order of numbers is called the _____ scale.

ANSWERS

1.1.   independent variable; dependent variable
1.3.   dependent variable
1.5.   ratio
1.7.   nominal

Chapter 2

Thinking about Influences on Behavior

The previous chapter gave us one important purpose for statistics: determining whether an independent variable had an effect or not. Now we continue our ascent, by considering the two major concepts that are used to answer this question—the concepts of "error" and the "effect of the independent variable."

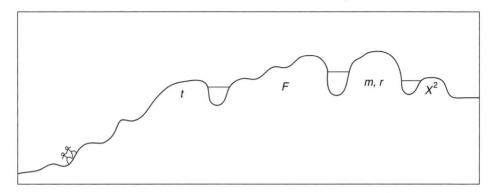

SCORES AND INFLUENCES

We will use our hypothetical experiment from Chapter 1 as an example throughout this book. The independent variable was mood, and the dependent variable was how long each participant helped. Thus, each number is a measure of behavior. We will call each number a *score*. The scores are reproduced in Table 2.1. To understand statistics, we need to ask "What influences scores?" What makes a score high or low? To get yourself thinking, try to imagine some things that might influence a score—things that might make one participant help for a shorter or longer period of time. Also, pick out some of the most extreme scores and imagine what might have influenced them. A space for your ideas is provided.

Write down influences here:

How many influences did you think of? Did you consider individual differences in willingness to help (some people may always be willing to help a lot, other less willing)? Time of day (which might influence how much time people have available to help)? Sex of the con-

TABLE 2.1.   Amount of Time in Minutes That Each of 12
             Hypothetical Participants Helped Another Person

CONTROL GROUP		EXPERIMENTAL GROUP	
1.	8	7.	10
2.	9	8.	16
3.	12	9.	12
4.	7	10.	14
5.	13	11.	11
6.	11	12.	15
Mean (average)	10	Mean (average)	13

federate or participants? What they did last night? Did you have the feeling that you could go on forever?

Keep in mind that each of these influences can make a score larger or smaller. For example, an individual who is always willing to help may have a high score, whereas someone not willing may have a low score. The most extreme scores had the strongest influences acting on them.

⅄   **CONCEPTUALIZATION:**

CATEGORIZING INFLUENCES

We could turn each of these influences into an independent variable and study it, if we had enough time. But we don't. Instead, researchers use techniques for controlling the influences, such as randomization or balancing.

Rather than thinking about controlling the influences, however, let's think about these influences from a statistical point of view. Statistics categorizes the influences into three categories. These somewhat abstract categories are the main point of this chapter. They are crucial because statistics is based on these categories.

---

1.   **Independent variables** are things we actually vary in our experiment.

Extraneous variables are all other possible influences on behavior. There are two different types of extraneous variables:

2.   **Nuisance variables** are influences that would effect each group about equally (even out) in the long run. Nuisance variables cause **error.**
3.   **Confounds,** in contrast, are variables that would effect one group more than the other, in the long run.

Note the phrase "in the long run" in the last two categories. That means that if we were able to continue the experiment for a long time, with lots and lots of participants, then the difference becomes clear. Nuisance variables are undesirable, although we can live with them. Nuisance variables cause error, and for simplicity we will call the influence of nuisance variables "error." On the other hand, confounds are really, really bad. Consider the following examples.

EXAMPLE OF A NUISANCE VARIABLE

Suppose that construction noise could be heard while we ran our helping experiment. It varied from loud and obnoxious to nonexistent, and when it was loud it made people less willing to help because they wanted to leave. If loud noise was just as likely to occur for both experimental and control participants, then it would be a nuisance variable. Its effects would even out in the long run. The error it adds would make our experiment less effective that is, less likely to reveal real differences in behavior.

EXAMPLES OF CONFOUNDS

However, what if the experimental participants were in a room much closer to the noise than the control participants? Or, what if the experimental participants were much *further* from the noise? In each case, the noise would influence one group more than the other. Noise would be a confound, and it would ruin our experiment for the following reason. If the statistics said there was a difference in how our groups behaved, we wouldn't know if it was because of the independent variable or the noise (the extraneous variable). *Confound* means to "mix up"—to mix up the causes in an experiment. If the statistics said there was no difference in behavior, we also wouldn't know if the independent variable really had no effect, or if there was an effect but the confound canceled it.

DONE! Ϫ

BETWEEN-GROUP VERSUS WITHIN-GROUP INFLUENCES

Try answering this question: For each of the three categories of influence on scores, is the influence a between-groups influence or within-groups influence?

Between- or Within-Groups Influence?

1. Independent variables:

2. Nuisance variables:

3. Confounds:

This is a rather difficult question. The answers are as follows, and the reasons behind the answers will become clear soon. Independent variables are varied between groups, so they are a between-group influence. Nuisance variables, on the other hand, causes differences primarily within groups (they cause error). Confounds, on the other hand, affect one group more than the other, and are a between-group influence.

As we continue, we will use only two of the abstract categories. One will be the effects of the independent variable, the **IV effect.** The other will be the effects of nuisance variables, which we will call **error.**

We will usually ignore confounds. This is because statistics have no way of separating confounds from IV effects (both produce between-groups effects). Careful researchers (i.e humans!) are necessary to spot confounds. We will return to our discussion of confounds after we understand some statistics.

This leaves us with our two main categories, which we will continue to work with:

IV effects: a **between-groups** influence
Error: a **within-groups** influence

ᛘ   **CONCEPTUALIZATION:**

IV EFFECTS AND ERROR

Now we will get more specific about the influences on a score, using our two categories. The thinking is simple-minded, yet, it is an essential part of statistics.

Remember that each score in our experiment is a measure of one individual's behavior. We will assume that the two things that influence (or determine) each individual's score are the IV effect and error. Each influence is a specific amount—a number. Let's begin with the IV effect. We assume that the IV effect is the same for every single person within a group. Because this assumption is important, let's emphasize it:

In the world of statistics, the **IV effect** is assumed to be exactly the same for every participant within a condition.

We can translate this idea into math in the following way. Because the IV effect is the same for everyone within a group, we can use the *means* (averages) of the groups to measure the IV effect.[1] In a two-group experiment, the IV effect is simply the difference between the two groups—the experimental mean minus the control mean:

IV effect = Experimental mean − Control mean

In our helping experiment,

IV effect = 13 − 10 = 3

This effect will be the same for everyone in the experiment: 3 for every experimental participant and 0 for every control participant. You can see this in Table 2.2. The first column heading for each group is for the control mean, which we will use as the starting point. The second column lists the IV effect.

Error, in contrast, varies from person to person. It is the part of the score *not* determined by the IV effect. There is a column for error for each group in Table 2.2.

---

[1] To calculate a mean, simply sum all scores and then divide the sum by the number of scores.

TABLE 2.2. Two Influences That Add Together to Make the Scores

	CONTROL GROUP					EXPERIMENTAL GROUP			
	START	IV EFFECT	ERROR	SCORE			START	IV EFFECT	ERROR	SCORE
1.	10	0	−2	=8	7.		10	3	−3	=10
2.	10	0	−1	=9	8.		10	3	+3	=16
3.	10	0	+2	=12	9.		10	3	−1	=12
4.	10	0	−3	=7	10.		10	3	+1	=14
5.	10	0	+3	=13	11.		10	3	?	=11
6.	10	0	?	=11	12.		10	3	?	=15
Mean				=10	Mean					13

Error is the part of a score that is unique to an individual.
In math, it is the difference between an individual's score and the group mean.

For example, participant 10 had a score of 14 (see Table 2.2). The error in this score was 1, because that is the difference from the experimental mean of 13 (14 − 13 = 1).

Thus, in our way of thinking, each score is determined as follows. We will assume that every person's score starts out (before any influence) at the control mean of 10. For the control group, each score is the control mean, plus an IV effect of 0 (since this is the control group), plus the error, as shown in Table 2.2. For example, for participant 2, the score starts out at 10, plus an IV effect of 0, plus an error for this individual of −1, for a total of 9.

For the experimental group, each score is the control mean, plus the IV effect of 3, plus the error. For example, for participant 8, the score starts out at 10 (the control mean), plus an IV effect of 3 for the experimental group, plus an error for this individual of +3, for a total of 16. Read several more scores in the table until you follow this. Then figure out the error effects for participants 6, 11, and 12. Answers are provided in a footnote. After calculating the error values, check your results.[2]

This simple-minded way of conceptualizing scores is the basis of statistics! There are only two categories of influence in the world of statistics: between-group IV effects and within-group error.

Let's ponder this for a moment. You can think about the IV effect as being the average effect of the IV on individuals. In our example, it is the average effect of mood on time spent helping. The neat thing in the simple view is this: Everything else is error. Error might include individual differences in willingness to help, time of day, noise as a nuisance variable (as discussed earlier), and anything else that might influence one score differently than the others. This idea is important so it is restated:

You can think of error as deviation from the mean,
or being different from the average.

We will use "deviations from the mean" to measure error in the next chapter.

DONE! ⅄

---

[2] You should get +1 for participant 6, −2 for participant 11, and +2 for participant 12.

THE TRAIL AHEAD

The concepts of IV effect and error will be essential to us along our path. A central issue that we will address is this: Is the IV effect that we measure a real effect, or was it caused by chance? The answer to this question tells us if the experiment "worked or not" If the IV effect is real, then it did cause actual differences in people's behavior. The main statistics we will use to answer this question are fractions that compare the IV effect to the error. They compare the between-group influence to the within-group influence. For example, the *t*-statistic will be this fraction:

$$t = \text{Between-group influence/Within-group influence} = \text{IV effect/error}$$

This comparison will become more meaningful as we proceed.

REVIEW

Define the following terms:

IV	IV effect
Extraneous variable	Error
Nuisance variable	Between-group
Confound	Within-group

Big Question: What stays the same for every participant in a group and what changes?

EXERCISES

2.1. Research was conducted on the relationship between test prep courses and students' scores on the Graduate Record Exam (GRE), an entry test for graduate school. The participants were 12 college graduates with bachelor's degrees in psychology from a Florida university. The experimental group consisted of 6 participants who attended the same local 8-week test prep course. The other 6 students made up the control group that did not take part in any test preparation courses. The scores on the actual GRE test for all 12 participants follow:

CONTROL GROUP		EXPERIMENTAL GROUP	
1.	1000	7.	1100
2.	1100	8.	1280
3.	1030	9.	1040
4.	1120	10.	1160
5.	1070	11.	1000
6.	980	12.	1200

Decompose the data (refer to Table 2.2) to determine if the independent variable caused a difference in the dependent variable.
a. What is the IV? What is the dependent variable (DV)?
b. Compute the mean for the each group.
c. Compute the IV effect.

    d. Compute the error for each participant's score.

    e. What are some possible confounds that may also have influenced the GRE scores?

2.2. You are running an experiment on visual spatial relations in which the participant's view of the computer screen is very important to the outcome of the experiment. Your first group is run on a computer in the basement of your psychology department in a dark, quiet room and the participants' view of the computer screen is very good. The second group is run upstairs in the psychology department in a corner of the break room where fluorescent lights make it difficult for subjects to see the computer screen. You find that participants in the first group did significantly better on the task versus the second group.

    a. You conclude from this that there is a significant IV effect for the first group. What is wrong with this conclusion?

    b. What should you do to ensure that you minimize extraneous variables for both groups?

    c. Let's say that you run both groups in both environments. Would the difference in environment be a confound or a nuisance variable?

2.3. IV effects (the effects of different treatments on different groups) is a _____ group influence, whereas error (differences due to individual differences) is a _____ group influence.

2.4. _____ is the part of a score that is unique to an individual.

2.5. Fill out the missing IV effect, error, and score information for items a–i. Consult Table 2.2 if you need help.

CONTROL GROUP				EXPERIMENTAL GROUP			
START	IV EFFECT	ERROR	SCORE	START	IV EFFECT	ERROR	SCORE
12	0	−1	11	12	6	−1	17
12	0	+1	13	12	6	a.	b.
12	0	+2	14	12	6	+1	19
12	c.	d.	e.	12	f.	+3	g.
12	0	−5	h.	12	6	i.	18
Mean = 12				Mean = 18			

2.6. Professional Weight Loss Centers is trying to decide between two different types of weight loss programs—a high carbohydrate diet versus a high protein diet over an 8-week period.

HIGH CARBOHYDRATE	HIGH PROTEIN
1. 13	11. 19
2. 10	12. 7
3. 13	13. 11
4. 15	14. 9
5. 9	15. 7
6. 10	16. 6
7. 5	17. 3
8. 15	18. 1
9. 10	19. 3
10. 10	20. 4

    a. What is the IV? What is the DV?

    b. What is the mean for each group?

    c. Compute the IV effect.

    d. What is the error for each participant's score?

    e. What are some possible confounds in this study that may have also influenced the participants' weight loss?

2.7. Warren works for a consumer-testing laboratory and his current project is trying to figure out which plant food works best to promote growth of hydrangeas. The first group of plants receives Polly Pickle's Perfect Plant Food (PPPPF) and the other group receives Red Tater's

Rambunctious Plant Stuff (RTRPS). The plants are left to grow for 7 days and then inches grown were measured.

	PPPPF	RTRPS
	1. 2	11. 10
	2. 3	12. 11
	3. 4	13. 12
	4. 5	14. 13
	5. 2	15. 12
	6. 3	16. 9
	7. 1	17. 10
	8. 2	18. 11
	9. 3	19. 12
	10. 5	20. 10

a. What is the IV? What is the DV?
b. What is the mean for each group?
c. Compute the IV effect.
d. What is the error for each participant's score?
e. What are some possible confounds in this study that may have also influenced the plants' growth?
f. What if you found out that in order to help his friend Red Tater, Warren put Polly's plants into the dark during the experiment?

2.8. A group of researchers believes that seeking prenatal care during pregnancy results in babies with a higher birth weight. The researchers took a sample of 16 babies born in Tampa, Florida, during a 2-week period. In group 1, all mothers sought prenatal care; in group 2, none of the mothers sought prenatal care during their pregnancies.

GROUP 1 (PRENATAL CARE)	GROUP 2 (NO PRENATAL CARE)
1. 6.38	9. 4.25
2. 5.50	10. 5.50
3. 8.44	11. 6.15
4. 9.00	12. 6.00
5. 9.50	13. 7.56
6. 7.19	14. 5.63
7. 7.50	15. 8.93
8.. 8.06	16. 5.50

a. What is the IV? What is the DV?
b. What is the mean for each group?
c. Compute the IV effect.
d. What is the error for each participant's score?
e. What are some possible confounds in this study that may have also influenced the babies' birth weight?

2.9. In a research methods class, 12 students in each of two different labs are compared on the score of the first class test.

JASON'S LAB		MELANIE'S LAB	
PARTICIPANT	SCORE	PARTICIPANT	SCORE
1.	91	13.	82
2.	80	14.	76
3.	76	15.	55

JASON'S LAB		MELANIE'S LAB	
PARTICIPANT	SCORE	PARTICIPANT	SCORE
4.	51	16.	100
5.	26	17.	84
6.	92	18.	42
7.	82	19.	90
8.	78	20.	100
9.	35	21.	35
10.	40	22.	80
11.	99	23.	42
12.	78	24.	90

a. What is the IV? What is the DV?
b. What is the mean for each group?
c. Compute the IV effect.
d. What is the error for each participant's score?
e. What are some possible errors in this study that may have also influenced the outcome?

ANSWERS

2.1. a. IV = test prep; DV = GRE scores
    b. See below.
    c. $1130 - 1050 = 80$
    d. See below.
    e. individual IQ differences; test-taking skill differences

	CONTROL GROUP					EXPERIMENTAL GROUP			
	START	IV EFFECT	ERROR	SCORE		START	IV EFFECT	ERROR	SCORE
1.	1050	0	−50	1000	7.	1050	80	−30	1100
2.	1050	0	50	1100	8.	1050	80	150	1280
3.	1050	0	−20	1030	9.	1050	80	−90	1040
4.	1050	0	70	1120	10.	1050	80	30	1160
5.	1050	0	20	1070	11.	1050	80	−130	1000
6.	1050	0	−70	980	12.	1050	80	70	1200
Mean				1050		Mean			1130

2.3. between; within
2.5. a. −3; b. 15; c. 0; d. +3; e. 15; f. 6; g. 21; h. 7; i. 0
2.7. a. IV = type of plant food; DV = number of inches grown in 7-day period
    b. mean for PPPPF = 3.00; mean for RTRPS = 11.00
    c. IV effect = $11.00 - 3.00 = 8.00$
    d. Construct chart:

	START	IV EFFECT	ERROR	SCORE		START	IV EFFECT	ERROR	SCORE
1.	3	0	−1	2	11.	3	8	−1	10
2.	3	0	0	3	12.	3	8	0	11
3.	3	0	+1	4	13.	3	8	+1	12
4.	3	0	+2	5	14.	3	8	+2	13
5.	3	0	−1	2	15.	3	8	+1	12

	START	IV EFFECT	ERROR	SCORE		START	IV EFFECT	ERROR	SCORE
6.	3	0	0	3	16.	3	8	−2	9
7.	3	0	−2	1	17.	3	8	−1	10
8.	3	0	−1	2	18.	3	8	0	11
9.	3	0	0	3	19.	3	8	+1	12
10.	3	0	+2	5	20.	3	8	−1	10

Error for each group must always equal zero!!!!
e. Did all plants receive same amount of water and sunlight? Were both plants in the same environment?
f. The experiment would be confounded because we would confuse the effect of plant food with sunlight deprivation. This would also be a dishonest and fraudulent practice!

2.9. a. IV = which person's lab; DV = score on first test
b. mean for Jason's lab = 69; mean for Melanie's lab = 73.
c. IV effect = 73 − 69 = 4
d. Construct chart:

	START	IV EFFECT	ERROR	SCORE		START	IV EFFECT	ERROR	SCORE
1.	69	0	+22	91	1.	69	4	+9	82
2.	69	0	+11	80	2.	69	4	+3	76
3.	69	0	+7	76	3.	69	4	−18	55
4.	69	0	−18	51	4.	69	4	+27	100
5.	69	0	−43	26	5.	69	4	+11	84
6.	69	0	+23	92	6.	69	4	−31	42
7.	69	0	+13	82	7.	69	4	+17	90
8.	69	0	+9	78	8.	69	4	+27	100
9.	69	0	−34	35	9.	69	4	−38	35
10.	69	0	−29	40	10.	69	4	+7	80
11.	69	0	+30	99	11.	69	4	−31	42
12.	69	0	+9	78	12.	69	4	+17	90

e. We may have sampling error just pulling from these two samples. We should pull samples from all labs to make sure we don't make a sampling error.

Chapter 3

DESCRIBING INFLUENCES ON BEHAVIOR

Remember what the IV effect and error are? The IV effect is the difference between the means for our two groups of participants, as you saw. The second category, error, involves differences between individual scores and the group mean. It is equivalent to the amount of *spread* in the scores. Spread can be measured in several ways, including as deviations from the mean. The purpose of this chapter is to expand the ideas of the mean and of spread.

The mean and measures of spread can be used to describe almost any behavior. Such descriptions are called descriptive statistics. (How's that for an intuitively meaningful term?) **Descriptive statistics** can be used to describe many quantities, including psychological concepts, consumer characteristics for a business, or socioeconomic variables for the government.

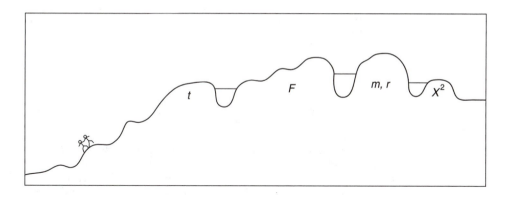

THE MEAN AS CENTRAL TENDENCY

The main descriptor that people want is a measure of **central tendency**—one number that captures what a given group or sample is like, overall. The **mean** provides the most straightforward measure of central tendency. (It is also called the *average*.) To calculate the mean, simply add the scores and divide by the number of scores. This is done for the control scores of our example in Table 3.1. You can see that I've added the scores up, producing a sum of 60 in the second row from the bottom. Then I divided by the number of scores, 6, to get the mean. Look this over, and then calculate the sum and mean for the experimental group. Do this before moving on and check your work.[1]

[1] The sum is 78 and the mean (78/6) is 13.

TABLE 3.1.   Each Participant's Response to the Request for Help

CONTROL GROUP		EXPERIMENTAL GROUP	
X_1	8	X_1	10
X_2	9	X_2	16
X_3	12	X_3	12
X_4	7	X_4	14
X_5	13	X_5	11
X_6	11	X_6	15
Sum = 60		Sum =	
Mean = 10		Mean =	

USING SYMBOLS

Did you notice the symbols in Table 3.1, for example, X_1? We now develop the idea of symbols. Symbols are very useful for us because they allow us to define math precisely. Symbols are also recyclable; we can use the same symbols over and over with new sets of numbers. But most important for you, symbols serve as an efficient summary of how to calculate a statistic. Once you have learned a statistic, you can use the symbolic definition as a quick reminder of how to calculate it (say, next year).

Let's consider the symbols that could be applied to Table 3.1. First, notice that individual scores can also be represented by the variable X. Each X represents a score, and the subscript numeral (1–6 in Table 3.1) designates which score it is

X_1 is the first score.
X_2 is the second score.
X_i means any score, where the i can be replaced by any number.

Thus, X_i is a generic symbol for any score. We need generic symbols (variables) in order to provide general descriptions.

Let's look at Table 3.2, which is Table 3.1 with some changes made. There are new symbols, but don't worry about them yet. Also, although we haven't used generic X_i's yet, we will later.

TABLE 3.2.   Table 3.1 with a Few More Symbols

CONTROL GROUP		EXPERIMENTAL GROUP	
X_1	8	X_1	10
X_2	9	X_2	16
X_3	12	X_3	12
X_4	7	X_4	14
X_5	13	X_5	11
X_6	11	X_6	15
Sum = $\sum_{i=1}^{n} X_i = 60$		Sum = $\sum_{i=1}^{n} X_i =$	
Mean = $\bar{X}_1 = 10$		Mean = $\bar{X}_1 =$	

Now for one of the new symbols:

The symbol for the mean is $\bar{X}$.

To indicate which group the mean is for, we use subscripts. We will call the control group "group 1" since it is the first group, and the experimental group "group 2."

The means for the control and experimental groups are $\bar{X}_1$ and $\bar{X}_2$.

Now let's calculate the mean. The general formula is

$$\bar{X} = \frac{\sum_{i=1}^{n} X_i}{n}$$

The formula is easy if you take it step by step. At the bottom on the right side is n, which is the number of scores in the set (6 in the present cases). The numerator (or top part) has the Greek capital letter sigma, Σ, which means summation.

Σ means add up whatever is inside. The symbols below and above sigma tell you when to start and stop: $\sum_{start}^{stop}$ variable

You usually start with the first score in a group (1) and go to the last score (n). What would you get by doing this with the control group: $\sum_{i=4}^{6} X_i$?

Write out the meaning as you calculate and check your work.[2]

A PROBLEM WITH THE MEAN

Usually, the mean works pretty well. For example, Table 3.3 shows three sets of scores representing salaries of people living on a hypothetical block near Seattle. The salaries on the left side (set 1) are well represented by the mean, which is shown at the bottom. But what about set 2, in which a certain wealthy business-person bought a house on the block? One person's extreme score replaces a more normal salary. Check this out. What if you told your servant that you would pay him the mean of the salaries on the block? Would the salary become expensive in the second case? Does the mean really represent the salaries on the block? And what happened in set 3? Calculate the mean and decide. The low score in set 3 has less of an effect than the high score in set 2, but it still distorts the mean.[3]

---

[2] You should get 31.
[3] The mean for set 3 is 30,834. This is considerably less than 37,833.

TABLE 3.3.   Three Sets of Salaries and Their Means

	SET 1		SET 2		SET 3
X_1	$40,000	X_1	$40,000	X_1	$40,000
X_2	42,000	X_2	7,000,000	X_2	2
X_3	30,000	X_3	30,000	X_3	30,000
X_4	50,000	X_4	50,000	X_4	50,000
X_5	28,000	X_5	28,000	X_5	28,000
X_6	37,000	X_6	37,000	X_6	37,000
$\overline{X}$	37,833	$\overline{X}$	1,197,500	$\overline{X}$	?????

The lesson is that:

> The **mean** is greatly influenced by extreme scores!

THE MEDIAN

An alternative measure of central tendency—the **median**—works well in situations like this. The median is simply the middle score.

> ## To Calculate the Median:
>
> 1. Arrange the scores in order from least to most.
> 2. With an odd number of scores, take the middle score. With an even number, take the middle of the middle two scores, by adding the two scores and dividing by 2.

How would the median do as a measure of central tendency for the three sets of salaries? For your convenience, the scores are arranged in order in Table 3.4. Calculate the three medians and then check your results.[4]

TABLE 3.4.   Salaries Arranged for Calculating Medians

	SET 1		SET 2		SET 3
X_1	$28,000	X_1	$28,000	X_1	$2
X_2	30,000	X_2	30,000	X_2	28,000
X_3	37,000	X_3	37,000	X_3	30,000
X_4	40,000	X_4	40,000	X_4	37,000
X_5	42,000	X_5	50,000	X_5	40,000
X_6	50,000	X_6	7,000,000	X_6	50,000
Median					

THE MODE

One other measure of central tendency is the **mode.** The mode is the most frequent score. In the set (0, 1, 1, 2), the mode is.1. The mode works best when you have a lot of

---

[4] Medians: $38,500 for set 1 and set 2; $33,5000 for set 3.

scores; it doesn't apply well to our sets of salaries. The problems at the end of this chapter provide better data for finding the mode.

CENTRAL TENDENCY AND THE IV EFFECT

The mean and median measure the central tendency of one group of scores. What does the IV effect measure? It measures how the central tendency has been changed by the independent variable. The IV effect is the difference between two means. You can also calculate the IV effect from the difference between two medians. In the chapters ahead, we will need to think about both central tendency itself, and about *differences* in central tendency (the IV effect). Our main goal will be to test to see if the difference in central tendencies is a real effect or one that could be attributed to chance.

CENTRAL TENDENCY ISN'T EVERYTHING

The mean and other measures of central tendency measure only the *central* tendency in a set of scores. They tell us only about the middle. However, individual behavior varies in many ways and it is important to consider this variation. For example, an opinion poll might say that the mean rating of a group leader's performance is "good." But this is only the mean, it doesn't say anything about the variety of opinions, including people who rated performance as "bad" or "excellent." What if one group of six gave the ratings (excellent, bad, very good, poor, excellent, bad) and another group gave the ratings (good, good, good, good, good, good)? Would you want to consider the ratings of these two groups to be the same because they have the same mean?

To know the whole story, we have to consider the entire set of response scores, that is, the *distribution* of scores.

LOOKING AT A SET OF SCORES: FREQUENCY DISTRIBUTIONS

Thinking is often aided by good tables and good illustrations. How can we illustrate a distribution of scores? In this section, we will illustrate a distribution of heights of adult females, taken from 2 years of a survey used in my Research Methods course. I asked the students to report their height. Let's start with the distribution of 10 scores (heights), taken from the front row of one class. We start by creating a **frequency distribution,** which sorts the scores into categories. The frequency distribution is shown in Table 3.5. It is simply a table, in which the rows are categories or "bins" for scores. The frequency of each category is tabulated as "ones" and summarized on the right (in parentheses).

TABLE 3.5. A Frequency Distribution

HEIGHT		TOTAL
60		(0)
61	1	(1)
62	1	(1)
63	11	(2)
64	11	(2)
65		(0)
66	1	(1)
67	111	(3)
68		(0)

Look carefully at Table 3.5. Note, for example, that the category for 67 inches had three students in it , while the others had 0, 1, or 2. Perhaps students of similar heights sat together. A recipe for making frequency distributions is provided at the end of this chapter, in the Reference section. If the idea seems unclear, go to that section and work out some problems.

Our next step is to make the distribution more graphic. We graph the distribution as a **histogram,** as shown in Figure 3.1. In essence, the histogram is simply the distribution turned on its side, with ×'s instead of 1's. The "tops" of the categories are connected to make a polygon (see Figure 3.1. and the Reference section at the end of the chapter for a step-by-step procedure). The result is that the score categories are arranged horizontally, along the bottom, and the height in the graph (how tall a bar is) represents frequency. This way of looking at a distribution, with tall bars meaning high frequencies, is very important.

> In a **frequency histogram,** the values of the scores are listed from left to right along the bottom, going from lowest to highest.
>
> The *frequency* of the scores—how often they occur—is the height of the polygon, with frequent scores being higher.

As you can see in Figure 3.1, the most frequent category (67 inches) is the highest in the figure. Other categories are lower. Frequency distributions are especially helpful when looking at large samples of scores, as you will now see.

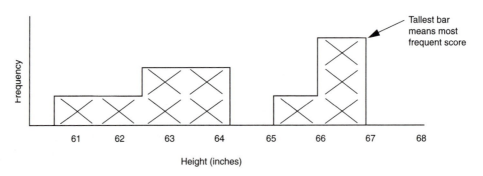

FIGURE 3.1. A frequency histogram.

In Figure 3.2, the entire set of scores is shown. This figure is also a graph of a frequency distribution (a frequency histogram). Instead of ×'s, only a bar graph is used. The frequencies can be read off from the horizontal axis (abscissa). To make the graph simpler, I have grouped pairs of heights (e.g., 60 and 61 inches) in the same category. Again, height in the graph means frequency, so taller bars mean scores that occur more often.

What are the most frequent scores? (Check your work.[5]) You can see that frequency is highest in the middle, and gets much lower toward the "negative side" (the lower scores) and toward the "positive side" (the higher scores).

---

[5] 64–65 inches.

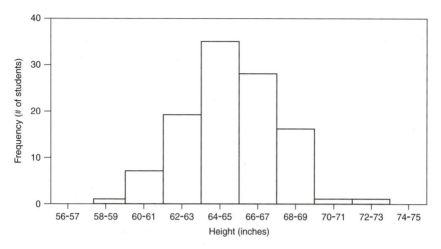

FIGURE 3.2. A frequency distribution of women's heights in two Research Methods classes (n = 111).

FREQUENCY DISTRIBUTIONS HAVE SHAPES

As larger numbers of scores are used in a frequency distribution, an interesting thing happens—the shape often becomes more idealized. You can often tell important things from the shape of a frequency distribution. The distribution of Figure 3.2 resembles an important shape termed a **normal distribution.** If more scores were used, the distribution would approach that shown at the top of Figure 3.3, which is also a normal distribution.

> A **normal distribution** is special type of distribution that is symmetrical and bell shaped.

In the **normal distribution,** the frequency of scores increases toward the middle and decreases toward the negative side and positive side. We will use this distribution as we continue to develop the idea of statistics.

The next two distributions in Figure 3.3 are *skewed* distributions, meaning that they point (skew) in one direction. You can think of *skew* as direction of pointing. **Negative skew** means pointed toward the negative side (left, or lower scores). This shape could indicate that there is a *ceiling effect.* For example, if a test was way too easy, most scores would bunch toward the top. There may be a few low scores, however, perhaps for students who hadn't been in class (mentally or physically).

Positive skew means pointing toward the higher side. This shape indicates that there are some extremely high scores. If we made a frequency histogram of salaries in a region, the distribution would be likely to be positively skewed, caused by the small number of people with very high salaries (above, say, $100,000). Most people's salary would be near the other end, perhaps bunching between $30,000 and $60,000. Because it reduces the effects of extreme salaries, medians should be used to represent the central tendency of salaries (or other skewed distributions).

The last shape is a **bimodal distribution.** Remember that the mode is the most frequent score. *Bimodal* means that there are two high points. If I had included both males

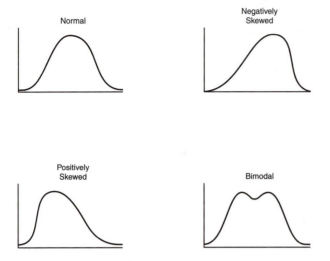

FIGURE 3.3.   Different shapes of frequency distributions.

and females in the distribution of heights, the frequency histogram would be bimodal—there would be a mode for females and one for males. Bimodal distributions often indicate that you are really dealing with two different populations, each one causing one of the modes.

In summary, the overall shape of a distribution is informative. Make sure that you can read frequency distributions. In particular, be sure you can tell which scores are where, and which are most frequent. If you aren't sure, reread this section and do the exercises 3.3 and 3.5–3.8 at the end of the chapter before proceeding. We will be building on distributions as we continue.

MEASURING THE SPREAD OF THE DISTRIBUTION

Our next task is to summarize how spread out the distribution is. How much do the scores vary from left to right, or low to high? Remember that central tendency tells us only about the center. Another measure is needed to represent the width or spread of the distribution. We will consider three measures, beginning with the simplest.

TOTAL SIZE OF THE DISTRIBUTION: THE RANGE

The range measures the total "width" of the distribution, from the lowest score to the highest.

Range = Highest score − Lowest score.

As you can see, the range is simple to calculate. However, it will be strongly influenced by extreme scores. For example, the ranges for the salaries in Table 3.4 are $22,000 for set 1 and $6,972,000 for set 2. What is the range for set 3? (Check your work.[6])

---

[6] The range is 50,000 − 2 = 49,998.

The range is a convenient measure of spread, but it is greatly influenced by extreme scores.

A BETTER MEASURE: VARIABILITY ABOUT THE MEAN

A better way to measure the spread of a distribution is in relation to the center of the distribution. We will use the mean as our measure of the center. Usually, about half of the scores go down from the mean and about half go up. The amount they go up or down is variability about the mean.

Variability is how much scores change, from high to low. Variability is usually measured in relation to the mean.

We will make this idea more precise by defining variability in terms of **deviations**—the differences between individual scores and the mean.

Deviation scores. You obtain a deviation by subtracting the mean from an individual score. This is an idea you have used before.

Deviation from the mean $X_i - \bar{X}$.

Using Deviations Let's practice with the data from our experiment on helping behavior. In Table 3.6, I've done the calculations for the control group; you should complete the deviations for the experimental group. For now, ignore the bottom two rows.

Deviations from the mean are an important component in statistics. However, we do not yet have a single number to summarize the spread of an entire distribution of scores. One way to get that single number would be to use absolute deviations and take their mean. That is, first make each deviation positive (its absolute value). Then take the mean of these values. At the bottom of the table, I have calculated the mean of the absolute deviations for the control group. This *average deviation* is a reasonable summary of the spread of scores; it tells us how much spread there is in each score, on the average. Calculate the average deviation of the experimental group (Check your work.[7])

TABLE 3.6. The Helping Data Arranged for Calculating Deviations

	CONTROL GROUP				EXPERIMENTAL GROUP		
	SCORE	MEAN	DEVIATION		SCORE	MEAN	DEVIATION
X_1	8	10	−2	X_1	10	13	−3
X_2	9	10	−1	X_2	16	13	
X_3	12	10	2	X_3	12	13	
X_4	7	10	−3	X_4	14	13	
X_5	13	10	3	X_5	11	13	
X_6	11	10	1	X_6	15	13	
Sum of absolute values		=	12	Sum of absolute values		=	
Mean of absolute values		=	2.0	Mean of absolute values		=	

[7] 2.0

The average deviation is a very important concept. Take a minute to think about it. I have rewritten the concept in the following box, and room is provided for you to rewrite it in your own words.

> The **average deviation** is the average amount of deviation between each score and the mean.

In essence, the average deviation is our measure of variability. Measuring variability will be very important in most of our statistics. And the meaning of the average deviation is fairly obvious. However, if we work with the numbers just a bit more, we get a summary of spread that makes mathematicians happy because it is elegant and easier to calculate. It is called the *standard deviation* and it is the one we will use.

STANDARD DEVIATION (SD)

The **standard deviation** (SD) is a mathematically useful formula for the average deviation. It permits mathematical wonders that we can take advantage of. It is often abbreviated as *s* in other statistics books, but I use SD because it is more meaningful.

The SD is like the average deviation with two differences: We square the deviations before adding them and then unsquare them at the end. The steps for calculating SD are as follows:

> ### Calculating the Standard Deviation (SD) of a Sample
>
> 1. Make a table with four columns:
>   A. Put the scores in column 1 and the group means in column 2.
>   B. Calculate the deviations from the mean and put them in column 3.
>   C. Square each deviation and put these squared deviations in column 4.
> 2. Sum the squared deviations.
> 3. Divide by $n - 1$ to get the mean squared deviation. This is called the **variance.**
> 4. Unsquare the variance by taking its square root.

These steps are applied to the data for the control group in Table 3.7. Go over each step of the calculations to be sure you understand them. Note that in step 3, we divide by $n - 1$ rather than n. This is a correction for using a small set of numbers, called a *sample.* (The concepts of samples and populations are covered in the next chapter.)

After you are comfortable with the calculations, apply them to the data for the experimental group in Table 3.8. Be sure to do each step. Write down what you are doing as you do it, to help you remember what you did. The answers are given in a later paragraph.

Don't use the standard deviation key on your calculator—it is guaranteed to prevent you from learning. At the end of this chapter, in the Reference section, the formula for the standard deviation is presented. It says the same thing as the step-by-step recipe given earlier, but more concisely.

Did you arrive at a variance of 5.6 and a standard deviation of about 2.4? (I say "about" because I've rounded the standard deviation, as I did for the control group. If fuller precision is preserved, the standard deviation is 2.366. Sometimes calculations will differ slightly because of rounding.) If your answers were not within this "rounding error," check your work!

TABLE 3.7. Data for the Control Group, Arranged for Calculating Standard Deviation

	1. SCORE	2. MEAN	3. DEVIATION	4. SQUARE
		CONTROL GROUP		
X_1	8	10	−2	4
X_2	9	10	−1	1
X_3	12	10	2	4
X_4	7	10	−3	9
X_5	13	10	3	9
X_6	11	10	1	1
Sum of squares (Add!)			=	28
Variance (Divide by $n − 1$)			= SD^2 =	5.6
Standard deviation (Take square root)			= SD =	2.4

Note: $n − 1 = 6 − 1 = 5$.

TABLE 3.8. Data for the Experimental Group, Ready for Calculating Standard Deviation

	1. SCORE	2. MEAN	3. DEVIATION	4. SQUARE
		EXPERIMENTAL GROUP		
X_1	10	13		
X_2	16	13		
X_3	12	13		
X_4	14	13		
X_5	11	13		
X_6	15	13		
Sum of squares			=	
Variance			= SD^2 =	
Standard deviation			= SD =	

Note: $n − 1 = 6 − 1 = 5$.

REMEMBER THE MEANING: AVERAGE DEVIATION

Once you have the calculations down, take a minute to think about what the standard deviation really is. It is, in essence, the average deviation of the scores from the mean. You can see that the standard deviation I calculated was very similar to the average deviation in Table 3.6 for the control group. Your standard deviation for the experimental group should also be close to the average deviation of 2.0 for the experimental group. In summary, the standard deviation is very much like the average deviation. By thinking of the average deviation, the meaning of standard deviation may be easier to remember.

Now is a good time to consolidate your thinking. Use this space to write down your understanding of the standard deviation.

VARIABILITY AND ERROR

Take a deep breath and get ready to ponder a remarkable connection. Remember when we divided each score into the IV effect and error? If not, review Chapter 2 (Table 2.2) now!

The fact to note is this: Our definition of deviation from the mean is identical to the previous definition of error—the difference between an individual score and the mean. This means that variability is equivalent to error, and that it is a within-group influence. Variability is the part of each individual's score that is error! Thus, the standard deviation is useful for summarizing the spread in a distribution and the error within a group or a distribution.

> **Variability** (deviation from the mean) is equivalent to **error.**

In your own words, elaborate on the meaning of each term and on their relationship to each other.

Variability	Standard Deviation	Error

VIEWING DATA FROM AN EXPERIMENT

In this chapter, we are continuing to develop the critical concepts of IV effects and error. As you will see in future chapters, the IV effect is meaningful in relation to the amount of error. Because of this, graphs that illustrate experimental data often provide both the IV effect (the means) and a measure of error (e.g., the standard deviations). This is done in Figure 3.4. The points represent the means and the bars above and below the points (the *error bars*) illustrate the size of the standard deviation.

FIGURE 3.4.   A graph of the means from our helping experiment, with bars indicating the standard deviations.

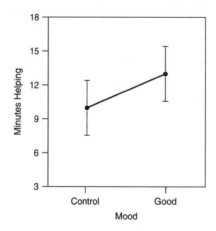

Figure 3.4 indicates that as mood varies, so does the amount of helping. However, the standard deviation is almost as large as the effect of mood. What does this indicate about our experiment? Is the effect of mood a real effect? Stay tuned—we will be able to answer the question after you learn some more concepts.

REFERENCE

Symbolic Definition of Standard Deviation

(Use this for samples; it has the $n - 1$ correction.)

$$SD = s = \sqrt{\frac{\Sigma (X_i - \bar{X}_1)^2}{n - 1}}$$

Standard Deviation for Populations

(Use this for entire populations.)

$$SD = s = \sqrt{\frac{\Sigma (X_i - \bar{X}_1)^2}{n}}$$

Steps for Making Frequency Distributions and Histograms

1. Calculate the range (highest–lowest).
2. Decide how many categories to count. Usually seven is a good number, but sometimes you will want more (for a finer grained distribution) and sometimes less (for a coarse distribution).
3. Divide the range by the number of categories. This gives you your category size.
4. Make a table with one row for each category. The first category is "(Lowest score) to (Lowest score plus category size)." The second category is "(Top of first category) to (Top of first category plus category size)," and so on. The table should resemble Table 3.5 (although there is only one score in each category in Table 3.5).
5. Count the number of scores in your data within each category.
6. Make the graph. Put the categories along the abscissa (horizontal axis) and plot either ×'s (one for each score) or the frequencies (to correspond to the ordinate or vertical axis). See Figures 3.1 and 3.2 for examples.
7. To make a polygon, outline the top of the distribution.

REVIEW

Define the following terms:
Mean

Median

Variability

Range

Average deviation

SD

EXERCISES

3.1.   The number of e-mails received in one working business day by eight top executives at two large corporations are shown here:

	CORP A		CORP B
X_1	45	X_1	23
X_2	34	X_2	72
X_3	22	X_3	36
X_4	28	X_4	29
X_5	34	X_5	48
X_6	19	X_6	23
X_7	34	X_7	65
X_8	16	X_8	56

For each corporation, compute the following:
a. Mean
b. Mode
c. Median
d. Range
e. Which corporation has the largest spread or variability in e-mails received?

3.2.   For each of the six members of the Smith family, the average number of hours of television watched during a typical weekend was calculated and the results are given:

X_1	4
X_2	10
X_3	7
X_4	1
X_5	12
X_6	8

a. Calculate the mean.
b. Calculate the average deviation.
c. Calculate the variance.
d. Calculate the standard deviation.

3.3.   A frequency distribution of the number of vacation days taken by the 34 employees at Timeoff Associates is presented here:

NO OF VACATION DAYS	NO OF EMPLOYEES (FREQ)
9	2
10	7
11	5
12	4
13	3
14	4
15	7
16	2

a. Create a frequency polygon for the frequency distribution.
b. What shape is this distribution?

3.4.   A group of 10 females and a group of 10 males were asked to fill out a questionnaire that assesses the amount of awareness on a 15-point scale of an ideal body type. The scale goes from 1 to 15 with 1 being "least aware of body type" and 15 being "most aware."

MALES	FEMALES
9	13
9	14
9	15
9	15
8	14
10	14
11	14
9	14
8	14
8	13

  a. What is the mean for each group?
  b. What is the mode for each group?
  c. What is the median for each group?
  d. What is the range for the test? What is the range for males? What is the range for females? What is the range for both groups?

3.5. A troop of Girl Scouts is selling cookies and you have gathered the following data:

BOXES SOLD		BOXES SOLD	
X_1	25	X_{11}	100
X_2	100	X_{12}	125
X_3	200	X_{13}	125
X_4	400	X_{14}	200
X_5	50	X_{15}	525
X_6	25	X_{16}	200
X_7	35	X_{17}	100
X_8	200	X_{18}	150
X_9	100	X_{19}	45
X_{10}	45	X_{20}	50

  a. What is the mean?
  b. What is the variance?
  c. What is the SD?
  d. How would you describe this distribution?

3.6. A stockbroker wants to know how his clients are doing in the way of profit margin.

PROFIT	PROFIT
-1000	800
1000	1000
500	1500
500	1000
500	1000
300	1000
1000	500
500	4500
700	

Compute the following for his clients' data:

a. Mean, median, and mode

b. Range

c. Variance, SD

d. What does this distribution look like?

3.7. You work for the U.S. Forestry department and you are charting the amount of reforestation in comparison to deforestation in 10 sections of a national park. The R/D ratio is given here in per-100K trees:

R/D	R/D
11	2
11	10
1	10
10	10
0.6	11
6	11

a. What are the mean, median and mode of this data?

b. What is the range of this data?

c. What is the variance, SD of this data?

d. What does this distribution look like?

e. What is the best measure of central tendency in this case? Which is most representative of the data?

3.8. A psychotherapist wants to make a frequency distribution of number of drinks per day for a group of clients trying to moderate their drinking. Her data is shown here:

NUMBER OF DRINKS	FREQUENCY
0	2
1	2
2	1
3	1
4	1
5	1
6	3
7	3
8	5
9	7
10	2
11	2
12	1

a. Create a frequency polygon for the frequency distribution.

b. What shape is this distribution?

ANSWERS

3.1. a. A = 29; B = 44

b. A = 34; B = 23

c. A = 31; B = 42

d. A = 29; B = 49

e. Corp B

3.3. b. bimodal

3.5. a. mean = 140 boxes

b. variance = 16257.90

c. SD = 127.61
d. This distribution is bimodal.

SCORE	DEVIATION	SQUARE	SCORE AND FREQUENCY
25	−115	13225	25xx
100	−40	1600	35X

SCORE	DEVIATION	SQUARE	SCORE AND FREQUENCY
200	60	3600	45xx
400	260	67600	50xx
50	−90	8100	100xxxx
25	−115	13225	125xx
35	−105	11025	150x
200	60	3600	200xxxx
100	−40	1600	400x
45	−95	9025	525x
100	−40	1600	
125	−15	225	
125	−15	225	
200	60	3600	
525	385	148225	
200	60	3600	
100	−40	1600	
150	10	100	
45	−95	9025	
500	−90	8100	
140			
Sum of squares		308900	
Variance		16257.8947	
SD		127.50645	

3.7. a. mean = 7.8; mode = 11.5; median = 2
b. range = 11−0.6 = 10.4
c. variance = 17.75; SD = 4.21
d. This distribution is negatively skewed.
e. The mode would be most representative of this data.

R/D RATIO	DEVIATION	SQUARE	SCORE AND FREQUENCY
11	3.2	10.24	0.6x
11	3.2	10.24	1x
1	−6.8	46.24	2x
10	2.2	4.84	6x
0.6	−7.2	51.84	10xxxx
6	−1.8	3.24	11xxxx
2	−5.8	33.64	
10	2.2	4.84	
10	2.2	4.84	
10	2.2	4.84	
11	3.2	10.24	
11	3.2	10.24	
Mean =	7.8		
Sum of squares		195.28	
variance		17.7527273	
SD		4.21339854	

Chapter 4

LOOKING AT POPULATIONS

The mean and standard deviation are useful for describing groups of scores. Now we begin to add some high-level concepts to our tool belt. In particular, we need to be able to work with large groups of scores, called **populations.** The ideas you learn here will be essential as we continue to ascend the mountain.

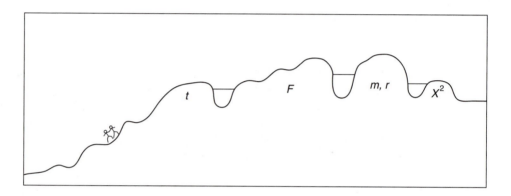

SAMPLES AND POPULATIONS

So far, we have been considering fairly small sets of scores. These are **samples,** which are drawn from larger **populations.**

> A **population** is the entire set of participants or measurements in which a researcher is interested.
> A **sample** is any subset of the population.

Populations might involve all people, all adult females, all left-handed persons, and so on. Populations are usually large, but they are sometimes small. The population of all people who have hiked Statistics Mountain is small (but growing).

Samples are selected from the populations, for example, we might select a sample of 20 lefties. We normally do our experiments with samples, because we don't have enough time to test an entire population.

Samples also vary in size and sometimes can be very, very large. When they are extremely large, they are functionally equivalent to populations. However, very large samples are usually available only in rare cases, such as when health statistics have been gathered at hospitals. Psychologists typically deal with only small samples.

If we do use a small sample, what kind of conclusion would we want to draw? Which of the following conclusions sounds more important to you?: "Twenty people are more likely to help when they are in a good mood, but who knows about the rest of the world" or "People in general are more likely to help when they are in a good mood." Most psychologists want to draw conclusions about people in general. We can make such conclusions in a principled manner, thanks to statistics. However, this creates one of the complexities of statistics:

How can we use samples to draw conclusions about populations? The solution begins with the normal distribution.

> We gather and analyze data from **samples** (often small ones), but we draw conclusions about **populations.**

ⵣ   **CONCEPTUALIZATION:**

NORMAL DISTRIBUTIONS AND STANDARD NORMAL DISTRIBUTIONS

A remarkable thing is often discovered when a very large sample of scores (a population) is measured: The scores form a **normal distribution.** For example, consider the heights of babies. How tall (long) is the average 9-month-old girl? What is an unusually short size? An unusually tall one? Try to figure the answer out from the frequency polygon shown in Figure 4.1. This is a slightly simplified version of the actual population data for female infants. (Check your work.[1])

Note the normal shape of the distribution shown in Figure 4.1. As you learned in the previous chapter, it is symmetrical and bell shaped. Something else is extremely important: The shape can be divided into regularly sized regions that form a pattern that can be used over and over, much like a dress pattern can be used over and over. The pattern is called the **standard normal distribution.**

Let's begin by looking at the pattern. The crucial aspect is the vertical bars. Note that there is one bar in the middle, at the mean. In most cases, we use the mean as the starting point. It is the center of the distribution, marked with a 0 on the standard deviation scale. From the mean of 70 cm, we can go down one standard deviation (-1 SD), which is 2.5 cm in the present case. This puts us at 67.5 cm. These units are called **standard units,** or **z scores.** Thus, a score of 75 would have a z score of what? (Check your work.[2])

Here's a remarkable fact: About 34% of the scores will be in the region between the bars marked 0 and 21. That is, about 34% of the baby heights will be in this range (67.5 to 70 cm). What if we went up from the mean? Where would we go to and what percent would be in that region? Check the next paragraph.

Going up, we would go from the mean of 70 cm to 72.5 cm (11 SD). Again, 34% of the scores would be there. Mark these percentages in the figure.

We can then go out one more standard unit, to the second standard deviation. These occur at 65 and 75 cm. Fourteen percent of the scores occur between the first and second standard deviations, on each side. Beyond the second standard deviations, about 2% of the scores occur on each side. To summarize:

---

[1] You should have found the average height to be 70 cm (27.6 inches). Unusually short begins where the left side of the curve gets low, somewhere around 65 cm; unusually tall begins on the right, somewhere around 75 cm.

[2] 75 is 2 standard units up, or a z score of $+2$.

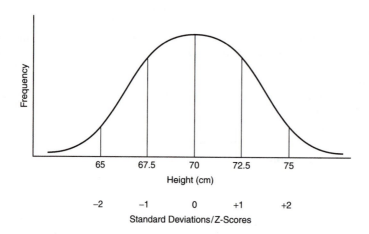

FIGURE 4.1.   A frequency distribution of heights of 9-month-old girls.

The **standard normal distribution** is normal in shape.

The standard deviations (SDs) mark regions with percentages of scores:
   34% between the mean and first SD (or standard unit or z score)
   14% between the first and second SD (or standard unit or z score)
   2% of the scores are beyond the second SD (or standard unit or z score)

It is important for you to be familiar with the standard normal distribution. Start learning to reproduce it now. Find some blank paper and draw it from memory. Mark the first and second standard deviation in each direction, and indicate the percentages of scores within each region. Keep doing this until you are familiar with the percentages.

DONE!   ⅄

RECYCLING DISTRIBUTIONS

Because standard normal distributions are so normal, and because the standard deviation is so standard, we can recycle the distribution shown in Figure 4.1 by applying it to other sets of data. In fact, by changing just one thing, we can fit this pattern to any somewhat normal population of scores. (Tailors would love to be able to do this with clothes.) An example follows that helps to explain this.

An Example

A nice unused standard normal distribution is shown in Figure 4.2. How can we apply it to the data for heights of females in Research Methods courses (Figure 3.2)? Let's begin by labeling the SDs (as ±1, ±2). Label each one. The SDs are standard units that apply to any standard normal distribution.

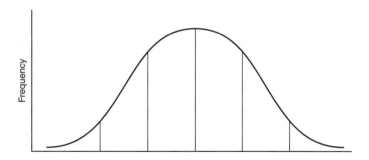

FIGURE 4.2.   A frequency distribution for you to label.

Now we need the second set of labels—the values for each unit from the data. These labels depend on the actual values in the data. We need the mean (which is 65.9 inches) and the standard deviation (which is 2.5 inches), and we need to apply those to Figure 4.2. Can you do this without further instructions? Note that we are now using inches (whereas centimeters were used for babies). If you have problems applying the values, use the instructions that follow.

Labeling a Standard Normal Distribution

1. You need the mean and standard deviation (SD).
2. Put the mean in the middle.
3. Subtract one SD from the mean and put this value under −1 SD (on the left). Add one SD to the mean and put this value under +1 SD (on the right).
4. Subtract two SDs from the mean and put this value under −2 SD (left). Add two SDs to the mean and put this value under +2 SD (right).

You can now calculate percentages of heights within each region. For example, what percentage of heights is between 60.9 inches and the mean of 65.9 inches? (Check your work.[3])

In the example you worked, you have applied the normal distribution to a new set of data! The only thing you changed from the previous figure was the standard deviation, which determines the actual values at each vertical bar. Thus, the SD allows us to convert an actual set of scores into this standardized pattern. The standard deviation provides the crucial conversion factor.

The **standard deviation** is the conversion factor
The SD allows us to convert any distribution into a standard normal distribution.
Summarize in your own words:

---

[3] Your labels on your graph should be as follows: −2 SD/60.9 in., −1 SD/63.4 in., mean/65.9 in., +1 SD/68.4 in., +2 SD/70.9 in. The percentage of heights between 60.9 in and 65.9 in is 48.

USING DISTRIBUTIONS

Standard normal distributions will be very useful to you. Become familiar with them: Continue to memorize their shape and the percentages in each of the main regions. Practice recalling the standard normal distribution during television commercials or while doing mundane chores. Practice drawing them in any empty, legal white space. Standard normal distributions are an essential part of your tool belt and you will be using them as you climb the mountain.

CUMULATIVE DISTRIBUTIONS

It is also helpful to view normal distributions in one other way. Instead of looking at them from the middle (mean) outward, which we have done so far, you can also look at them from left to right. In this view, the scores **cumulate.** This is shown in Figure 4.3. The basic idea is that you begin with the lowest scores at the left, and add up the percentages as you go to the right. We are now concerned with "the percentages of scores under (left of) a certain score." Thus, the leftmost tail, up to 22 SD, is 2%, and the next region (22 to 21 SD), adds 14%, cumulating to 16%. What will be the cumulative total up to the mean? It would be 50%. Finish labeling the distribution. Cumulative percentages are usually called *percentiles*. To practice this way of viewing the scores, use Figure 4.3 to answer the following questions:

1. What percentage of scores is under 11 SD? Remember that this includes *all* scores under 11 SD.
2. What percentage of scores is under 12 SD? (Check your work.[4])

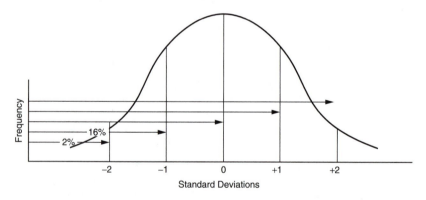

FIGURE 4.3.   A cumulative frequency distribution for you to label.

BEING PRECISE: A MORE EXACT NORMAL DISTRIBUTION

In this chapter I rounded the percentages of scores between each standard deviation in the standard normal distributions to make learning easier. For most purposes, the rounded percentages will serve you well. Keep them in memory.

For technophiles, the exact percentages are shown in Figure 4.4, along with standard deviations up to 63.

[4] The answers are 84% and 98%, respectively.

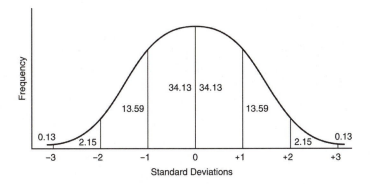

FIGURE 4.4.   The exact standard normal distribution. Percentages shown are percentages between each standard deviation.

REVIEW

Define the following terms:
Sample

Population

Standard normal distribution

z scores (standard units)

percentages for each standard unit

Cumulative distributions

EXERCISES

4.1.   Court records in a small town show that the number of miles over the speed limit for convicted speeders is normally distributed with a mean of 15 mph and a standard deviation of 4 mph.
   a. Draw and label a standard normal distribution.
   b. What percentage of speeding tickets is between 11 and 19 mph?
   c. What percentage of speeding tickets is between −2 and −1 SD?
   d. What is the cumulative percentage of tickets up to the mean of 15 mph?
   e. What is the cumulative percentage up to +2 SD?
4.2.   Professor Mason has just finished grading midterm exams for the 100 students in her Abnormal Psychology course. The mean grade turns out to be 76 and the standard deviation is 9.
   a. Draw and label a standard normal distribution.
   b. What percentage of exam grades is between −1 and +2 SD?
   c. What percentage of exam grades is between 67 and 76?
   d. What is the cumulative percentage of grades up to −1 SD?
   e. What percentage of grades falls above 94?
4.3.   What percentage of scores in a standard normal distribution falls *above* +1 SD?
4.4.   Professor Perone has just finished grading midterm exams for the 100 students in his Research Methods class. The mean is 75 and SD = 10.
   a. Draw and label a standard normal distribution.
   b. What percentage of the grades falls between 65 and 85?

  c. What percentage of grades falls between −2 and +1 SD?
  d. What is the cumulative percentage of up to +1?

4.5. Professor Schulz is running an experiment in which time to recognize certain types of visual stimuli is the dependent variable. The mean recognition time is 600 ms and SD = 150.
  a. Draw and label a standard normal distribution.
  b. What percentage of the responses falls between 750 and 900 ms?
  c. What percentage of reponses falls between −1 and +1 SD?
  d. What is the cumulative percentage up to −1 SD?

4.6. A dietician wants to set up a distribution for the mean number of fat grams consumed per day by her clients. The mean nmber of fat grams consumed per day = 25 and SD = 10.
  a. Draw and label a standard normal distribution.
  b. What percentage of the clients falls between 25 and 45?
  c. What percentage of the clients falls between the mean and +2 SD?
  d. What is the cumulative percentage up to −2 SD?

4.7. In your physics class, you received a score of 95 on your first exam. The mean of the class is 80 and the SD is 15.
  a. Draw and label a standard normal distribution.
  b. What percentage of the scores falls between 50 and 65?
  c. What percentage of the scores falls between −1 SD and +2 SD?
  d. What percentage of your classmates did worse than you on the test?

ANSWERS

4.1. a. −2 SD = 7; −1 SD = 11; mean or 0 SD = 15; +1 SD = 19; +2 SD = 23
  b. 68%
  c. 14%
  d. 50%
  e. 98%

4.3. 16%

4.5. a. −2 SD = 300 ms; −1 SD = 450 ms; 0 SD = 600 ms; +1 SD = 750 ms; +2 SD = 900 ms
  b. 14%
  c. 68%
  d. 16%

4.7 a. −2 SD = 50; −1 SD = 65; 0 SD = 80; +1 SD = 95; +2 SD = 110
  b. 14%
  c. 82%
  d. 84%

Chapter 5

How Accurate Are Sample Means?

In the previous chapter we saw that we gather data from samples, even though we want to make conclusions about populations. We summarize our samples with the mean and standard deviation. We now consider an important question in statistics: "How accurate is a given sample mean?" Specifically, "How close is the sample mean to the mean of the population?"

This question brings us to a higher level of thinking, and the "jump" in thinking is an essential step in statistics. We will use a total of three levels of thinking, two of which we have already covered. The lowest level involves the raw scores—the X's. Recall that we can find the IV effect and error in each of those scores. We take one jump upward when we calculate sample statistics, which summarize our samples—the means and IV effect, and the standard deviations (or error). You should be comfortable with that jump by now.

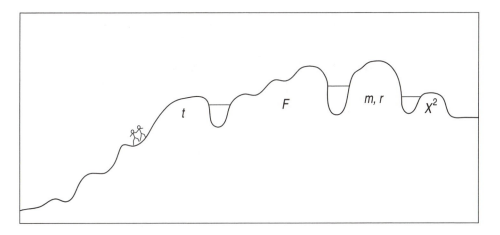

This chapter is about the next jump upward. This is perhaps the most difficult, and it does make some people dizzy at first. The jump begins with the question, "How accurate are sample means?" In this jump, we summarize summaries of statistics; that is, we summarize means, IV effects, and error. Once we learn to do this, we will be ready for our final climb to the top of the mountain.

TWO DETERMINANTS OF ACCURACY OF SAMPLE MEANS

Sample means are likely to have at least some error; that is, they differ from the population mean by some amount. This error is termed **sampling error.** There are two crucial determinants of the accuracy of a sample mean (two factors that reduce sampling error). One is the **sample size,** or n. How accurate would the mean of a sample of size

1 be? Probably not very good. A sample size of 10 would be better, and a sample size of 100 would be even more accurate.

The second determinant is **variability.** Imagine taking a sample of size 2 from this small population: [1, 1, 1, 2, 2, 2, 2, 2, 1, 1]. The mean of the population is 1.5. Sample means should also be fairly accurate; they would have to range between 1.0 and 2.0.

But what about this population: [1, 143000, 2, 500, 665200, 7305002, 5, 44969, 15, 484]? Would samples of the same size (2) be accurate? Probably not! I took two random samples; one had a mean of 332,600.5 and one of 252.5. Neither was close to the population mean of 815,917.8.

These examples suggest that there are lawful relationships governing the accuracy of a sample mean. (These relationships can be easily proven with mathematics.) To summarize:

The Accuracy of a Sample Mean

1. Increases with larger sample sizes.
2. Increases when the population has less variability. (Large sample size and low variability also decrease sampling error.)

Let's put these relationships to work. First, how can we measure sample size? Second, how can we measure variability? What statistics could be used?

For sample size, how about using n? Second, for measuring variability, I would be happy if you suggested our best measure, the standard deviation.

Indeed, the accuracy of a sample mean is measured by taking the standard deviation and then reducing it by a factor of n—the square root of n. This is the **standard error.**

Standard Error

$$\text{Standard error} = \text{SE} = \frac{\text{SD}}{\sqrt{n}}$$

AN EXAMPLE

Consider the sample of 10 heights in Figure 5.1. The mean and standard deviation are also shown. What is the standard error? Calculate it in the box provided and check the paragraph following the box for the answer.

FIGURE 5.1.   The frequency polygon for 10 heights. With mean and SD shown above it.

> Calculate the standard error:

The answer is 2.22 divided by the square root of 10, or 0.7. This means that our mean (of 64.4 in.) is likely to be wrong by 0.7 inches, on the average. In fact, this particular mean was wrong by 1.5 inches (remember that the mean for the entire sample was 65.9 in.). The error in this case was more than average. That happens because of chance—because of nuisance variables that contribute in a random manner to error.

🏃 **CONCEPTUALIZATION:**

LOOKING AT A DISTRIBUTION OF SAMPLE MEANS

The standard error is a measure of the variability of the mean. It tells us the sample means will vary, sometimes being lower than a true population mean and sometimes higher, because of error (chance). It provides a nice, convenient measure. However, it is also important to look at distributions (remember the last chapter?). This time, the distribution is of sample means, and it is called the sampling distribution of the mean. This is a crucial concept to learn. It is a theoretical concept, not one you will actually calculate, although you could image yourself calculating it.

Sampling Distribution of the Mean

This value is generated by taking samples over and over again from the same population.
1. Choose a sample size and then take every possible sample of that size from the population.
2. Calculate the mean of each sample and plot it in a frequency histogram.

Thus, we are "sampling" over and over and generating a distribution—hence, the term sampling distribution.

Take a wild guess as to what shape the means will form when they are plotted in a distribution. Yes, they will form a normal distribution! If we calculated the standard deviation of these means, we would find that it is the same as the standard error, because the standard error is a standard deviation of means.

Let's generate a sampling distribution of the mean from data introduced earlier (the adult female heights from two Research Methods classes). The distribution of *individual* heights is reproduced in Figure 5.2; note that it resembles a normal distribution in shape. What happens when we repeatedly take means from this sample?

Imagine that we repeatedly took samples of 10 heights from the entire set of scores, until we had every possible sample. Each time we take 10 scores, calculate their mean, plot their mean in the frequency histogram, and then replace the scores in the

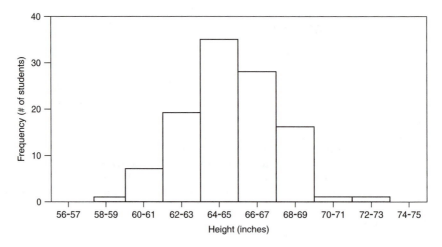

FIGURE 5.2.   A frequency distribution of women's heights in two Research Methods classes [*n* = 111).

pool (sampling with replacement). It will take a while to do this. However, we can be assured that the resulting frequency distribution will be a standard normal distribution like that shown in Figure 5.3. Moreover, it will have the same mean as our original set of data. These facts are proven by mathematics. (The proof is called the *central limit theorem*. Interestingly, this theorem also tells us that even if the population is not normally distributed, the sampling distribution of the mean will be normal as long as the sample size is reasonable.)

The SD calculated from the entire set of individual scores was 2.48; what is the standard error of the sample means? Calculate and check in the next paragraph.

Let's focus now on Figure 5.3, which shows the sampling distribution of means of heights. Don't be mislead by the *width* of the shape in Figure 5.3, because width is irrelevant. We could make the shape wider or smaller, it doesn't matter. What is crucial is the value of the standard error (SE), which you should have calculated as 0.78. (SE = 2.48/(square root of 10) = 0.78.) This means there is only 0.78 inches between each SE. Read the values that are shown in the figure, and enter the other two. Note how small the range of each interval is. For example, what percentage of scores is between 65.9 and 66.7? Calculate and check in the following paragraph.

The percentage is 34, because this is a standard normal distribution.

Thus, we see that the standard error of the mean is considerably less than the original SD. This is because the SE concerns variability of *means,* rather than variability of

FIGURE 5.3.   A sampling distribution of means of heights.

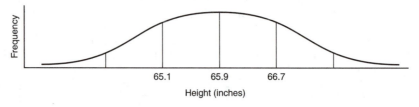

individual scores. The SD concerns variability of individual scores. We will be using sampling distributions of means and SEs when we do statistics shortly.

DONE! ⟨

SUMMARIZE WHAT YOU HAVE LEARNED

Now is a good time to review the concepts you have just learned. Use your own words. Be verbose to aid your learning.

Steps Needed to Create a Sampling Distribution of the Means

What is the meaning of the term *standard error*?

What happens to the SE as error increases?

(*Hint if necessary:* The size of the SE is directly related to the size of the SD, which in turn increases with the amount of error. Therefore. . . .)

PUTTING THE PIECES IN PERSPECTIVE

We have covered all of the concepts you need to do something very important. First, however, let's look at the pieces in perspective. Our close-up of Mount *t* (Figure 5.4) provides perspective. It also reveals a major reason for the difficulty of statistics: Statistics requires many concepts, at many levels of abstraction. You must begin at the basic level of individual scores and samples. This level is fairly concrete. However, you then calculate sample statistics (mean and standard deviation) from your samples. This is somewhat abstract. Even more abstract is the next step, of calculating the standard error. These statistics summarize your summaries of samples. It takes work to become familiar with the more abstract levels. To embellish the ideas in your mind, add the abbreviations that go with each term, as well as definitions and perhaps pictures that are meaningful to you. Then, on another piece of paper, try to reproduce this set of terms along with their definitions. Be sure to learn to distinguish similar concepts from each other, and become able to produce each step in the chain of abstraction.

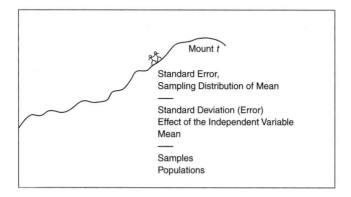

FIGURE 5.4.   The concepts that serve as the foundation of the *t*-test.

These concepts provide your foundation for learning statistics. Review your foundation, solidify it by writing definitions and comments in your own words, and then get ready to use it.

REVIEW

Define the following terms:
  Sampling error

  Sample size (n)

  Standard error as a measure of the variability of means

  Standard error = SE = $\dfrac{\text{SD}}{\sqrt{n}}$

  Sampling distribution of the mean

EXERCISES

5.1. Consider two samples of eight students' midterm exam grades from Professor Mason's Abnormal Psychology course. (Refer to Exercise 4.2.)

SAMPLE 1	SAMPLE 2
Mean = 82	Mean = 69
SD = 5.1	SD = 11

a. Compute the standard error for each sample.

b. If we would repeatedly take samples over and over of Professor Mason's students' exam grades and compute means, what is this type of distribution called? What shape would this distribution be?

5.2. Research has shown that the mean age at which women give birth to a first child has risen to 25.6 years with a standard deviation of 3.2 years. Samples of 50 women were drawn to form a sampling distribution of means.

a. Compute the standard error of the sample means.

b. Draw and label the standard normal distribution with the standard error.

c. What percentage of women give birth between 26.05 and 26.5?

5.3. The following data is taken from two samples of 25 students' final exam grades from Professor Perez's British Literature class:

SAMPLE 1	SAMPLE 2
Mean = 95	Mean = 75
SD = 7	SD = 3

a. What is the SE of each sample?

b. If we took a sample of 25 over and over again from this same pool of students and computed the means and SD, what would be the shape of the distributions and how close would these means and SD come to the true value?

5.4. The following data is taken from two samples of Florida drivers stopped for possible DUI violations. The first sample is from Officer Folsom's stops and the second from Officer Rinck's. Each person's blood alcohol level is recorded below. Florida State law considers drivers intoxicated at 0.08 blood alcohol level.

OFFICER FOLSOM	OFFICER RINCK
0.08	0.10
0.07	0.11
0.05	0.35
0.20	0.15
0.11	0.21

a. Calculate the mean and SD of each group.

b. Calculate the SE of each group.

c. What if you had the same means and SD, but you had a sample size of 25 each? Calculate the SE for each group in this instance. Do larger sample sizes reduce error?

5.5. Dr. Gjurashaj has sampled 25 students of each gender in her class to see how many children, on average, each gender would like to have. The results are shown below.

MALES	FEMALES
Mean = 5	mean = 2
SD = 2.58	SD = 3.33
N = 25	N = 25

a. Calculate the SE for each sample.

b. If we had sample sizes of 100, then what would the SE be for each group? Would this increase or decrease the SE?

5.6. Professor McDermott is doing a study on stress levels in older (>25 years old) and younger (<25 years old) college students. The data follows for her two samples. The stress levels range from 1 to 10 on a self-report questionnaire.

OLDER	YOUNGER
Mean = 5	Mean = 7
SD = 1.0	SD = 2.0
N = 100	N = 100

a. What is the SE for each sample?
b. If we had sample sizes of 36, what would happen to the SE? Would it increase or decrease?

5.7. Professor Tracy is doing a study involving onset of smoking. Taking samples of 100 participants to form a sampling distribution of the means, he found that mean onset = 13 years with a standard deviation of 2.5 years.
a. What is the SE of the sample means?
b. Draw and label the standard normal distribution with the standard error.
c. What percentage of children begins to smoke between 12.5 and 13 years?

5.8. You work for a consumer-testing lab and you are testing how many years of wear a carpet can take before it disintegrates. You are tetsting two different carpets made by two big carpet manufacturers, the Carpet Company and the Blue Rug Company. You have taken samples of 256 trials several times for each manufacturer's carpet. The mean for the Carpet Company's carpet = 25.2 years, SD = 2.5 years; the Blue Rug Company's mean = 35.2 years, SD = 1.5 years.
a. What is the SE of the sample means for each company?
b. Draw and label the standard normal distribution with the standard error for each company.

ANSWERS

5.1. a. sample 1, SE = 1.8; sample 2, SE = 3.89
b. sample distribution of means; standard normal distribution

5.3. a. SE(1) = 1.4; SE(2) = 0.6
b. The distribution would be a normal, bell-shaped curve and the mean and SD would move closer and closer to the true value. Accuracy of a sample mean increases with larger sample sizes and also increases when population has less variability.

5.5. a. SE = 0.32 (males); 0.37 (females)
b. SE = 0.16 (males); 0.16 (females); larger sample size cuts SE in half!

5.7. a. SE of sample means = 0.25
b. −2 SE = 12.5; − 1 SE=12.75; 0 SE = 13.00; + 1 SE = 13.25; + 2 SE=13.50
c. 48%

Chapter 6

Answering the Researcher's Question by Turning It Upside Down

We are ready to return to the main problem researchers face—determining whether the experiment worked. "Did the independent variable cause one group of participants to behave differently than the other group of participants?" Answering this question means drawing a conclusion, or making an inference; therefore, this type of statistic is known as **statistical inference.**

To understand the inference process, we need to take some time to set it up. Get ready for some mental work. To begin, how do you think the researcher would like to answer the question about whether the experiment worked or not? Most researchers would like to hear a loud "Yes!" This is the sensible way to view the question.

However, because statistical inference uses mathematics based on chance, we need to do a strange thing: We need to turn the researcher's thinking upside down. We need to assume that the experiment did not work at all—that the IV had absolutely no effect. This is called the **null hypothesis.** This will be the starting point for our final ascent of the mountain. We will use the null hypothesis to determine, in a precise way, whether the experiment worked. The going will sometimes be tough, but the reward is a rather remarkable perspective.

Our thinking involves a total of three levels, making the two types of jumps we have discussed. Remember that we start at the bottom with the raw X's in our sample. Then we summerize the samples with means and standard deviations, at the second level. The third level require summaries of the sample summaries. At this level, we will use something similar to but distinct from the standard error. We will use the standard error of the difference. "Differences between sample means" is the focus. What would be a typical difference between means, under the null hypothesis? You will see.

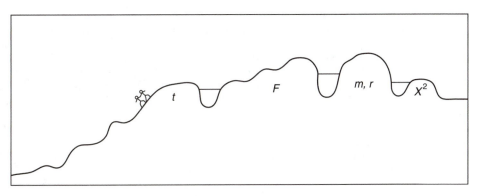

THE NULL HYPOTHESIS

Our first step is to get the idea of the null hypothesis firmly in mind:

Null Hypothesis

The IV had no effect at all; any differences in the means occurred because of chance alone.

   Chance is another word for error; any differences in sample means are due to error (nuisance variables).

We need the null hypothesis because it allows us to use probability theory, which you can think of as the theory of pure chance. The theory of pure chance says that nothing more is at work than chance, which is error, which is caused by nuisance variables.

   Thinking in terms of the null hypothesis is likely to be somewhat strange, but it is absolutely necessary. To prepare your mind for it, you can chant the following four or more times:

"I understand only nothingness—only the null hypothesis—chance, error, nuisance. I can reach somethingness only through nothingness."

If you have the null hypothesis firmly in mind, we can now carry it out to its full extent.

AN EXPERIMENT WITH NOTHINGNESS

We will assume that the null hypothesis is true—that the IV has no effect at all, and that only chance is working. We will create a **sampling distribution** based on the null hypothesis.

   To make this more concrete, let's begin with the idea of conducting an experiment with an IV that has no effect at all (null hypothesis is true). For example, let's say we will measure helping behavior, but the only independent variable we manipulate is the brand of socks that our male confederate (the experimenter's helper) is wearing. The socks will be the same material, color, and cut, but different brands (i.e., made by different companies). We will pretest the socks to make sure they are equally comfortable, and we will cover up the socks by having the confederate wear long pants. In addition, to eliminate experimenter bias, we will put the socks on the confederate and keep the brand secret. We will assume that our procedure was effective and that there was no experimenter bias. In the experiment, the confederate wears one brand with one sample of participants and another brand with another sample.

   We do the experiment—the confederate asks for help and the participants respond. Then we calculate the means of our samples, and calculate the standard deviations. Then we calculate the *difference* between the two sample means (the IV effect). Thus:

For each sample, we calculate:
  1. Means: $\bar{X}_1 - \bar{X}_2$.
  2. Standard deviations: SD_1 and SD_2.
  3. IV effect: $\bar{X}_1 - \bar{X}_2$.

If the null hypothesis were true, what would be the most likely difference? What types of differences would you expect to occur most often? If our independent variable really has no effect (and it seems unlikely to), the most likely difference will be zero or near zero. Of course, because of chance (error, nuisance variables), the actual difference will vary somewhat, being greater than zero sometimes and less than zero sometimes.

Now is a good time to summarize what we have been doing, to consolidate the idea. You are allowed to include something about this seeming silly, but be assured that these ideas are learned by every person who comes to understand statistics. We continue to develop our ideas in the next section.

Your Summary

CONCEPTUALIZATION:

EXPANDING THE NULL HYPOTHESIS: THE SAMPLING DISTRIBUTION OF THE DIFFERENCE BETWEEN MEANS

Now let's continue to develop the idea by being a little more theoretical. Assume that we can repeat our experiment, over and over and over, with new samples of participants. (Either our experimenter is very patient, or we start doing the experiment by computer simulation.) Each time we do the experiment, we calculate the difference between the means. After repeating the experiment thousands of times, we plot these differences in a frequency distribution. This is the **sampling distribution of the** *difference* **between the means.**

Sampling Distribution of the Difference between Means

The Sampling distribution of the difference between means is a frequency distribution of: differences between sample means (IV effects).

It can be produced by computer simulation. Under the null hypothesis, the mean of the differences is zero.

This type of distribution will become very important, so let me introduce it to you carefully, with some repetition. An example is shown in Figure 6.1. Keep in mind that each score in this distribution is a difference between two sample means. Note that the shape of the distribution is normal; it is another standard normal distribution.

The standard units at the bottom of Figure 6.1 (-2, -1, 0, $+1$, and $+2$) are **standard errors of the difference** (between means). This is abbreviated as SE_{diff}. SE_{diff}'s are like standard errors in that they can be calculated from standard deviations. The formula is easy and is presented later. The SE_{diff} measures the variability of the difference between means (the variability of the IV Effect).

The actual values of the SE_{diff} are also given in Figure 6.1, above the standard units. In this example, the value of the SE_{diff} is 0.5, as you can see. The value of the

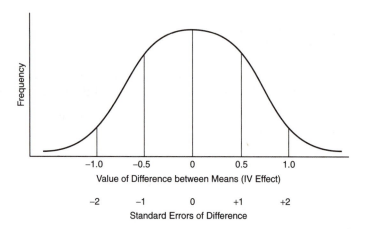

FIGURE 6.1.   A sampling distribution of differences between means.

SE_{diff} provides a conversion factor between actual values and standard units, in the same way that the standard deviation does. Therefore, by using standard units, we can use the same figure with another set of data, with the only change being the size of the SE_{diff}. We can use the SE_{diff} to calculate percentages in each region, as with any other standard normal distribution. Thus, what percentage of differences (IV effects) falls between -0.5 and 0? (Check your work.[1])

The distribution we are studying has a long name, so read it slowly (better yet, copy it while thinking about each word):

Sampling distribution of the difference between means.

Sampling distribution of the difference between means.

We will abbreviate it as SDODBM you can pronounce it *sdod-a-bun*. Review its properties and understand them.

Properties of the SDODBM

1. Like any standard normal distribution, the SDODBM can be divided into regions and percentages.
2. The standard units that mark the regions are standard errors of the difference.
3. The regions can also be marked by actual values that depend on the data.
4. This is a distribution of differences between means, and it is based on the null hypothesis. Therefore, the mean of the standard units and of the actual values of the difference between means is always zero.

DONE!   𝞥

---

[1] The answer is, 34.

🧍 CONCEPTUALIZATION:

USING THE SDODBM

We are ready to use the SDODBM to solve the original problem of determining if the experiment worked. Are you rested and ready?

To start, let's revisit a familiar idea that you should have stored in the back of your mind—the researcher's hypothesis—the hypothesis that the IV had a real effect. You will need it shortly.

Now let's return to the SDODBM, which is based on the null hypothesis. The null hypothesis says the IV had no effect. In the SDODBM shown in Figure 6.1, the SEdiff— the amount differences between means deviate from zero by chance alone—was 0.5. For variety, let's now use the SDODBM shown in Figure 6.2, with a SE_{diff} of 2.0 minutes. Thus, the data are minutes, and the average deviation of differences between means is about 2.0. As always, the modal (the most frequent difference between means) is zero.

Here's what we will do: We will consider some possible outcomes of our experiment and ask how well they fit into the SDODBM under the null hypothesis. As a start, let's say the difference between sample means in an experiment was 1.0 minutes. That is marked *a* in Figure 6.2. Here's the big question we have to ask:

"Is this difference likely to occur by chance?" Or, in other words, "Is the null hypothesis a reasonable explanation of the effect?"

How would you answer this question for *a*? The answer is a big "Yes!" It is very likely to occur by chance, because it is in the middle of the SDODBM, along with lots of other differences that would occur under the null hypothesis. Difference *a* is quite typical.

However, what if the difference between means was 5.0 minutes? This difference is marked *b* in the figure. Is this difference likely to occur by chance? What do you say?

The answer is that it *could* occur by chance, but only rarely. In fact, differences greater than ± 2 SE_{diff} (more than 4.0 minutes) occur less than 5% of the time. That is, differences occur to the left of -2 SE_{diff} or right of $+2$ SE_{diff} occur less than 5 times out of 100. The null hypothesis is *not* a good explanation of this difference.

If such a difference occurs only rarely by chance, what is a better explanation of

FIGURE 6.2. Another sampling distribution of differences between means, with some possible outcomes shown.

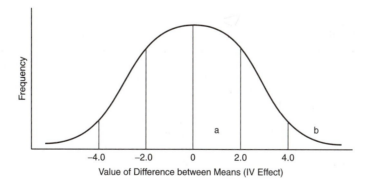

it than the null hypothesis? Look back in your mind. Is there another hypothesis? If you found the researcher's hypothesis, you are doing well. (If not, find it!) The researcher's hypothesis says that the difference was caused by the IV because the IV really does have an effect.

So, the crucial question all depends on where a difference (IV effect) occurs within the distribution. Does it fall in a likely region like *a* or in an unlikely region like *b?* It can be summarized in this way:

The Crucial Question

We plot a *difference* within the SDODBM.

If it falls in the likely region, we say it is due to chance; the null hypothesis is a reasonable explanation.

If it falls in the extreme outer regions, we say it is unlikely to be due to chance. We reject the null hypothesis. We conclude the difference is caused by the IV.

Write the crucial question in your own words:

DONE!   𝝠

A BORDERLINE BETWEEN THE LIKELY AND UNLIKELY REGIONS

Wouldn't it be nice to have a clear borderline as to where the likely and unlikely regions are? In fact, a borderline has been set for you and all other researchers, as a widely agreed on convention. The "likely" region includes the middle 95% of the scores—any difference within this region will be called "likely" and the null hypothesis is a reasonable explanation. The outer regions on each end (the outer 5%) are the unlikely regions; they are called the **regions of rejection** (of the null hypothesis). The place where this unlikely 5% region begins is designated the **critical value.** Figure 6.3 shows the critical value in one general case. The value is close to 2 SE_{diff}'s and in fact rounds to 2. Look Figure 6.3 over carefully, noting where the likely and unlikely regions are. Also, notice that this figure shows standard errors of the differences—the lower scale from Figure 6.2, rather than actual values (upper scale). When expressed in standard errors, the ideas are standardized and can apply to any set of experimental data. We will learn to use the standardized scale in the next chapter. For now, we will use the value of the differences (upper scale) in making our decisions.

In summary, when the difference occurs in the likely region, the null hypothesis is a reasonable explanation. When the difference occurs in the regions of rejection (labeled "unlikely" in Figure 6.3), it could have occurred by chance only rarely, and the researcher's hypothesis provides a better explanation of it. We therefore reject the null hypothesis, and accept the researcher's hypothesis that the IV had a real effect.

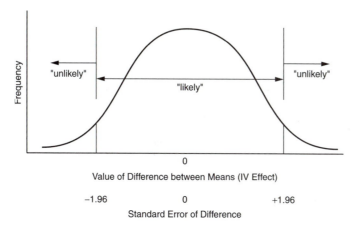

FIGURE 6.3. The likely and unlikely regions within a sampling distribution of the difference between means.

LET'S TALK ABOUT OUR DECISION

Our decision, about whether or not the null hypothesis is a reasonable explanation, is so important that it is expressed in multiple ways in statistics. Some of the most important ways are listed in the following box. I use somewhat informal phrases that are easier for students. Statisticians have special phrases that they use; these phrases are contorted and difficult for most people to think about, but they honor the true meaning of statistics. In particular, when the null hypothesis appears reasonable, statisticians say that you "fail to reject the null hypothesis." You fail to reject it because it is a reasonable explanation. You will see the statistically correct phrase in many statistics books and especially in advanced texts.

Read each of the boxed phrases and compare numbered lines between boxes. Use them to elaborate your understanding. Also note that more is said about lines 5 and 6 below the boxes.

Ways of Saying that the Null Hypothesis Is a Good Explanation

1. The differences can be explained by chance.
2. The null hypothesis is a reasonable explanation.
3. "We fail to reject the null hypothesis." (Statistically correct terminology)
4. The IV had no effect.
5. The probability of a difference this large is greater than 0.05 under the null hypothesis.
6. $p > 0.05$.

Ways of Saying the Researcher's Hypothesis is a Good Explanation

1. The differences are due to the IV.
2. The null hypothesis is wrong.
3. "We reject the null hypothesis." (Statistically correct terminology)
4. The IV had an effect.
5. The probability of a difference this large is less than 0.05 under the null hypothesis.
6. $p < 0.05$.

PROBABILITY STATEMENTS

Lines 5 and 6 in the boxes above are probability statements. Line 5 is a precise probability statement about the situation. Go over line 5 in each box carefully, comparing what is said and noticing the differences. Draw pictures if it helps. Line 6 in each box is a summary of line 5 that is used in journal articles to say the same thing. The letter "*p*" is used to mean probability, which ranges from 0 to 1.0.

PRACTICE

We are solving the big problem! We have a way to determine if the experiment worked. However, because the road was complicated and a long chain of logic was involved, the ideas are likely to take some time to sink in. Take a short break, and then let's practice with the SDODBM.

Let's begin by making a SDODBM.

Constructing a SDODBM

1. You need the SE_{diff}. Remember that the mean is always zero.
2. Put the mean (0) in the middle and add the standard units ($\pm SE_{diff}$'s).
3. Subtract one SE_{diff} from 0 and put this value under -1 SE_{diff} (on the left). Add one SE_{diff} to 0 and put this value under $+1$ SE_{diff} (on the right).
4. Subtract two SE_{diff}'s from 0 and put this value under -2 SE_{diff} (left). Add two SE_{diff}'s to 0 and put this value under $+2$ SE_{diff} (right).
5. Draw the critical border of the likely region at -2 SE_{diff} and $+$ SE_{diff}.

Let's assume that the SE_{diff} turned out to be fairly large ($SE_{diff} = 15$). What would the SDODBM look like? Try drawing it and labeling it completely (use space provided for Figure 6.4). Then answer the following big questions for these experiments, using the actual values scale. (Check your work.[2])

1. IV effect is -7. ($SE_{diff} = 15$)
2. IV effect is 50. ($SE_{diff} = 15$)
3. IV effect is -14.5. ($SE_{diff} = 15$)

FIGURE 6.4.   You draw this one. Be sure to label the diagram completely!

---

[2] *Question 1:* This difference is likely; accept the null hypothesis. *Question 2:* This difference is unlikely; reject the null hypothesis. *Question 3:* This difference is likely, accept the null hypothesis.

CALCULATING THE SE$_{diff}$

The SE$_{diff}$ is calculated by combining the error in your two samples. For mathematical reasons, it is easiest to use the *variances*. The variance is the SD before you squared it, SD^2. Note that this formula applies when your sample sizes, the two n's, are equal. (A more complex formula is given later that applies to unequal n's.)

Formula for SE$_{diff}$

$$SE_{diff} = \sqrt{\frac{SD^2_1}{n_1} + \frac{SD^2_2}{n_2}}$$

(with equal sample sizes)

Two problems to work on follow. Calculate the SE$_{diff}$'s and construct the SDODBM. Remember to think about whether you need SDs or SD's. After finishing the problems, check your work.[3]

- *Case A:* Control SD^2 = 2, n = 3; experimental SD^2 = 3, n = 3.
- *Case B:* Control SD = 3, n = 4; experimental SD = 4, n = 4.

Now plot these IV effects in each case and decide if they look likely. (Check your work.[4]) In both cases A and B, plot:

- *Case 1:* IV effect = 2.5.
- *Case 2:* IV effect = 4.

PERSPECTIVE

Once you are ready, let's look at the detailed view of Mount t (Figure 6.5) and use it to visualize our thinking process. Recall that we had to calculate statistics at three levels, beginning with individual scores and samples, proceeding to sample statistics, and then summaries of sample statistics. This is the route up the mountain shown. One path involves the IV effect and one involves error. Near the top we have the IV effect (difference between means) and the standard error of the difference (SE$_{diff}$). What do we do next using the SE$_{diff}$?

We finish the top of the mountain by adding . . . guess what?

The SDODBM. We use the SE$_{diff}$ to construct the SDODBM. Let's say our SE$_{diff}$ had a value of 6. Construct the SDODBM on top of the mountain, using SE$_{diff}$ = 6.

After we have the SDODBM, we need to think about where our difference between means, the IV effect, falls. Note that it is represented as a flag in Figure 6.5. Let's say the IV effect was 2. What should we do with the flag? How about planting it, exactly where it goes in the SDODBM. What is the crucial question we ask?

We ask if the IV effect is likely to occur by chance or if it appears to be real. Answer this crucial question and check your work.[5] Finally, note that you have used samples, but can now make conclusions about the populations named at the bottom right of the figure.

---

[3] *Case A:* SE$_{diff}$ = sqrt(2/3 + 2/3) = sqrt(4/3) = sqrt(1.333) = 1.15. *Case B:* Square SDs before using them; SE$_{diff}$ = sqrt(9/4 + 16/4) = sqrt(25/4) = sqrt(6.25) = 2.5.

[4] Case 1, reject the null with case A but not case B. Do the same in case 2.

[5] The "flag" would fall near the middle of the SDODBM. The null hypothesis is a reasonable answer.

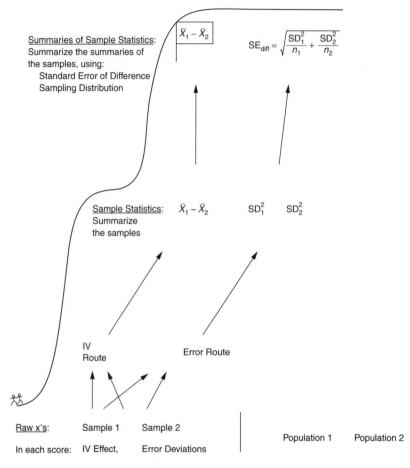

FIGURE 6.5.   Route for statistical inference.

⚘ CONCEPTUALIZATION:

ANOTHER VIEW: THE BIG DECISION

Now you get an opportunity to gain perspective by learning about correct and incorrect statistical decisions. Because the decision process is based on probabilities, we will "probably" make errors—some proportion of our decisions will be wrong. There is no simple way around this. There are two possible errors. Thinking about them helps us to understand the decision process.

TYPE I ERRORS

The first type of error can be seen in the sampling distributions in Figures 6.2 and 6.3. To understand this error, first set your mind properly:

To Understand Type I Errors

Assume that the null hypothesis is true; the IV really had no effect.

Now try answering this question: "Given that the null hypothesis is true, how often will the difference be in the unlikely region—that is, how often will we mistakenly conclude that the IV had an effect?"

As you can see in the sampling distributions, the difference (under the null hypothesis) *will* occur in the region of rejection 5% of the time. That is, there will be a fairly big difference, because of chance alone, 5% of the time. When the difference is this big, a researcher would conclude that the IV had an effect, even though this is a mistake (because the null hypothesis is true). This error should happen 5% of the time.

This type of error has the fancy name Type I error. To help remember this error, I call it "*one* of the unusual 5% of scores that were far out by chance." To help you remember it, you might want to rephrase this in your own terms. In fact, why not do so now?

Type I error:

TYPE II ERRORS

To understand this type of error, you need to reset your mind:

To Understand Type II Errors

Assume that the IV did have an effect and that the null hypothesis is false.

This type of error cannot be seen in the figures you have seen, but we know it must occur sometimes. The error is that IV causes an effect, but the effect is too small to detect in our decision process.

For example, suppose that we were studying an independent variable that had a really small effect. Suppose the variable was whether a first-grade teacher mentions to students, one day near the end of the term, that math was fun or not fun. One group hears that math is fun and one hears otherwise. Then, 11 years later we analyze the SAT math scores of all participants.

Let us further suppose that the true effect of that IV was only one SAT point (out of a mean of 500 and a SD of 100). This is a very small effect. There also will be error, meaning that obtained IV effects (the differences between the means of the samples) vary around 1, sometimes being more and sometimes being less. What would the SDODBM based on the null hypothesis look like? What would you conclude if the IV effect were one? Create the SDODBM and answer this question and then check your answers in the following paragraph.

By design, the SD of the SAT is 100. If there were 30 participants in each group, you calculate the standard error of the difference as

$$SE_{Diff} = \sqrt{\frac{100^2}{30} + \frac{100^2}{30}} = 25.82$$

Thus, the SDODBM would look like Figure 6.6. Remember to look at the actual values along the horizontal axis, upper row. What about an obtained difference of 1? Where would you plot the difference? Plot the difference. Would we have to say the null hypothesis was reasonable?

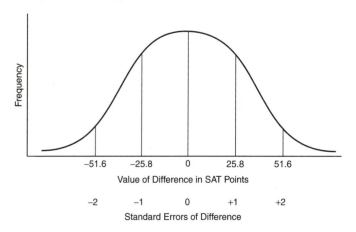

FIGURE 6.6.   A sampling distribution of differences between means for our SAT example.

The difference of 1 would be plotted near the center (just to the right of center) of the SDODBM. Therefore, we would have to say the null hypothesis was reasonable. Even though there was a real difference, the difference was not large enough to detect in our experiment, because it was not in the region of rejection. In fact, it was far from the region of rejection.

Thus, the definition of a Type II **error** is that there is a real effect, but that the null hypothesis was a good explanation because the IV effect was not large enough to be in the region of rejection.

To help remember what a Type II error is, I call Type II errors the case in which "the statistics were *too* conservative." Statistics are conservative in cases like these because a small IV effect was not detected. You can use your own words.

Type II error:

Type II errors illustrate an important asymmetry in statistical inference: We cannot reject the researcher's hypothesis with any certainty—we can't ever "prove" the null hypothesis. It is always possible that there really is an IV effect but it is small. This is why statisticians say you cannot prove the null hypothesis, and why statisticians prefer the phrase "fail to reject the null hypothesis."

In contrast to the researcher's hypothesis, we can reject the null hypothesis with some certainty (with a given probability). This is because the SDODBM tells us exactly how likely a given result is under the null hypothesis.

A 2 × 2 DECISION BOX

We can put errors and statistical decision making into perspective by using a 2 × 2 decision box, as follows. In a 2 × 2 design (Figure 6.7), there are four possibilities. One dimension (at the top) is the true state of the world (which mortal researchers never really know). The second dimension is the researcher's decision to accept or reject the null hypothesis. Putting these two dimensions together, we come up with four possible outcomes; two are correct and two are errors. An excellent exercise is to create this box from memory and think about what each outcome means. Try it the next time you are waiting in line.

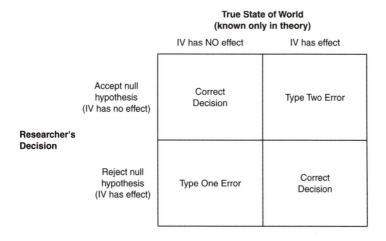

FIGURE 6.7. Conceptualizing statistical decisions in a 2 × 2 box.

Before leaving this topic, I will mention an analogy suggested by a student that is helpful in remembering Type I and II errors (thanks, Takako!). The situation is that you are infatuated with a member of the opposite gender, but you don't know his/her real feelings (in the same way that you never know for sure if the IV effect is real or not). When your friend smiles, you could interpret it as "the person really has special feelings for me." You could be correct, or you could be making a Type I error—concluding there was a real effect when the smile occurred because of chance alone. In contrast, you could conclude that the smile occurred only because of chance; the person does not have special feelings for you. You could be correct, or you could be making a Type II error—concluding that the smile was not real when in fact it was. As an exercise, put this into the 2 × 2 box provided in Figure 6.8. You are invited to add some of your own

FIGURE 6.8.   Makes statistics meaningful!

notations (and even revisions) to increase the meaningfulness of this analogy. Remember, you are doing this for education.

DONE!   ⅄

POWER: AVOIDING TYPE II ERRORS

One final concept fits in here because of its relation to Type II errors: the concept of statistical *power.*

> **Power** is the ability to detect an IV effect when it is there. Phrased in terms of error, power is the ability to avoid a Type II error—avoiding acceptance of the null hypothesis when there was an IV effect.

This concept is especially important when you are working with an independent variable that has a small effect or perhaps no effect. If the IV effect is small, it is easy to make the error of concluding that the null hypothesis was reasonable.

To see this problem, we need to engage in one more foray into theory. To start, we need a clear idea of the actual IV effect. (There is a complexity here: When we work with samples, we never know the actual IV effect—our samples merely estimate the effect. Nevertheless, we can theorize—we can pretend.)

Here is our scenario. Assume that when the null hypothesis is constructed (i.e., the SDODBM is generated from error, based on the hypothesis of no difference). The SDODBM is shown as a solid line, as at the bottom of Figure 6.9. Then, let's suppose that there was a small but real IV effect, and that if we generated a SDODBM, its would have a mean that was different from zero. Further, let's suppose that the SDODBM based on that IV effect would be like the dashed distribution shown at the top of Figure 6.9. (This SDODBM is made of dashed lines because it is based on conjecture, in contrast to the null hypothesis, which is based on the actual mathematical theory of pure chance.)

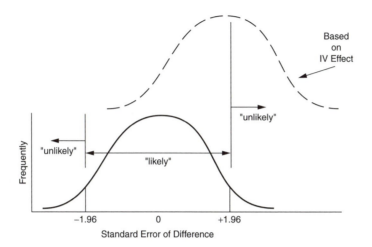

FIGURE 6.9. The likely and unlikely regions within a sampling distribution of the difference between means.

Notice the big vertical line in Figure 6.9; it is the relevant border between the likely and unlikely regions of the null hypothesis. Now look at the upper SDODBM (for the IV effect) and ask yourself what happens to most of the differences in this distribution. Think about this and then read on.

In this case, most of the differences in the upper distribution fall in the likely region, so the null hypothesis is accepted as reasonable most of the time. This occurs even though there was a real IV effect! These are all Type II errors.

Power is the ability to avoid Type II errors and (correctly) reject the null hypothesis. In the upper figure, power corresponds to the area to the right of the line—the unlikely region, where the correct decision of rejecting the null hypothesis is made. As you can see, there is relatively little power in this scenario.

Another example of low power was the SAT example used earlier to illustrate Type II errors. Try adding the SDODBM for the IV effect in that case by going back to Figure 6.6. Remember that the "actual" IV effect in that case was 1.

In contrast to these examples, it would be preferable to have high power—large "unlikely" areas in the SDODBM for the IV effect. This would mean there was a high probability of rejecting the null hypothesis.

When conducting experiments, we must be aware of the possibility that power can be low. Power is likely to be low if the IV effect is small, or if the error (in the form of the standard error) is high. Power can be quantified numerically (see an advanced statistics book). However, Figure 6.9 is sufficient for illustrating the concept, and the figure should tell you to "Watch out for low power!" The possibility of low power is a major reason why we can never prove the null hypothesis. If we accept the null hypothesis as reasonable, it might be that there was an IV effect but power was low and we made a Type II error. We develop these issues further in the next chapter. We will also discuss ways to increase power.

REVIEW

Define and elaborate on the following terms:
Statistical inference

Null hypothesis

Sampling distributions

Sampling distribution of the difference between means

Standard error of the difference, SE_{diff}

Properties of SDODBM

The crucial question

Region of rejection

Critical value

Ways of saying the answer to the crucial question

Type I error

Type II error

2×2 Decision box

EXERCISES

6.1.
SAMPLE A	SAMPLE B
Mean1 = 23	Mean2 = 18
SD1 = 4	SD2 = 6
N1 = 9	N2 = 6

a. Compute the IV effect.
b. Compute the SE_{diff}.
c. Draw and label the SDODBM.
d. If we took two more samples that had an IV effect of 3, what region would this fall into? What does this mean for the null hypothesis?
e. What type of error would we be committing in Part (d) if we truly knew the IV has an effect?

6.2.
SAMPLE A	SAMPLE B
Mean1 = 273	Mean2 = 317
SD1 = 30	SD2 = 50
N1 = 10	N2 = 10

a. Compute the IV effect.
b. Compute the SE_{diff}.
c. Draw and label the SDODBM.
d. IV effect of 40; accept or reject null hypothesis? Explain.
e. IV effect of -15; accept or reject null hypothesis? Explain.

6.3. Let's revisit our Chapter 5 data, in which we were figuring out SEs for each group. The following data is taken from two samples of 25 students' final exam grades from Professor Perez's British Literature class.

SAMPLE 1	SAMPLE 2
Mean = 95	Mean = 75
SD = 7	SD = 3

a. Compute the IV effect.
b. Compute the SE_{diff}.

    c. Draw and label the SDODBM.

    d. If we took two more samples that had an IV effect of 10, what region would this fall into? What does this mean for the null?

    e. What type of error would we be committing in part (d) if we truly knew the IV does not have an effect?

6.4.   Dr. Gjurashaj has sampled 25 students of each gender in her class to see how many children, on average, each gender would like to have. The results are shown here:

MALES	FEMALES
Mean = 5	mean = 2
SD = 2.58	SD = 3.33
$N = 25$	$N = 25$

    a. Compute the IV effect.

    b. Compute the SE_{diff}.

    c. Draw and label the SDODBM.

    d. If we took two more samples that had an IV effect of 1, what region would this fall into? What does this mean for the null?

    e. What type of error would we be committing in part (d) if we knew the IV truly does have an effect?

6.5.   Dr. Hewson takes a sample of the left half of his class and the right half of his class on IQ scores. He figures the SD and means for each half. Here are the data:

LEFT HALF	RIGHT HALF
Mean = 125	Mean = 115
SD = 10	SD = 10
$N = 36$	$N = 25$

    a. What is the IV effect?

    b. What is the SE_{diff}?

    c. Draw and label the SDODBM.

    d. Is the IV effect significant?

    e. If we took two more samples that had an IV effect of 5, what region would this fall into? What does this mean for the null?

    f. What type of error would we be committing in part (e) if we knew the IV truly does have an effect.

6.6.   A group of students is taking the LSAT, an entrance test for law school, when suddenly, one of the students suffers a seizure and the test must be interrupted. The students were allowed to make up the time they missed, but the State Bar Association wants to know if the interruption caused students to score less well than they would have without the disruption. Another group taking the test upstairs in an identical room was not interrupted. The State Bar Association hires you to check these statistics and tell them if the two groups are from the same population.

DISRUPTED GROUP	NONDISRUPTED GROUP
Mean = 120	Mean = 135
SD = 10	SD = 5
$N = 100$	$N = 100$

    a. What is the IV effect?

    b. What is the SE_{diff}?

    c. Draw and label the SDODBM.

    d. Is the IV effect significant?

    e. What is your conclusion as to the effect of the disruption on scores?

6.7.   The mean LSAT score for the entire group that took the LSAT that year was 131, with SD = 5. Calculate the SEOD between the disrupted group in Problem 6.6 (mean = 120; SD = 10, $N = 100$) and the mean and SD of the LSAT for the entire group with a sample group of $n = 100$. Also draw and label the SDODBM. Is the IV effect significant? Is the disrupted group likely to be from the same population as the overall sample group?

6.8.   What if we took the entire group from Problem 6.7 minus the disrupted group for the sample size and calculated the SEOD? There were 10,000 students sitting for the exam. Draw and label the SDODBM. IS the IV effect significant now? Is the disrupted group likely to be from the same population as the overall sample group?

ANSWERS

6.1.   a. $23 - 18 = 5$
       b. 2.79
       c. -2 SEOD $= -5.58$; -1 SEOD $= -2.79$; 0 SEOD $= 0$; 1 SEOD $= 2.79$; 2 SEOD $= 5.58$
       d. Do not reject (accept) null hypothesis; it is likely these two samples came from the same population.
       e. Type II error

6.3.   a. IV effect $= -20$
       b. sqrt $(49/25 + 9/25) = 1.52$
       c. -2 SEOD $= -3.04$; -1 SEOD $= -1.52$; 0 SEOD $= 0$; $+1$ SEOD $= 1.52$; $+2$ SEOD $= 3.04$
       d. We would still be able to reject the null; it is not likely the two samples came from the same population.
       e. Type I error

6.5.   a. IV effect $= -10$
       b. SE diff $= 2.60$
       c. -2 SEOD $= -5.20$; -1 SEOD $= -2.60$; 0 SEOD $= 0$; $+1$ SEOD $= 2.60$; $+2$ SEOD $= 5.20$
       d. Yes; it is not likely that these two samples came from the same population.
       e. It means that we do not reject the null; it is likely these two samples came from the same population.
       f. Type II error

6.7.   SEOD $= 1.12$; -2 SEOD $= -2.24$; -1 SEOD $= -1.12$; 0 SEOD $= 0$; $+1$ SEOD $= 1.12$; $+2$ SEOD $= 2.24$.
       IV effect $= 11$ and it is a significant effect beteen the two groups. These two samples are not likely to be from the same population.

Chapter 7

A Recipe for Answering the Researcher's Question

In the previous chapter, you studied a major statistic, called the *t*-test. I didn't use the name *t*-test, however, to reduce technicality. I wanted to emphasize the thoughtful, meaningful nature of statistical decisions. Be sure that you have a good handle on this thought process. This means doing the problems in Chapter 6 successfully, understanding all of the terms, and, most importantly, understanding all of the steps in thinking. Once you have done so, the technical aspects such as the *t* formula will be easier. We will now cover the formula, which makes the *t*-test easy to do. Then we will examine concepts that expand the generality of the test and allow you to tailor it to individual cases.

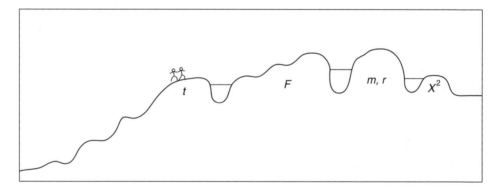

THE BIG PICTURE

The big question concerns whether an experiment worked or not; that is, did the IV have an effect? In essence, the big question concerns where a difference between means—an IV effect—falls in the sampling distribution of the difference between means (SDODBM). Does it fall in a region that is likely by chance or unlikely? Finding the answer to this question requires us to compare two familiar quantities, the IV effect and error.

> The *t*-test is a comparison between: the size of the IV effect and the size of the likely region under the null hypothesis.
>   The size of the likely region is determined by the standard error of the difference, which is in turn determined by the error in an experiment.
>   Therefore, the *t*-test is a comparison between the IV effect and error.

Figure 7.1 illustrates this process. Look at it carefully. Recall that there are two number scales along the horizontal axis: Actual values are given on the upper scale and stan-

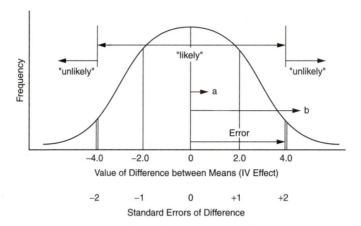

FIGURE 7.1.   The sampling distribution of differences between means that we used in the previous chapter.

dard units ($SE_{diff's}$) are given on the lower scale. The SE_{diff} is 2.0 and the two IV effects are represented by *a* and *b* in the figure (as in the previous chapter). I've added arrows to indicate the sizes of IV effects *a* and *b*. There are also arrows to indicate the size of the likely region (error) and the beginnings of the unlikely regions.

In literal terms, the *t*-test compares the size of an IV Effect arrow to the size of the error arrow. It does this with a fraction:

$$t = \frac{\text{Size of IV effect}}{\text{Size of error}}$$

There is an important benefit of this relation—the *t*-test becomes standardized, with the standard units corresponding to SE_{diff}'s. This means that you don't have to plot actual values of the IV effect (the upper row in Figure 7.1); you can instead simply plot the *t* value, which is the same as the number of SE_{diff}'s. Thus, you can use the somewhat simpler SDODBM shown in Figure 7.2. This is a sampling distribution of both *t* and the DBM.

FIGURE 7.2.   The sampling distribution of differences between means and the sampling distribution of *t*.

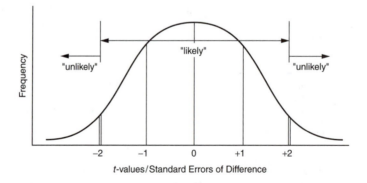

Use this sampling distribution for the two cases that follow. Calculate the *t* values and plot them using the *t* values along the horizontal axis. (Don't use the actual values of the IV effect, because this is standardized.)

- Case A: IV effect = 8, SE_{diff} = 16; *t* = ?
- Case B: IV effect = 40, SE_{diff} = 16; *t* = ?

The *t* for case A should be in the same place as the *a* in Figure 7.1; and the *t* for case B should be in the same place as the *b* in Figure 7.1.

In short, the *t* **formula** standardizes the IV effect by calculating how many SE_{diff}'s it is away from zero. If you need help remembering this, copy the following several times while saying that "the *t* standardizes the scale":

s***t***andardize

Also remember that the size of *t* is related to both the IV effect and error.

The value of *t* will be large when the IV effect is much larger than the error.

Researchers usually want a large t because it means their experiment produced a real difference rather than a difference based on chance.

Look again at Figure 7.1. As you can see, IV effect a is much smaller than the error, so this difference is consistent with the null hypothesis. However, IV effect b is larger than the error, so the null hypothesis will be rejected. Difference b appears to be real.

🧍 **STEP-BY-STEP METHOD TO LEARN:**

CALCULATING T VALUES

The symbolic formula is given below. Learn to apply it by using it.

The Formula for a *t*-Test

$$t = \frac{\text{IV effect}}{SE_{diff}}$$

$$t = \frac{\overline{X}_1 - \overline{X}_2}{\sqrt{\dfrac{SD_1^2}{n_1} = \dfrac{SD_2^2}{n_2}}}$$

Read the following step-by-step method and then calculate the *t* value for the data set given in Table 7.1. The answers are in a paragraph that follows.

TABLE 7.1.   Calculating the *t*-Test for Our Familiar Helping Experiment

	1. SCORE	2. MEAN	3. DEVIATION	4. SQUARE
		CONTROL GROUP		
X_1	8			
X_2	9			
X_3	12			
X_4	7			
X_5	13			
X_6	<u>11</u>			
Sums	=			=
Variance	= SD^2 =			=

	1. SCORE	2. MEAN	3. DEVIATION	4. SQUARE
		EXPERIMENTAL GROUP		
X_1	10			
X_2	16			
X_3	12			
X_4	14			
X_5	11			
X_6	<u>15</u>			
Sums	=			=
Variance	= SD^2 =			=

DIFFERENCES BETWEEN GROUPS
IV effect
SE$_{diff}$
t

STEP-BY-STEP METHOD FOR CALCULATING *t*

This method builds on the method for calculating the standard deviation by using a table with deviations. Learn to make this type of table from memory. It will help you remember the steps for *t*.

You can check your calculation of the SD^2 values against the calculations for Tables 3.7 and 3.8 in Chapter 3. For both groups, SD^2 = 5.6. The IV effect = 10 − 13 = −3.

Calculating the Value of *t*

1. Make a table like Table 7.1, with five columns (one for participant numbers) and lots of rows (enough for each participant plus seven additional rows).
2. Calculate the variances (the SDs squared). Remember how to calculate variances:
   A. Scores in column 1, group means in column 2, deviations in column 3, and squares in column 4.
   B. Sum squared deviations and divide by $n − 1$.
3. At bottom of table, calculate IV effect and standard error of difference.
4. *t* = IV effect/standard error of difference.

The SE_{diff} = square root of $(5.6/6 + 5.6/6)$ = sq.rt. $(0.0933 + 0.0933)$ = sq.rt. $(1.866) = 1.366$. The $t = -3/3.66 = -2.196$.

It turns out that this value is just inside the likely region for this sample size (as will be explained). The null hypothesis is a reasonable explanation. There may be no real IV effect, or the IV effect was too small to detect in this experiment.

Now it's your turn. On your own paper, make a table and calculate t for this small experiment: Control group: 5, 10, 15; Experimental group: 20, 25, 30. Before calculating the t, look at the numbers and try to guess if the value of t will be large or small. (Check your work.[1])

DONE! ⅄

EXPANDING THE IDEA OF t

We have been learning to think about t in the simplest case. If you have a good understanding, it is time to go on. The core idea will be the same, but we will develop the idea to see more of its grandeur.

$t_{obtained}$ AND $t_{critical}$

When we make a statistical decision, we use the t value obtained from the data, which you have been learning about. This is call $t_{obtained}$. For example, for our familiar experiment the $t_{obtained}$ was -2.196.

You also need a value that marks the end of the likely region (the end of the error arrow). It is called $t_{critical}$. This value changes with the sample size. For convenience, you can get this value from a t table, which provides the values calculated by mathematicians. This is explained soon.

$t_{obtained}$ is obtained from the data.

$t_{critical}$ is the critical point at which the likely region ends.

---

t WITH DIFFERENT SAMPLE SIZES

What kind of sample provides a better, more accurate mean: a large sample or a small one? As noted in Chapter 5, a larger sample is more accurate; a mean based on 32 participants is more accurate than one based on 2 participants. The same thing is true for t values: t values calculated from larger samples are more accurate. The likely region is smaller with larger samples because the means are more accurate. This fact is taken into account in the t-test by using different SDODBMs for each sample size.

As the sample size becomes smaller, the size of the likely region—the amount of error in a SDODBM—becomes larger.

---

[1] The answer is -3.67.

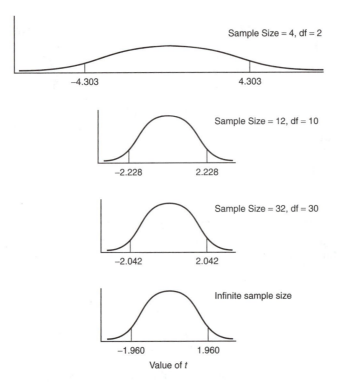

FIGURE 7.3   Four sampling distributions of the difference between sample means, differing in total sample size. Values for $t_{critical}$ are provided.

You will soon learn a convenient way to measure sample size. This measure takes into account the total size of the samples, including both groups of participants. Some SDODBMs for different total sample sizes are shown in Figure 7.3. Note that the size of the likely region changes, as you can see by looking at the values of $t_{critical}$ along the horizontal axis. Degrees of freedom (df) are also shown but don't worry about them yet.

One other important point is illustrated in Figure 7.3. Note that the SDODBM for a total sample of 32 is quite similar to the SDODBM for an infinitely large sample. This indicates that somewhat large samples are almost as good as populations. Thus, 32 people can be as good as several million, statistically speaking.

MEASURE OF TOTAL SAMPLE SIZE: DEGREES OF FREEDOM

Obviously, we need to consider the total size of our samples. For mathematical reasons, the best measure of sample size is called **degrees of freedom** (df). It is calculated from the two sample sizes:

Calculating Degrees of Freedom

Degrees of freedom $= \mathrm{df} = (n_1 - 1) + (n_2 - 1)$

$\mathrm{df} = n_1 + n_2 - 2$

TABLE 7.2. Illustration of the Statistical Meaning of Freedom

| | CONTROL GROUP | |
	CASE 1	CASE 2
X_1	4	4
X_2	??	8
X_3	??	??
Mean	6	6

The name and the formula follow from this question: How many scores are free to change when a sample statistic such as the mean has been calculated? Look at Table 7.2. Each sample has three participants, and the mean has been calculated. Can you figure out the value of the missing scores?

You can't figure out the value in the first case, but in the second you can. Do it if you haven't. This demonstration indicates that the last score is *not* free to vary; its value is constrained when a mean is calculated. Because that last score is determined, the number of scores that are *free to vary* (degrees of freedom) in one sample is $n = 1$. Combining the two samples gives you the formula for df in the *t*-test.

FINDING $t_{critical}$ IN A *t*-TABLE

Once you have the measure of total sample size, df, you use a *t* table to find $t_{critical}$. Table 7.3 is a *t* table. The values in the table come from a mathematical formula (see, e.g., *Statistics*, by H.L. Hays).

Let's use the table. Look first at the two columns on the left under "Two-Tailed Test." The df are shown in the first column and the values of $t_{critical}$ in the second column. If you wanted the critical value with 20 degrees of freedom, you would find "20" in the left column and the critical value, 2.086, would be next to it. Find this.

Now look up and down the columns. Notice that the values of $t_{critical}$ decrease as sample size (df) increases. That is because, as sample size increases, the accuracy of sample means increases and the SDODBM becomes more narrow (as you saw in Figure 7.3). The bottom row is for infinitely large samples—populations.

The two columns on the right under "One-Tailed Test" are explained next.

PUTTING THE IDEA TO USE

Now it is time to apply the concept of degrees of freedom and use the *t* table. Remember the formula (df $= n_1 + n_2 - 2$) and the sample size in our familiar experiment (6 in each group). Calculate the degrees of freedom and look up the critical *t* value. Recall that $t_{obtained}$ was -2.196. Make your statistical decision and write down the thinking process (use illustrations if it helps). (Check your work.[2])

---

[2] The df $= 6 + 6 - 2 = 10$, and $t_{critical}$ is 2.228 in a two-tailed test. Because this is larger than the obtained value of 2.196 (in an absolute sense), we know that the obtained value was inside of the critical value. Therefore, the null hypothesis is a reasonable explanation of this result; it could have occurred by chance. The result was not statistically significant and $p > 0.05$.

TABLE 7.3. *t*-Table of Critical Values for *t*

CRITICAL VALUES OF *t* (5% CRITERION)			
TWO-TAILED TEST		ONE-TAILED TEST	
df	VALUE	df	VALUE
1	12.706	1	6.314
2	4.303	2	2.920
3	3.182	3	2.353
4	2.776	4	2.132
5	2.571	5	2.015
6	2.447	6	1.943
7	2.365	7	1.895
8	2.306	8	1.860
9	2.262	9	1.833
10	2.228	10	1.812
11	2.201	11	1.796
12	2.179	12	1.782
13	2.160	13	1.771
14	2.145	14	1.761
15	2.131	15	1.753
16	2.120	16	1.746
17	2.110	17	1.740
18	2.101	18	1.734
19	2.093	19	1.729
20	2.086	20	1.725
21	2.080	21	1.721
22	2.074	22	1.717
23	2.069	23	1.714
24	2.064	24	1.711
25	2.060	25	1.708
26	2.056	26	1.706
27	2.052	27	1.703
28	2.048	28	1.701
29	2.045	29	1.699
30	2.042	30	1.697
40	2.021	40	1.684
60	2.000	60	1.671
120	1.980	120	1.658
∞	1.960	∞	1.645

CONDUCTING THE *t*-TEST: SUMMARY

The box on page 81 provides a summary of the steps necessary to conduct a *t*-test. The next box provides space to summarize the steps in your own words. Remember that the thinking is based on the null hypothesis.

ONE-TAILED TESTS

In the SDODBM we have used so far, the unlikely region falls on either side—in either "tail." That means that the IV effect can be positive or negative. For example, in Chapter 6, when testing the effects of the confederate's socks on helping, we might not know

---

Conducting the *t*-Test

A. Calculate the obtained *t*
   1. Make a table like Table 7.1, with five columns (one for participant numbers) and lots of rows (enough for each participant plus seven additional rows).
   2. Calculate the variances (the SDs squared).
   3. At the bottom of table, calculate IV effect and standard error of difference.
   4. *t* = IV effect/standard error of difference.

B. Calculate the Degrees of Freedom (df = $n_1 + n_2 - 2$)

C. Compare the obtained *t* to the critical *t*
   1. Get $_{\text{critical}}$ *t* from the *t* table using your df.
   2. If $t_{\text{obtained}} > t_{\text{critical}}$, conclude you have a real effect. If $t_{\text{obtained}} <= t_{\text{critical}}$, conclude the effect may be due to chance.

Conducting the *t*-Test

---

which brand of socks would produce more helping (if there was an effect at all). When we subtract one sample mean from the other, the value could be positive or negative. However, we often think we know whether the IV effect should be positive or negative. For example, we might expect that the IV good mood would lead to an increase in helping behavior. This means that an experimental group in a good mood would produce more helping than a control group. In such a case, we can concentrate our unlikely region on one side of the SDODBM—in one tail. This is shown in Figure 7.4. The consequence is that the value of t_{critical} is less than previously. This new case is called a **one-**

FIGURE 7.4   The likely and unlikely regions within a one-tailed sampling distribution of the difference between means.

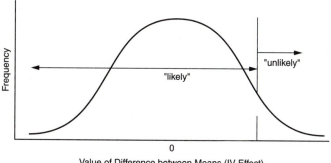

0

Value of Difference between Means (IV Effect)

0   +1.64

Standard Error of Difference

tailed *t*-test. The values of $t_{critical}$ for a one-tailed test are shown in the second pair of columns in Table 7.3.

The original way of dividing the unlikely region into two is called a **two-tailed *t*-test.** It is the more general way of conducting t-tests. It is also more conservative, in that you need a somewhat larger IV effect to be able to reject the null hypothesis.

Summary of One-Tailed *t*-Test

1. Formulate directional hypothesis prior to the experiment.
2. Calculate the *t* value and degrees of freedom using the *t* formula.
3. Compare the obtained *t* to the critical *t* for a *one-tailed test*.

USING THE ONE-TAILED TEST

Using the *t*-value and the degrees of freedom from our familiar experiment, look up the critical value for a one-tailed test. What is the statistical decision in the one-tailed case? (Check your work.[3])

Use this space to summarize the one-tailed *t*-test:

VARIATION IN THE VALUE OF *p*

In making statistical decisions, we use the critical region (the unlikely region, or the region of rejection of the null hypothesis). The widely agreed on size of the critical region is 5%, or 0.05. However, this region is not necessarily fixed. As you saw, you can use a one-tailed test under the appropriate circumstances. Furthermore, a region of rejection that is smaller than 5% is sometimes appropriate, and occasionally a larger region is appropriate. Therefore, you will see different values of *p* reported in scientific articles. For example, you might see "$p < 0.01$" in an article. This means that when a small region of rejection is used, the effect of the IV is real. The advantage of a smaller region is that it reduces Type I errors (calling a null result a real effect because the *t* was large by chance; see Chapter 6). This means that you can have more confidence in rejecting the null hypothesis. Small *p* values are most likely to be used in very precise areas of re-

---

[3] With df = 6 + 6 − 2 = 10, $t_{critical}$ is 1.812 in a one-tailed test. Because this is smaller than the obtained value of 2.196, we know that the obtained value was outside of the critical value, and we can reject the null hypothesis. The result was statistically significant and $p < 0.05$ This conclusion differs from that with a two-tailed test. However, note that we must decide whether to do the one- or two-tailed test before the experiment is conducted. If we decide after the results are collected to change the type of test, we are making an error known as "data fishing," which is discussed shortly.

search such as Psychophysics, where participants may do many thousands of trials of a task, producing very accurate means.

Larger p values might be used when you really need to avoid Type II errors—when you want a *powerful* test. For example, if you were trying to show that an IV effect does *not* occur, you would want to make sure you used a powerful test (i.e., one with few Type II errors). To be more concrete, let's say you were testing whether a new chemical was unhealthy. The IV effect in this case is the chemical and you are testing for bad effects. You would want to avoid missing an effect that really was there, so you could increase your power by using a larger p value. This reduces Type II errors—concluding that the chemical had no effect when in fact it did.

For convenience, most computer statistical programs now report the exact value of p that your obtained t merits—that is, they tell you exactly where in the SDODBM your difference falls, in terms of p values. For example, you might see "$p = 0.002$," meaning that your obtained t was located at the 0.002 point of the sampling distribution. Because this value is less than 0.05, you have a real effect. In fact, this effect would be real even if your critical region began at 0.01. If your obtained t had a p-value of 0.06, however, you could not reject the null hypothesis if your critical region was the conventional 0.05.

REPORTING *t*-TESTS IN ARTICLES

When you read a journal article, you will often find results of *t*-tests reported in the results sections. You may well be reporting *t*-tests yourself. The report often looks like this:

"The effect was significant, $t(28) = 3.44$, $p < 0.05$, two-tailed."

The conclusion was that the null hypothesis was rejected because the IV effect appeared to be real. The word "significant" is shorthand for this. (However, be careful of the meaning of "significant," as will be explained shortly.) The "(28)" is the number of degrees of freedom, "3.44" is the obtained t, and "$p < 0.05$" indicates that a critical region of reject of 5% was used. Because the test may be one or two tailed, the number of tails is indicated. In recent articles, you may also see the exact value of p reported (e.g., "$p = 0.002$"), because this is what statistical programs produce, as noted earlier.

WHAT HAPPENS WITH A BORDERLINE *p*-VALUE?

Experiments involve a lot of work. Imagine that you worked very hard on an experiment, you calculated your t value, and, like our familiar experiment, it was not significant in the two-tailed test. What should you do, switch to a one-tailed test? The answer is, "No, no, no!" Changing your test after the fact is cheating because the mathematics of the test is based on chance, under the assumption that the type of test is decided before the test is conducted. Changing the test from two tailed to one tailed is like placing a poker bet *after* the cards have been laid down.

Researchers do sometimes face the problem of a close t value. Such values are sometimes called *marginally significant*. If the effect being tested is an important IV effect, marginally significant is not good enough. What do you do? You must proceed in a way that does not bias your statistical decision process.

The best way to get a more definitive t value is to run more participants in your experiment. The additional participants will reduce the size of the standard error of difference (because you divide by the square root of n). This will also make your estimates of the means and the IV effect more accurate. Sometimes this will result in a significant *t*. However, at other times the *t* will remain non-significant, and possibly become further from the unlikely region. This is likely to happen when the IV effect really is zero or near zero and your formerly close *t* value was close because of chance (Type I error).

This process must be done in an unbiased way. It is not legal to run two participants and check your *t*, run two more and check, and so on. It is cheating to continually check only for a significant *t*. The way to be unbiased is to look for *either* a significant *t* or a clearly non-significant *t*. That is, you stop and make your decision if the *t* is large ($p < 0.05$) or small (giving you a large *p* value, say, $p > 0.40$; in this case, you accept the null hypothesis as reasonable). In this way, you do not unbalance the statistical decision process and its basis in probability theory.

THE MEANING OF STATISTICAL DECISIONS

You should now be able to calculate the *t*-test and make a statistical decision. You should be beginning to feel comfortable with the basic idea. Once you have done this and are rested, it is time to learn more about statistical inference by considering further aspects of its meaning. The meaning of a statistical decision is actually quite precise, and it is important to distinguish its meaning from other possible interpretations. The goal of this section iso consider the meaning of the *t*-test more precisely. Let me begin with three cautions. Then I will be more constructive about the meaning of *t*.

"SIGNIFICANCE" IS A LOUSY TERM

As noted, journal articles often contain the phrase "the effect was statistically significant." However, it is important to know that the meaning of "significance" is *very limited:*

> **"Statistically significant"** means only that the result was unlikely to occur by chance; "significance" says *nothing* about the importance of the result.

Some statistically significant results turn out to be unimportant. For example, a result might be a tiny effect, and unimportant because of its size, even though the null hypothesis was rejected. The reason "significant" is used is partly historical—because the *t*-test was so useful, it was used before it was fully understood—and partly because researchers have not been able to find a good replacement term. Some researchers have suggested that "reliable" be used, to indicate that an IV effect is likely to produce a real effect again, in a replication, because it is a real effect rather than an effect of chance. However, this term also has problems. The important point for you is that "significance" has the very limited meaning given above.

A BIG *t* MEANS LITTLE

In the same way that statistical significance can be misleading, the size of a *t* value can be misleading. A large *t* can be obtained with a tiny, unimportant IV effect. The main way to get a large *t* is to use a huge sample, because it results in a small standard error of difference. Other concepts are more meaningful than a large *t*.

YOU NEVER PROVE THE NULL HYPOTHESIS

This idea was mentioned in Chapter 6 and it bears repeating. Remember the Type II error? This error occurs when the IV effect is too small to detect in an experiment. The IV effect was in the likely region, so we did not reject the null hypothesis even though it was incorrect. Because we can make this error, we can never prove the null hypothesis. We can accept it as a reasonable explanation, keeping in mind that someone else could come up with a more sensitive experiment that would result in rejection of the null hypothesis. As the statisticians say, never "accept the null hypothesis as true or proven." It is most accurate to say that you "fail to reject the null hypothesis."

RELATIONS RELEVANT TO STATISTICAL DECISIONS

So what exactly does a significant *t*-test mean? To understand this, we need to discuss two concepts that are somewhat related to *t*-values. One concept is *effect size*, which is the measure of how large an IV effect is. The second concept is *power*, which is the ability to avoid accepting the null hypothesis when an IV effect occurs (introduced in Chapter 6). The concepts are related but also distinct. Once you can distinguish between these ideas and *t* values, you will have a good handle on the meaning of the *t*-test.

EFFECT SIZE

Effect size is a meaningful measure of how large the effect in an experiment is. The critical feature of effect size is that it compares the size of the IV effect to the variances (the standard deviations squared) in the samples, which do not depend on sample size. (In contrast, the *t*-test compares the IV effect to standard error, which is misleading because it depends on sample size—you can get a small standard error by using a large sample size.) We want effect size to depend on the IV effect, not on sample size. To see this, compute the *t* values for the two cases in Table 7.4. Ask yourself why they are different. Is one effect size larger? Then read the following paragraph.

TABLE 7.4. Calculating the *t*-Values in Two Cases

	CASE A		CASE B	
	CONTROL	EXPERIMENTAL	CONTROL	EXPERIMENTAL
Mean	26	20	26	20
SD	4	4	4	4
n	8	8	32	32

The IV effects were the same in these two cases ($26 - 20 = 6$). Yet, one t value was much larger (6.0 in case B versus 3.0 in case A; check the calculations[4]). Why was one value much larger? Because it had a larger sample size, which produces more accurate means and a smaller, more accurate SDODBM. This is not relevant to effect size. Instead, effect size is calculated with a formula developed by Jacob Cohen:

[4] Case A: $6/\sqrt{(4^2/8 + 4^2/8)} = 6/\sqrt{(4)} = 6/2$; case B: $6/\sqrt{(4^2/32 + 42/32)} = 6/\sqrt{(1)} = 6/1$.

Cohen's *d*

$$d = \frac{\overline{X}_1 - \overline{X}_2}{\sqrt{\dfrac{SD_1^1}{2} + \dfrac{SD_2^2}{2}}}$$

Apply the formula to our two cases in Table 7.4 and read on.

As you can see, the value of *d* is 1.5 in each case (check your work[5]); this tells us that these two effect sizes are equal. The effect size statistic can be especially useful when comparing results of different studies. Given a value of *d*, you will also want to ask, how large of a value is "large." Table 7.5 gives general conventions. As you can see, the effect we calculated was large in size.

TABLE 7.5.   Convention for Interpreting Effect Size

EFFECT SIZE (*d*)	INTERPRETATION
0.20	Small
0.50	Medium
0.80	Large

POWER

The other distinct concept is power. Recall that **power** is the ability to avoid acceptance of the null hypothesis when an IV effect occurs (Type II error). The concept is illustrated in Figure 7.5. Recall that the dashed distribution is a fictitious SDODBM

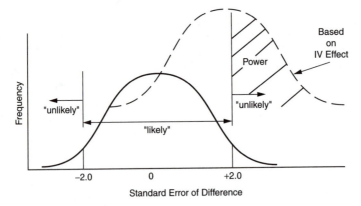

FIGURE 7.5.   The likely and unlikely regions within a sampling distribution of the difference between means, with 30 df. Power corresponds to the area indicated under the curve.

[5] The two cases are the same because the SDs are used but the n's are not:

$$d = 6/\sqrt{(4^2/2 + 4^2/2)} = 6/\sqrt{(16)} = 6/4 = 1.5.$$

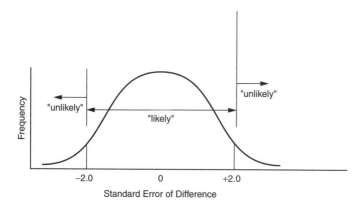

FIGURE 7.6.   Your drawing with a larger IV effect.

based on the assumption that there was an IV effect. The bottom distribution is the SDODBM based on the null hypothesis, with 30 df. Power corresponds to area to the right of the decision border in the figure. It is the proportion of times that a real IV effect will be concluded to be, in fact, real. Refer to the end of Chapter 6 if you need further review.

Power increases with two factors. First, it increases when the effect size is large. Large effect sizes would push the dashed distribution (the SDODBM for the IV effect) further away from the null distribution (further right in the present example). Second, power increases when the standard error becomes smaller. This has the effect of making both distributions more narrow and, consequently, more separate from each other.

To make this idea clear in your mind, redraw Figure 7.5 to illustrate what it would look like if power were increased (Figures 7.6 and 7.7). First, make the IV effect larger by moving the dashed SDODBM to the right (Figure 7.6). Second, redraw both SDODBMs with less error—make the distributions more narrow (Figure 7.7). Add labels, using pencil if you are unsure.

FIGURE 7.7.   Your drawing with a reduced error.

PUTTING THIS TOGETHER: *t*-VALUES AND RESEARCH DESIGN

We are now ready to bring the concepts together in the context of research design. Let's begin by focusing on the *t* formula and its relation to an experiment.

The *t* summarizes the relation between an IV effect and the error in an experiment, as shown in Figure 7.8. The IV effect increases directly with effect size. Error is

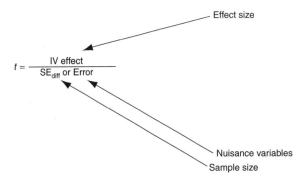

FIGURE 7.8.   Influences on *t* values.

measured by the standard error (SEdiff), and it is a function of two things: raw error, which is the effect of nuisance variables, and sample size (because the error of sample means increases with smaller samples). Because of these relations, the SDODBM, which is the distribution of *t* values, is meaningfully related to chance. However, to get a measure of effect size we need to remove the effects of sample size using Cohen's *d*.

One problem with our *t*-test is that it will sometimes have low power, meaning that Type II errors are likely. In theory, power can be increased, as you illustrated earlier. More practically, how do we increase power? These are considerations of experimental design, and they are meaningfully related to the *t* formula.

In the top part of the formula in Figure 7.8, we can increase power if we can make the IV effect larger. Sometimes this means using stronger manipulations of the IV or perhaps a more sensitive dependent variable. This would push the distribution for the IV effect further from the null hypothesis, as should occur in Figure 7.6. In the bottom part of the formula, we can do two types of things. First, we can reduce the effects of nuisance variables with methods of experimental control, such as holding extraneous variables constant. Second, we can increase sample size so that our sample means will be more accurate. Both of the changes make the SDODBM more narrow, as should occur in your second illustration (Figure 7.7).

To review, let's say that you are studying a weak but very interesting IV. How would you make your experiment powerful? Write your answers in the space provided and if you have problems reread the previous sections.

EFFECTS OF CONFOUNDS

Finally, remember *confounds?* Confounds are extraneous variables that influence one group more than the other in the long run. For example, as in Chapter 2, an extraneous noise may be much louder for the experimental group than for the control group. Because confounds influence one group more than the other, the effects of confounds would be reflected in the means and the differences between them. How do confounds influence the *t* formula? Answer and then read on.

```
[empty box]
```

Confounds influence the top part of the *t* ratio, making it larger or smaller than it really should be. A confound could turn a null effect into one that appears real, or it could turn a real effect into what appears to be a null effect. Thus, confounds are seriously misleading—they confound the investigator. That is why they are so bad.

SOME MORE DETAILS

You have now learned all of the big concepts, but there are a few important details remaining. They are covered here.

STANDARD ERROR OF THE DIFFERENCE, PART 2: UNEQUAL SAMPLE SIZE

The formula you have used for the SE_{diff} applies to experiments with equal sample sizes ($n_1 = n_2$). When your groups have differing sample sizes, a slightly more complex formula is necessary. This formula gives the proper weight to the error in each group:

Standard Error of Difference with Unequal Sample Sizes

$$\text{SE}_{\text{diff}} = \sqrt{\frac{(n_1 - 1)\,\text{SD}_1^2 + (n_2 - 1)\,\text{SD}_2^2}{n_1 + n_2 - 2}}$$

YOU'VE LEARNED ABOUT ONE TYPE OF *t*-TEST: *t*-TEST FOR INDEPENDENT SAMPLES

You have learned the most typical version of the *t*-test. It is for between-subject designs, in which you have two samples of participants. The samples should be independent from each other, meaning there is no relation between the participants in the two samples (e.g., each sample was randomly selected). In fact, the most precise name for the test you've learned is ***t*-test for independent samples.** A second type of *t*-test follows.

In the interest of consolidating this in your mind, write down the name of the first *t*-test. What is crucial about the groups? Add any other comments that will help to distinguish this statistic in your mind.

t-TEST FOR DEPENDENT SAMPLES

In some cases, there is a relation between two samples of participants—they depend on each other in some way, rather than being independent. For example, you might match pairs of participants, so that each participant in one sample is matched with another participant in the other sample on a relevant variable. In fact, you could use the most extreme form of matching: a within-participant design, in which each person participates in each condition. Thus, each participant is matched with him- or herself. In these cases, you use a simpler formula for the *t*-test. This is called the ***t*-test for dependent samples.** It is easier to compute than the *t*-test you have learned.

t-Test for Dependent Samples: The Procedure.   When there is a relation between the two samples, the analysis becomes easier because you work with pairs. Each pair is like a mini-experiment. The null hypothesis is that the difference between the pairs is zero. The researcher's hypothesis is that the difference is larger than zero.

The calculations are illustrated in Table 7.6. You begin by listing the pairs of scores (Score1 and Score2), and then calculating the difference between them, *D*. Then you calculate the mean difference and put it in column 4. Next, you calculate the deviation of each pair's difference from the mean difference (column 5), and square the deviations (column 6). You calculate the SD of the *D* values, using the sum of the squared de-

TABLE 7.6.   Calculating a *t*-Test for Dependent Samples.

PAIRS	1. SCORE 1	2. SCORE 2	3. DIFF (*D*)	4. MEAN *D*	5. DEVIATION	6. DEV. SQ.
X_1	4	2	2	2	0	0
X_2	5	4	1	2	−1	1
X_3	3	1	2	2	0	0
X_4	6	3	3	2	1	1
Sum = 18		10	8			2
Mn/Vr = 4.5		2.5	2			

$$SD^2 = 2/n - 1 = 2/3$$
then take square root to get SD:
$$SD = 0.8165$$

IV effect			= 2
SE_{diff}			= 0.8165/sq.rt.(4)
			= 0.8165|/2
			= 0.4082
t			= 2/0.4082 = 4.90

Note: We have pairs X_1 through X_4; each pair has two scores (Score1 and Score2), and a difference *D*. The degrees of freedom is as follows: df = *n* − 1 (where *n* is number of pairs). Use values for $t_{critical}$ from the *t* table.

viations and n-1 from the number of *pairs*. Then you calculate the standard error of the differences and the t from these formulas:

$$SE_{diff} = \frac{SD}{\sqrt{n}}$$

where the SD comes from the differences, and n is the number of pairs

$$t = \frac{\overline{D}}{SE_{diff}}$$

REVIEW

Define and elaborate on the following terms:
t formula

$t_{obtained}$ and $t_{critical}$

Effects of sample size on t distribution

Degrees of freedom

Finding t values in a table

One-tailed t-test

Two-tailed t-test

Statistical significance

Effect size

Power

Independent vs. dependent sample

t-test for dependent samples

EXERCISES

7.1. A consumer group wants to find out if the type of gasoline used in a car has an effect on the number of miles per gallon. Two brands of gasoline were tested in 10 exactly similar cars. The miles per gallon (mpg) are shown below for each car.

BRAND A	BRAND B
19	16
24	22
21	20
23	15
14	13

    a. Compute the mean and standard deviation for each brand.
    b. Compute the IV effect and standard error.
    c. Compute t.
    d. Compute degrees of freedom.
    e. Determine $t_{critical}$. Use a one-tailed test; level of significance $=0.05$. Compare to $t_{obtained}$. Does the brand of gas have an effect on the miles per gallon?

7.2.   The effects of radiation on time for mice to learn a specific behavior are being studied by a psychology graduate student. Samples of exposed and nonexposed mice are taught the behavior. The sample statistics are summarized here:

EXPOSED	NONEXPOSED
$N = 25$	$N = 25$
Mean = 15 minutes	Mean = 13.5 minutes
Variance = 2.0 minutes	Variance = 1.5 minutes
SD = 1.414 minutes	SD = 1.225

    a. Compute the IV effect and standard error.
    b. Compute t.
    c. Compute degrees of freedom.
    d. Is there evidence at the 0.05 significance level that exposed and nonexposed groups differ in the time required to learn the behavior?

7.3.   Sally works for a tobacco company that wants to know which type of stop-smoking drug is most effective so that it can market the most effective drug and replenish its market share lost from people who quit smoking.

DRUG X	DRUG Y
10	6
12	5
13	4
10	6
9	4
10	7
11	8
12	9
13	6
10	5

    a. What is the mean and SD for each type of drug?
    b. What is the IV effect and SE?
    c. What is t and df?
    d. Is one drug more effective than the other in helping people to quit?
    e. What could be a problem with the design of the study? What could be an ethical problem for the tobacco company in marketing an aid to quit smoking?

7.4.   We want to know if motorists in red vehicles receive more traffic citations than motorists in white vehicles. The data is in citations per year.

RED	WHITE
1	0
2	0
1	2
3	1
4	0

a. What is the mean and SD of each color of car?
b. Compute the IV effect and SE.
c. Compute *t* and df.
d. Does the color of car have an effect on the number of yearly citations?

7.5. In this problem, a maker of wood protectants wants to know if there is a difference in the amount of time lumber will last once it's treated with one of the two products. Protectant X and protectant Y are applied to several pieces of lumber and placed into a special weather aging environment that ages the wood several years in several days. We have five pieces of lumber treated with each product. Data is given in amount of years before the wood is destroyed by the elements

TYPE OF WOOD	PROTECTANTS
TYPE X	TYPE Y
27	33
25	35
27	35
26	33
25	34

a. Compute the mean and SD for each protectant.
b. Compute the IV effect and SE.
c. Compute *t* and df.
d. Is there a significant difference in number of years wood will last between the two protectants?

7.6. A group of researchers believes that seeking prenatal care during pregnancy results in babies with a higher birth weight. The researchers took a sample of 10 babies born in Tampa, Florida, during a 2-week period. In group 1, all mothers sought prenatal care. In group 2, none of the mothers sought prenatal care during their pregnancies.

GROUP 1 (PRENATAL CARE)	GROUP 2 (NO PRENATAL CARE)
6.38	4.25
5.50	5.50
8.44	6.15
9.00	6.00
9.50	7.56

a. What is the mean and SD of each group?
b. Compute the IV effect and SE.
c. Compute *t* and df.
d. Does prenatal care help to increase birth weight?
e. What would you do to make this a more powerful study?

7.7. You are a relationship counselor. You have a test for couples that tests their relationship satisfaction on a scale from 1 to 10. Each person is matched with his/her relationship partner. (*Hint:* See "*t*-test for Dependent Samples" in this chapter.)

PAIRS	FEMALE SCORE	MALE SCORE
X_1	3	5
X_2	4	5
X_3	8	10
X_4	9	9
X_5	6	7

a. What is the mean?
b. What is the IV effect?
c. What is the SD?
d. What is the SE?
e. What is the df?
f. What is $t_{obtained}$ and $t_{critical}$?
g. Is the difference between these matched pairs significant? The scores on the left are the female scores and the scores on the right are the male scores. What conclusions would you draw from your relationship tests?

ANSWERS

7.1.　a. mean of A = 20.2; mean of B = 17.2; SD of A = 3.96; SD of B = 3.7
　　　b. IV effect = 3; SE = 2.4
　　　c. 3/2.4 = 1.25
　　　d. df = 5 + 5 − 2 = 8
　　　e. $t_{critical}$ = 1.86; 1.25 < 1.86; therefore, accept null hypothesis that brand of gas does not effect mpg

7.3

				TYPE OF TEST DRUG				
		DRUG X					DRUG Y	
	Score	Mean	Devtn.	Square	Score	Mean	Devtn.	Square
1	10	11	−1	1	11　6	6	0	0
2	12	11	1	1	12　5	6	−1	1
3	13	11	2	4	13　4	6	−2	4
4	10	11	−1	1	14　6	6	0	0
5	9	11	−2	4	15　4	6	−2	4
6	10	11	−1	1	16　7	6	1	1
7	11	11	0	0	17　8	6	2	4
8	12	11	1	1	18　9	6	3	9
9	13	11	2	4	19　6	6	0	0
10	10	11	−1	1	20　5	6	−1	1
Mean = 11			Sum = 18		Mean = 6		Sum = 24	
SD = 1.414			Var = 2		SD = 1.63		Var = 2.667	
				SE_{diff} = 0.683				
				t = 7.32				

a. mean (drug X) = 11, SD = 1.41; mean (drug Y) = 6, SD = 1.63
b. IV effect = 6 − 11 = −5; SE = 0.683
c. $t = 7.32^*$; df = 10 + 10 − 2 = 18 (* means statistically significant)
d. $t_{critical}$ = 2.10. Yes, drug Y helps people quit in an average of 6 weeks versus drug X, which takes an average of 11 weeks
e. The major problem with this study is that it tells us how long it takes for people to quit, but it does not tell us how long people remain nonsmokers and that would be the more important effect. The major ethical problem here is that when you create a substance which addicts people and then provide a way to conquer that addition, a conflict of interest arises.

7.5

	SCORE	MEAN	DEVTN.	SQUARE			SCORE	MEAN	DEVTN.	SQUARE
1	27	26	1	1		6	33	34	−1	1
2	25	26	−1	1		7	35	34	1	1
3	27	26	1	1		8	35	34	1	1
4	26	26	0	0		9	33	34	−1	1
5	25	26	−1	1		10	34	34	0	0
Mean = 26			Sum = 4			Mean 34			Sum = 4	
SD = 1			Var = 1			SD = 1			Var = 1	

$$SE_{diff} = 0.632$$
$$t = -12.65$$

a. mean (X) = 26, SD = 1; mean (Y) = 34, SD = 1
b. IV effect = 34 − 26 = 8; SE = 0.632
c. $t = -12.65$; df = 8
d. $t_{critical} = -2.603$; $t(8) = -12.65^*$. There is a significant difference between number of years for protectant X and protectant Y. Protectant Y treated wood lasts an average of 8 years longer than wood treated with protectant X.

7.7. a. mean (diff) = −1.2
b. IV effect = −1.2
c. SD = 0.84
d. $SE_{diff} = 0.37$
e. df = 4
f. $t_{obtained} = -3.21$; $t_{critical} = -2.78$
g. $t(4) = -3.21^*$. The difference between male and female scores on the relationship questionnaire is significant. Males scored a mean of 7.2 and females scored a mean of 6.0. We could say that males are happier than females with their relationships. However, there may be other reasons for this difference, such as females rate their happiness lower even though it is equal to males. A self-report test like this is also very subjective.

Chapter 8

EXPANDING OUR THINKING TO n DIMENSIONS: ANALYSIS OF VARIANCE

Looking back, you should be able to appreciate that the t-test is an achievement with a lot of thought behind it. Would you like that thought to help you with our next statistic? Happily, it does! It will help us with the F-test, also called *analysis of variance.* In our journey, we will be crossing a bridge toward an understanding of analysis of variance.

In a very real sense, analysis of variance is a mind-expanded version of the t-test. It allows you to ask more sophisticated questions than the t-test, including multidimensional questions—questions about the effects of more than one independent variable. We begin by looking at the types of questions you can ask with analysis of variance. This in itself is an important thing to know. The discussion will begin with the people who invented the two tests because their personalities are related to the nature of the tests. Then we focus on the simplest type of F-test and cover the thinking behind it, step by step. Our emphasis is on understanding rather than efficient computation. Computers have mastered computation; the critical task for humans is understanding what the computations mean.

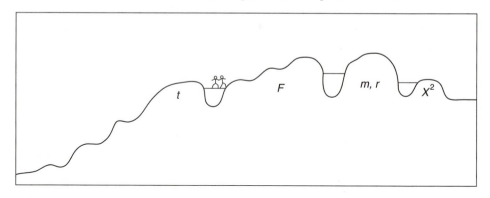

GOSSET AND FISHER

The person who invented the t-test, William Gosset, was employed by Guiness brewery. He had degrees in mathematics and chemistry, but his love was applying elegant formulas to practical problems. He liked formulas that he could compute in his head, and he often worked on the back of envelopes. He wrote under a pen name ("Student"), perhaps because his employers did not want the public to suspect that there was "error" in their "samples." Yet, Gosset was in fact employed to find a way to measure error in the samples of beer. He invented the t-test, which was a creative and elegant solution. However, it was not highly refined mathematically. Then along came Sir Ronald Fisher, who was reputed to think in n dimensions at once. He was a mathematical genius and very systematic. Fisher used the insights behind Gosset's invention and turned them into an elegant system of statistical analyses. The statistic is called the F-test, and the entire system is known as the **Analysis of variance,** which is often abbreviated as **ANOVA.**

ANOVA has a tremendous advantage over the *t*-test. The *t*-test is meant for pairs of means; it cannot handle experiments with more than two means. However, larger experiments are often very informative. In fact, larger experiments can provide considerable additional information with a minimal increase in the amount of time researchers and participants need to spend. ANOVA can handle larger experiments in an elegant manner.

For example, let's say we wanted to compare the effectiveness of different study methods. Our participants study a textbook chapter on a new topic and then we test their understanding. The dependent variable (DV) is the test score; the independent variable (IV) is the study method. Let's make the control group a "just read" condition. The other group could be a "read and underline" condition. But would we want to stop here? There are other study methods, such as "read and outline." Thanks to ANOVA, we can compare more than two groups at the same time. The expanded, better experiment is described in Figure 8.1. Note that we have one IV (study method) but it has three "levels" (three different conditions, or groups of participants, or samples). This is called a **multilevel design.**

IV$_A$: Study Method

Condition 1/Level 1	Condition 2/Level 2	Condition 3/Level 3
Just Read	Read and Underline	Read and Outline

FIGURE 8.1. Description of a Three-Level Design.

There is another way that we can expand our experiment that is perhaps even more important: We can use more than one IV. For example, it might be that the effectiveness of the study method depends on the topic that is studied. Perhaps one method is best for topics like history and another best for topics like mathematics. By using both types of topics, we can create a much more informative experiment. To do so, we term the study method "IV$_A$," where the "A" represents the first IV. Then we add the second IV, IV$_B$ (topic matter). It can have two levels, for example, B$_1$ (history) and B$_2$ (math). This is called a **factorial design** because the conditions in the experiment multiply—each IV is a factor that is multiplied to provide the full design. In the present case, the three levels of study method combine with the two levels of topic matter to yield six conditions, as shown in Figure 8.2. I've filled in two of the combinations; can you fill in the rest?

IV$_A$: Study Method

		Level 1	Level 2	Level 3
		Just Read	Read and Underline	Read and Outline
	Level 1:	A$_1$B$_1$	A$_2$B$_1$	
	History	Just Read,		
		History		
IV$_B$: Topic				
	Level 2:			A$_3$B$_2$
	Math			Read and Outline,
				Math

FIGURE 8.2. Description of a Factorial Design.

ANOVA allows us to analyze larger experiments like those shown in Figure 8.2. In fact, you can analyze any experiment, no matter how many IVs are used, as long as your computer is big enough. We will discuss factorial designs in Chapter 10, where you will see a completed Figure 8.2. In summary:

ANOVA can be used

1. Compare more than two groups
2. Analyze the effects of more than one independent variable.

Yet, ANOVA is simply an expansion of the basic ideas of the *t*-test. In this chapter, we cover the simplest form of ANOVA, which is equivalent to the *t*-test—ANOVA for one independent variable with two levels. We focus on ANOVA for between-participant designs because they are easiest. After you learn this basic ANOVA, you should find it easy to expand the idea to more than two levels and more than one independent variable in the two chapters that follow.

I begin by introducing some main pieces used in ANOVA, which are very similar to the "influences" in the *t*-test. Remember these influences? They were the **IV effect** and **error.** In Chapter 2, we saw that these influences appear in each score. Fisher's method for ANOVA involves breaking each score into these influences, which he called *sources of variability,* and then working directly with the variability.

INFLUENCES OF A SCORE, PART 1: REMINDER FROM THE *t*-TEST

In many ways, the *F*-test is like the *t*-test. Our thinking begins with individual scores, within which we can find IV effects and error. Then the IV effect and error become summarized at higher levels, and we calculate the statistic by dividing the IV effect by error.

Table 8.1 is the example you saw in Chapter 2 for decomposing scores. Look it over. As you can see, the IV effect came from the two sample means. The error came from the deviations of individual scores from the means. Note that we are now using the terms *sample 1* and *sample 2* in place of *experimental group* and *control group.* This is because we will soon have more than two groups.

TABLE 8.1.   Two Influences That Add Together to Make the Scores

	SAMPLE 1					SAMPLE 2			
	START	IV EFFECT	ERROR	SCORE		START	IV EFFECT	ERROR	SCORE
1.	10	0	−2	= 8	7.	10	3	−3	=10
2.	10	0	−1	= 9	8.	10	3	+3	=16
3.	10	0	+2	=12	9.	10	3	−1	=12
4.	10	0	−3	= 7	10.	10	3	+1	=14
5.	10	0	+3	=13	11.	10	3	?	=11
6.	10	0	+1	=11	12.	10	3	?	=15
Mean				10	Mean				13

The *t*-test is a comparison between the IV effect and error. However, for simplicity, I left one relationship out of our meaningful *t* formula. This relation does not change how we calculate the *t*-test, but it does add to how we think about it. The relation is that **sampling error** influences the size of the IV effect. Sampling error is error in means of samples (see Chapter 5.) Its place in the formula is

$$t = \text{IV effect } (+\text{Sampling error})/\text{Error}$$

Sampling error has always been there. Ultimately, it is caused by the same source as the error in the bottom—by deviations in individual scores. However, sampling error takes the form of error in sample means.

So, to summarize, there are two main categories of influences:

1. IV effect + Sampling error, which comes from differences between the means, $\overline{X}_1 - \overline{X}_2$
2. Error, which comes from deviations, $X_i - \overline{X}$.

🚶 **CONCEPTUALIZATION:**

INFLUENCES OF A SCORE, PART 2

Fisher reworked the definitions of these influences so they could be applied to experiments with more than two samples. We study his definitions now, and then arrange the numbers so ANOVA will be easy to calculate.

To provide a more flexible measurement of IV effects, Fisher added the idea of the **grand mean.** The grand mean is the mean of all scores in the experiment. It is helpful to think of it as the *starting point of all scores.* The reasons for this will soon be clear. In our familiar experiment, the grand mean is $(13 + 10)/2 = 11.5$.

> The **grand mean** is symbolized as
> $$\overline{X}_G$$
> It is the starting point of all scores.

Remember that the IVs are now designated A, B, and so on. The means of each level of A are designated as follows:

> **Means of levels** are symbolized as
> $\overline{X}_A$ in general, and for specific levels as $\overline{X}_{A1}$, $\overline{X}_{A2}$, and so on.

In calculating IV effects, Fisher used **differences from the grand mean.** Thus, in ANOVA,

$$\text{IV effect} = \overline{X}_{A_1} - \overline{X}_G \quad \text{or} \quad \overline{X}_{A_2} - \overline{X}_G$$

In an experiment with two conditions, the IV effect in ANOVA is half that with the *t*-test. You can see this in our example experiment. For the *t*-test, the IV effect was defined by the difference between the means $(13 - 10 = 3)$. Now, in ANOVA, the IV effect becomes $(13 - 11.5 = 1.5)$ and $(10 - 11.5 = -1.5)$.

Fisher's measure of error was the same as in the *t*-test. It uses **deviations from the sample mean:**

$$\text{Error} = X_i - \overline{X}_A$$

There is one more important point involving a "model." The model is based on Fisher's insight that we can find each of the influences—IV effect and error—within each and every score in an experiment. Thus, we can think of each score as being composed in the following way:

$$X_i = \overline{X}_G + (\text{IV effect}) + (\text{error})$$

Using symbols this is

$$X_i = \overline{X}_G + (\overline{X}_A - \overline{X}_G) + (X_i - \overline{X}_A)$$

This model may seem abstract, but it becomes easy to understand if we attach meaning to it. When applied to the first participant's score in our (now familiar) experiment, the model says

$$\overline{X}_G + (\text{IV effect}) + (\text{error}) = \text{Participant 1's score}$$

or

$$11.5 + (1.5) + (-3) = 10$$

The model can be applied to each score in the experiment, as it is in Table 8.2. Let's begin by thinking about what the model is: The model is simply a list of the influences on a behavioral score. Consider the first participant as an example. The model says that this person's score starts out at the grand mean. This starting point is the same as for every individual's score, as you can see for the other participants listed in the table. Then the score for participant 1 is influenced by the IV. This time, the effect is the same size as for every other person within the condition. The last influence is the error. The amount of error is unique for every individual; error creates the deviations from the sample mean. Put this model into practice by calculating the scores for the four unfinished participants in the table. You will find the influences for each participant in Table 8.4.

TABLE 8.2. Additive Model Applied to Our Experiment

	SAMPLE 1					SAMPLE 2			
	$\overline{X}_G$	IV	ERROR	SCORE		$\overline{X}_G$	IV	ERROR	SCORE
1.	11.5	+1.5	−3	= 10	7.	11.5	−1.5	−2	= 8
2.	11.5	+1.5	+3	= 16	8.	11.5	−1.5	−1	= 9
3.	11.5	+1.5	−1	= 12	9.	11.5	−1.5	+2	=12
4.	11.5	+1.5	+1	= 14	10.	11.5			= 7
5.	11.5	+1.5	−2	= 11	11.	11.5			=13
6.				= 15	12.	11.5			=11
$\overline{X}_{A_1} = 13$					$\overline{X}_{A_2} = 10$				

$$\overline{X}_G = 11.5$$

DONE! ⅄

⚘ CONCEPTUALIZATION:

THE MODEL

Our thinking is this: For each score there is a starting point—the grand mean—and two sources—the IV effect and error, which are simply added to the grand mean. You will see these two sources throughout the ANOVA study, so don't forget them.

There is one other important aspect of this model: the idea the two sources, IV effect and error, simply add together. This is one of those simpleminded, but very important, ideas. It is an important assumption. It means that each source is independent of the other sources; the IV effect and error do not influence each other when they are combined. We will call this the **additive model.** (The more general name is *general linear model.*)

It is important that you understand the additive model. Therefore, Table 8.3 provides another, somewhat smaller example for you to work. Begin with the sample means and calculate a grand mean, and then form the deviations. Enter them in them in the appropriate columns. Once you've completed the whole table, you will be ready to rearrange the numbers and then do the ANOVA. The answers are given in Table 8.4.

TABLE 8.3. Applying the Additive Model to a Smaller Experiment

	$\bar{X}_G$	IV	ERROR	SCORE		$\bar{X}_G$	IV	ERROR	SCORE
		SAMPLE 1					SAMPLE 2		
1.				= 7	5.				=3
2.				= 5	6.				=7
3.				= 4	7.				=6
4.				= 8	8.				=4
				$\bar{X}_{A_1} = 13$					$\bar{X}_{A_2} = 10$
				$\bar{X}_G =$					

This idea is quite abstract. Use this space to summarize the idea in your own words. Illustrations and formulas are allowed.

TABLE 8.4.   Completed Table 8.3

	SAMPLE 1					SAMPLE 2			
	$\overline{X}_G$	IV	ERROR	SCORE		$\overline{X}_G$	IV	ERROR	SCORE
1.	5.5	+0.5	1	= 7	5.	5.5	−0.5	−2	= 3
2.	5.5	+0.5	−1	= 5	6.	5.5	−0.5	2	= 7
3.	5.5	+0.5	−2	= 4	7.	5.5	−0.5	1	= 6
4.	5.5	+0.5	2	= 8	8.	5.5	−0.5	−1	= 4
			$\overline{X}_{A_1} = 6$					$\overline{X}_{A_2} = 5.5$	
			$\overline{X}_G = 5.5$						

DONE!   ⅄

REARRANGING THE DEVIATIONS

For our next step, let's begin by presenting a very helpful fact: If you add the deviations due to error and the IV, you get what is called the *total deviation*. We now define this relationship and use it to calculate ANOVA.

To understand the relationships between the deviations, let's start with our additive model:

$$X_i = \overline{X}_G + (\overline{X}_A - \overline{X}_G) + (X_i - \overline{X}_A)$$

Using math, we can subtract a grand mean from both sides of the equation. We simply subtract an $\overline{X}_G$ from the left side and erase it from the right side (since there was an $\overline{X}_G$ on the right already):

$$(X_i - \overline{X}_G) = (\overline{X}_A - \overline{X}_G) + (X_i - \overline{X}_A)$$

The part on the left side is the **total deviation;** it is the total deviation of an individual's score from the grand mean. Thus, in words our rearranged model is as follows:

The Model for ANOVA

Total deviation = IV effect + Error

SUMS OF SQUARED DEVIATIONS

In summary, each score has three important deviations. You know the meaning of the IV effect and error. Total deviations simply their total; it has no further meaning but it will be very useful. These three deviations will be important throughout the ANOVA. You will transform them into **sums of squares:** You will calculate the three deviations for each participant, square them, and then sum the squares across all participants (as will be explained). You end up with three sums of squares, one for each deviation. To make the calculation of sums of squares easy to learn, we will use **deviation tables.** Deviation tables are unique to this book; their purpose is to make the analysis of variance meaningful and easy to remember.

DEVIATION TABLES

The numbers from our familiar experiment have been arranged into a deviation table in Table 8.5. The table looks imposing but is actually very simple if you take it step by step.

To begin, note that sample 1 is now *above* sample 2. This is because we will want to sum numbers for both samples when we do ANOVA; we will simply sum certain columns. Next, note the three headings: Total, IV, and Error. These are our three types of deviation, and they produce the three types of sums of squares. Within each type of deviation, we do the same three things, producing three columns in each case. First, we list the deviation (columns 1, 4, and 7). Next, we do the subtractions and enter the resultant deviations (columns 2, 5, and 8). Finally, we square the deviations and enter the "squares" in the last set of columns (3, 6, and 9). The reason for using squares will become apparent shortly.

Study Table 8.5 carefully. In particular, look at the deviations under the "IV" column. They look pretty similar, don't they? Indeed, the IV effect is assumed to be the same for every participant. Look at the deviations under "Error" in column 8 They are different for every participant. Which participants contributed the most error? Those participants contributed more error because they were extreme within their group; their scores were more different from the group mean (meaning there was a stronger effect of nuisance variables).

TABLE 8.5.   Deviation Table for Our Familiar Experiment

	TOTAL			IV(BETWEEN)			ERROR (WITHIN)		
	1. TOTAL DEV	2. TOTAL DEV	3. TOTAL SQUARE	4. IV DEV	5. IV DEV	6. IV SQUARE	7. ERROR DEV	8. ERROR DEV	9. ERR. SQUARE
				Sample 1					
1.	$10 - 11.5$	-1.5	2.25	$13 - 11.5$	1.5	2.25	$10 - 13$	-3	9
2.	$16 - 11.5$	4.5	20.25	$13 - 11.5$	1.5	2.25	$16 - 13$	3	9
3.	$12 - 11.5$	0.5	0.25	$13 - 11.5$	1.5	2.25	$12 - 13$	-1	1
4.	$14 - 11.5$	2.5	6.25	$13 - 11.5$	1.5	2.25	$14 - 13$	1	1
5.	$11 - 11.5$	-0.5	0.25	$13 - 11.5$	1.5	2.25	$11 - 13$	-2	4
6.	$15 - 11.5$	3.5	12.25	$13 - 11.5$	1.5	2.25	$15 - 13$	2	4
				Sample 2					
7.	$8 - 11.5$	-3.5	12.25	$10 - 11.5$	-1.5	2.25	$8 - 10$	-2	4
8.	$9 - 11.5$	-2.5	6.25	$10 - 11.5$	-1.5	2.25	$9 - 10$	-1	1
9.	$12 - 11.5$	0.5	0.25	$10 - 11.5$	-1.5	2.25	$12 - 10$	2	4
10.	$7 - 11.5$	-4.5	20.25	$10 - 11.5$	-1.5	2.25	$7 - 10$	-3	9
11.	$13 - 11.5$	1.5	2.25	$10 - 11.5$	-1.5	2.25	$13 - 10$	3	9
12.	$11 - 11.5$	-0.5	0.25	$10 - 11.5$	-1.5	2.25	$11 - 10$	1	1
Sums of squares			____			____			____

Note also the words in parentheses at the top, "Between," which is next to IV, and "Within," which is next to "Error." These words have important meanings:

> **Between** refers to the fact that the basis of the deviations is between groups—the deviations are the differences between the means of the samples (and the grand mean).
> **Within** refers to the fact that error variability is within groups—the deviations are differences between individual scores and the sample mean.
> We use these terms through the rest of this chapter.

⅄ **CONCEPTUALIZATION:**

INFLUENCES AS SOURCES OF VARIANCE

We calculated three types of deviations—for the total, the IV effect, and error. Then we squared them. This turns them into variances. We do this because Fisher had the insight that the math is systematic if we use *variances*. This is the same type of squaring of deviations we did when we calculated the standard deviation and variance in Chapter 3. Let's consider the idea of variance further.

You know error as deviations from the sample mean, caused by nuisance variables. When we square them, the result is **error variance.** This is also called **within-group variance,** because the deviations are deviations of individual scores from the sample mean—they are entirely within the group. Error variance becomes the bottom of our statistical formula for the *F*-test, in the same way that error was the bottom of the *t* formula. Remember that error comes from nuisance variables, and researchers try to minimize error and error variance.

Now for a slightly tricky step: We turn the IV into a source of variance. This time, the variance is *good* variance, because it is due to the IV. This variance is *variance from the grand mean.* Column 6 of the deviation table (Table 8.5) shows the IV variance. Look at this column. In the small experiment that you worked out (Table 8.3), the IV variance came from the deviations you put in the IV column. When the deviations are squared, the result is termed variance due to the IV. It is also called **between-group variance,** because it is based on differences *between* sample means (and the grand mean).

As noted, researchers generally like between-group variance because it is caused by the IV. It will go in the top of the *F* statistic. The researcher usually want lots of variance due to the IV. To help keep this in mind, you can chant this rhyme several times:

> Variance within a bruise on my shin, but variance between—it is supreme.

The distinction involving between-group variance and within-group variance was foreshadowed in the first chapter, when we discussed differences in perceptions of banking among American and Japanese individuals. We contrasted between-country differences (between-groups variation) and within-country differences (within-group variation) (Figure 8.3.)

In addition to within- and between-group variation, we have the totals in columns 1, 2, and 3 of Table 8.5. These are simply the total of the within- and between-group vari-

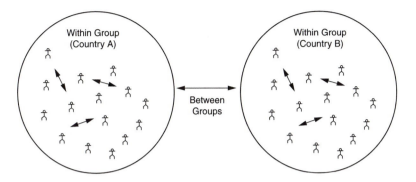

FIGURE 8.3.   An Illustration of Variation Between Groups (the Central Arrow) and within Groups (within Each Circle).

ances (or squares), and they produce the *total variance* (or total squares). The totals are always useful for checking our calculations, because within + between = total.

Now we can sum the variance (squares) in the experiment. Sum (add) the squares in columns 3, 6, and 9 of Table 8.5. In each of those three columns, sum the squares for all 12 participants and put the total at the bottom of the column. These are *sums of squares* or *SS*. Keep in mind what each of the three sums is for:

Sums of squares are variances for

1. Total
2. IV effects (Between-group variance)
3. Error (within-group variance).

In summary, the deviation table gives us the three sums of squares we need. Learn to make the deviation table and you have learned to do much of the ANOVA. The last major step is to relate the sums of squares to each other. Get ready to take that step.

DONE!   𝑋

𝑘   **CONCEPTUALIZATION:**

SOURCE TABLES

Now we are ready to finish the ANOVA. The ANOVA requires only the summed squares that you just calculated and some degrees of freedom. To keep things simple for now, I will provide the degrees of freedom.

The work remaining is to complete what is called a **source table** (also called an *ANOVA table* in some contexts). A source table is organized around the three sources of variance. It creates higher level summaries of the variances that correspond roughly to the higher level statistics you used in calculating *t*.

Table 8.6 has three rows for numbers, which are named after their sources: IV/between, Error/within, and Total. Enter your sums from Table 8.5 in the second column, labeled "Sums of Squares(SS)." (These totals should be 83 for total, 27 for IV, and 56 for error; if not, check your math!) Note that I have provided the third

TABLE 8.6.   Source Table

SOURCE	SUMS OF SQUARES (SS)	df	MS	$F_{obtained}$
IV/between		1		
Error/within		10		
Total (for checking)		11		$F_{crit} = 4.96$

column, degrees of freedom (df). There is a df for the IV, which I will explain later, and a df for error that is similar to the df in the *t*-test. If you add these two, you get the total df.

Once your sums of squares are put in the table, along with the df's I've put in, you are ready to complete the table and calculate *F*. Two steps are involved.

Steps for Completing a Source Table

Step 1. In each row, divide the sums of squares by the df. This gives you *mean squares* for the IV and for error. Enter this under the MS column in Table 8.6.

A **mean square** is the average (mean) of the variance (squares).

Step 2. Divide the means square for the IV by the mean square for error, and that ratio is your obtained *F*. Enter under $F_{obtained}$.

The formula you are using is:

Formula for *F*

$F = Ms_{between}/MS_{within}$ or, conceptually,

$F = $ IV variance/Error variance.

Now you are finished calculating *F*. You will compare $F_{obtained}$ to a critical value for *F* to see if your IV had a real effect. The F_{crit} is written at the bottom right of the table. $F_{obtained}$ should be 4.82. (if it is not, check!) When we compare these two, we see that we have to accept the null hypothesis; this difference falls within the critical region for *F*. (More details are presented later.) The completed table is shown in Table 8.7, but try your hand at Table 8.6 first. Figure 8.4 illustrates the concept of the source table.

TABLE 8.7.   Completed Source Table

SOURCE	SUMS OF SQUARES (SS)	df	MS	$F_{obtained}$
IV/between	27	1	27	$F_{obt} = 4.82$
Total (for checking)	83	11		$F_{crit} = 4.96$

DONE!

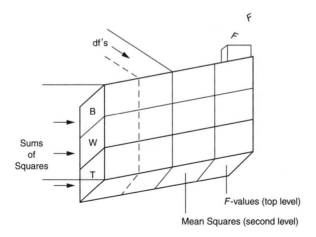

FIGURE 8.4.   The source table as an elevator. The first layer (the left side) is the sums of squares and df's from the raw data. The second level is the mean squares, and the top is the *F* value, which relates between variance to within variance. You can call this the *F elevator*.

CHECKING YOUR CALCULATIONS

Before moving on, let me mention the check we do on our calculations. In the Sums of Squares column, check to make sure that

Sums of squares total = (Sums of squares IV) + (Sums of squares error)

In the df column, check that

Total df = (df_{IV}) + (df_{error}).

Back when computer programs were not available and researchers always used calculators, even for huge studies, they were always happy when these quantities added up. When they did not, the researchers had to push thousands of calculator keys again.

SUMMARY: CALCULATE ANOVA IN TWO EASY TABLES

Thus, the calculations of ANOVA can be organized in terms of two tables. We use the deviation table to separate each score into its component influences and get sums of squares. The source table is then used to compare these variances in the form of the *F* ratio.

The steps for using these tables are summarized at the end of this chapter. You will be given practice calculating *F* ratios in the Exercises section at the end of the chapter. If you would like, start some exercises (calculate *F*) now. In the following sections, I have more to say about *F*.

ॐ   **DEEPER UNDERSTANDING:**

MEANING OF *F*

The *F* ratio provides a way to compare the variance due to the IV to the variance for error. Because there is sampling error in the top (sampling error of the means), the full meaning of the *F* is as follows:

Meaning of the *F* Ratio

F = variance due to IV ($+$error)/Error variance

Remember the null hypothesis? The null hypothesis says the IV has no effect at all. What does this mean in terms of *F* ratios?

Implications of the Null Hypothesis for the *F* Ratio

When the null hypothesis is true, the *F* ratio should usually turn out to be about 1.
The sampling error in the top of the *F* should cause about as much variance as the error in the bottom, which is error variance.

Of course, the *F* will vary above and below that because the amounts of error will vary by chance. The most frequent (modal) value should be 1, however.

When the IV has a real effect, it adds variance to the top. There should be more variance due to the IV than error. The *F* ratio should be greater than 1 (sometimes much greater).

DONE!   𝝙

F DISTRIBUTIONS

Figure 8.5 shows sampling distributions for the *F* under the null hypothesis. Note that the unlikely region begins at the far right—it is the area to the right of the vertical line, or beyond the critical value for F (F_{crit}). The unlikely region begins to the right because Fisher squared everything to make it positive, so that large values will always be at the right side. The critical region is in one tail of the distribution, so in this sense it is a one-tailed test. However, conceptually, the *F*-test is always a two-tailed test because the direction of the difference between the two groups does not matter; a positive and negative difference will provide the same result. **F distributions** are theoretically similar to the sampling distributions of the *t*. They are all based on the idea that the IV has no effect at all. Also, the distribution gets tighter with larger sample sizes, because larger samples produce more accurate means.

Degrees of Freedom and the *F* Table

Any statistical test requires a measure of sample size. In the *F*-test, there are two. One of them is related to the error variance and the number of scores in total (as in the *t*-test). If is df_{error}. It is also called the **df for the denominator** (bottom of *F* ratio) because it is related to the error variance. The other is df_{IV}. It is also called the **df for the numerator** (top of *F* ratio) because it is related to the IV effect. The sampling distribution for the *F* changes with both of the df's so you need to use both. Starting with the top one, they are defined as follows:

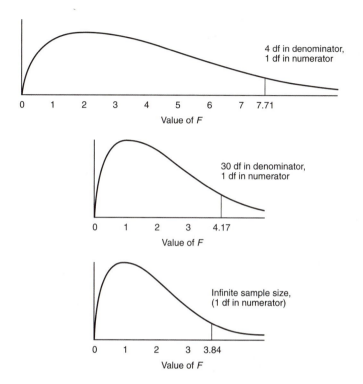

FIGURE 8.5. Three Sampling Distributions of the *F* Statistic, Differing in Total Sample Size. Critical *F* is Shown.

Calculating Degrees of Freedom

$$df_{IV} = df_{numerator} = \text{Number of levels} - 1$$
and
$$df_{Error} = df_{denominator} = \text{Total number of scores} - \text{Number of levels}.$$
There also is a df that is used only for checking calculations:
Total df is calculated from the total number of scores in the experiment, *N*:
$$df_{Total} = N - 1.$$

To find F_{crit}, use both df's to look it up in an *F* table. The values in an *F* table are calculated from a mathematical formula (see, e.g., *Statistics,* by W. L. Hays). A partial *F* table is shown in Table 8.8. Let's use it to find F_{crit} with 2 df for the IV effect ($df_{numerator}$) and 8 df for error ($df_{denominator}$). Begin by using the leftmost column to find the "8" for the $df_{denominator}$. Then find the column headed with "2" for the $df_{numerator}$. What is the value where the 8-row and 2-column meet? You should find it to be 4.46. That would be F_{crit}.

The completed *F* table, shown in Table 8.9, has more rows and columns. Use it to find F_{crit} for these two problems: $df_{IV} = 2$, $df_{error} = 20$; and $df_{numerator} = 8$, $df_{denominator} = 14$. (Check your work.[1])

---

[1] With 2 and 20 df, F_{crit} is 3.49. With 8 and 14 df, F_{crit} is 2.70.

TABLE 8.8.   Partial F-Table

	CRITICAL VALUES OF F $df_{numerator}$			(IV)
$df_{denominator}$(ERROR)	1	2	3	4
1	161.4	199.5	215.7	224.6
2	18.51	19.00	19.16	19.25
3	10.13	9.55	9.28	9.12
4	7.71	6.94	6.59	6.39
5	6.61	5.79	5.41	5.19
6	5.99	5.14	4.76	4.53
7	5.59	4.74	4.35	4.12
8	5.32	4.46	4.07	3.84
9	5.12	4.26	3.86	3.63
10	4.96	4.10	3.71	3.48

REPORTING *F*-TESTS IN ARTICLES

When you read a journal article, you will often find results of F-tests reported in the results sections. You may well be reporting F-tests yourself. The report often looks like this:

"The effect was significant, $F(1, 28) = 11.83$, $p < 0.05$, $MS_e = 870.04$."

The conclusion was that the null hypothesis was rejected because the IV effect appeared to be real. Again, remember that the word *significant* is shorthand for this, and that its meaning is limited to "the null hypothesis was an unlikely explanation." The "(1, 28)" indicates the degrees of freedom, which are 1 for the numerator and 28 for the denominator; "11.83" is the obtained F; and "$p < 0.05$" indicates that a critical region of rejection of 5% was used. The number of tails is not indicated, because it is always the same in the F-test (two tails conceptually, although there is one tail in the distribution). In recent articles, you may also see the exact value of p reported (e.g., "$p = 0.002$"), because this is what statistical programs produce, as noted earlier. Finally, the MS_e is the value of the mean square error from the source table. It is often reported because it can be used to tell how much variability is in the experiment, among other reasons (see an advanced text).

🏃 **DEEPER UNDERSTANDING:**

F'S AND *t*'S

You can calculate both a *t*-test and an F-test on the same two-sample experiment. As it turns out, the value you obtain for F will always be the same as the value for t squared. That is,

$$F = t^2$$

This is not surprising since Fisher squared his quantities. The important point is the similarity of these two conceptualizations. In both, the IV effect is compared to the amount of error in the experiment.

TABLE 8.9. Completed F-Table

Critical Values of F (5% criterion)

$df_{denominator}$ (ERROR)	$df_{numerator}$ (IV)												
	1	2	3	4	5	6	7	8	9	10	20	30	∞
1	161.4	199.5	215.7	224.6	230.2	234.0	236.8	238.9	240.5	241.9	248.0	250.1	254.3
2	18.51	19.00	19.16	19.25	19.30	19.33	19.35	19.37	19.38	19.40	19.45	19.46	19.50
3	10.13	9.55	9.28	9.12	9.01	8.94	8.89	8.85	8.81	8.79	8.66	8.62	8.53
4	7.72	6.94	6.59	6.39	6.26	6.16	6.09	6.04	6.00	5.96	5.80	5.75	5.63
5	6.61	5.79	5.41	5.19	5.05	4.95	4.88	4.82	4.77	4.74	4.56	4.50	4.36
6	5.99	5.14	4.76	4.53	4.39	4.28	4.21	4.15	4.10	4.06	3.87	3.81	3.67
7	5.59	4.74	4.35	4.12	3.97	3.87	3.79	3.73	3.68	3.64	3.44	3.38	3.23
8	5.32	4.46	4.07	3.84	3.69	3.58	3.50	3.44	3.39	3.35	3.15	3.08	2.93
9	5.12	4.26	3.86	3.63	3.48	3.37	3.29	3.23	3.18	3.14	2.94	2.86	2.71
10	4.96	4.10	3.71	3.48	3.33	3.22	3.14	3.07	3.02	2.98	2.77	2.70	2.54
11	4.84	3.98	3.59	3.36	3.20	3.09	3.01	2.95	2.90	2.85	2.65	2.57	2.40
12	4.75	3.89	3.49	3.26	3.11	3.00	2.91	2.85	2.80	2.75	2.54	2.47	2.30
13	4.67	3.81	3.41	3.18	3.03	2.92	2.83	2.77	2.71	2.67	2.46	2.38	2.21
14	4.60	3.74	3.34	3.11	2.96	2.85	2.76	2.70	2.65	2.60	2.39	2.31	2.13
15	4.54	3.68	3.29	3.06	2.90	2.79	2.71	2.64	2.59	2.54	2.33	2.25	2.07
16	4.49	3.63	3.24	3.01	2.85	2.74	2.66	2.59	2.54	2.49	2.28	2.19	2.01
17	4.45	3.59	3.20	2.96	2.81	2.70	2.61	2.55	2.49	2.45	2.23	2.15	1.96
18	4.41	3.55	3.16	2.93	2.77	2.66	2.58	2.51	2.46	2.41	2.19	2.11	1.92
19	4.38	3.52	3.13	2.90	2.74	2.63	2.54	2.48	2.42	2.38	2.16	2.07	1.88
20	4.35	3.49	3.10	2.87	2.71	2.60	2.51	2.45	2.39	2.35	2.12	2.04	1.84
21	4.32	3.47	3.07	2.84	2.68	2.57	2.49	2.42	2.37	2.32	2.10	2.01	1.81
22	4.30	3.44	3.05	2.82	2.66	2.55	2.46	2.40	2.34	2.30	2.07	1.98	1.78
23	4.28	3.42	3.03	2.80	2.64	2.53	2.44	2.37	2.32	2.27	2.05	1.96	1.76
24	4.26	3.40	3.01	2.78	2.62	2.51	2.42	2.36	2.30	2.25	2.03	1.94	1.73
25	4.24	3.39	2.99	2.76	2.60	2.49	2.40	2.34	2.28	2.24	2.01	1.92	1.71
26	4.23	3.37	2.98	2.74	2.59	2.47	2.39	2.32	2.27	2.22	1.99	1.90	1.69
27	4.21	3.35	2.96	2.73	2.57	2.46	2.37	2.31	2.25	2.20	1.97	1.88	1.67
28	4.20	3.34	2.95	2.71	2.56	2.45	2.36	2.29	2.24	2.19	1.96	1.87	1.65
29	4.18	3.33	2.93	2.70	2.55	2.43	2.35	2.28	2.22	2.18	1.94	1.85	1.64
30	4.17	3.32	2.92	2.69	2.53	2.42	2.33	2.27	2.21	2.16	1.93	1.84	1.62
40	4.08	3.23	2.84	2.61	2.45	2.34	2.25	2.18	2.12	2.08	1.84	1.74	1.51
60	4.00	3.15	2.76	2.53	2.37	2.25	2.17	2.10	2.04	1.99	1.75	1.65	1.39
120	3.92	3.07	2.68	2.45	2.29	2.17	2.09	2.02	1.96	1.91	1.66	1.55	1.25
∞	3.84	3.00	2.60	2.37	2.21	2.10	2.01	1.94	1.88	1.83	1.57	1.46	1.00

EFFECTS SIZE AND POWER

Does a large *F* mean that a result is large or important ? I hope your answer was a loud "No!" Remember that an accurate measure of effect size requires that we remove the effects of sample size using an effect-size statistic such as Cohen's *d* (see Chapter 7).

What is power? Power is the ability to avoid Type II errors—accepting the null hypothesis as reasonable when the IV really did have an effect. Which factors increase power?

Power is increased when the effect size is large, when nuisance variables are minimized, and when sample size is increased. Power is an especially critical issue when effect size is small, and this is as relevant for the *F*-test as for the *t*-test.

EFFECTS OF CONFOUNDS

Remember that confounds are extraneous variables that influence one group more than the other, in the long run. How do confounds affect an *F*? Think this out.

Confounds influence the top part of the *F,* making it larger or smaller than it really should be. A confound could turn a null effect into a one that appears real, or it could turn a real effect into what appears to be a null effect. Thus, confounds are seriously misleading—they confound the investigator. That is why they are so bad.

DONE! ⅄

WITHIN-PARTICIPANT DESIGNS

You have learned the ANOVA for a between-participant design, in which each group of participants receives a different treatment. In a different type of design—a within-participant design—participants receive multiple treatments. The principles would be the same but the formula somewhat different for this type of design. The analysis would be analogous to the dependent *t*-test covered in the previous chapter. Refer to an advanced statistics text for details.

⅄   **STEP-BY-STEP METHOD TO LEARN:**

FINAL SUMMARY: CALCULATING ANOVA

HOW TO CALCULATE *F* FOR A BETWEEN-PARTICIPANT DESIGN

1. **Get sums of squares from the deviation table:**
   A. Make a deviation table like that shown in Table 8.10. Include enough rows for the participants, the sample means, and the grand mean. Include 10 columns. The first column, marked 0, should have room for the participant numbers and the original scores (*X*'s).
   B. Calculate means for each sample and the grand mean and enter in column 0.
   C. Using the means, form the deviations in columns 1, 4, and 7, and put the results in columns 2, 5, and 8.
   D. Square the deviations and enter into columns 3, 6, and 9.
   E. Sum the deviations in columns 3, 6, and 9 to get sums of squares. Check that Total = IV + Error
2. **Summarize in source table:**
   A. Make a source table like that shown in Table 8.11 and enter the sums.
   B. Calculate the df's and enter them.
   C. In each row, divide SS by df to get mean squares (MS).
   D. Divide MS_{IV} by MS_{error} to obtain *F*.

TABLE 8.10.   Deviation Table for Two Samples of Six Participants

0. SCORES	TOTAL			IV(BETWEEN)			ERROR (WITHIN)		
	1. TOTAL DEV	2. TOTAL DEV	3. TOTAL SQUARE	4. IV DEV	5. IV DEV	6. IV SQUARE	7. ERROR DEV	8. ERROR DEV	9. ERROR SQUARE
				Sample 1					
1.									
2.									
3.									
4.									
5.									
6.									
$\overline{X}_A =$									
				SAMPLE 2					
7.									
8.									
9.									
10.									
11.									
12.									
$\overline{X}_B =$									
$\overline{X}_G =$									
Sums of squares =									

TABLE 8.11.   Source Table for Any Experiment with One IV

SOURCE	SUMS OF SQUARE (SS)	df	MS	$F_{obtained}$
IV/between				
Error/within				
Total (for checking)				

3. **Compare to F_{crit}:**
   A. Get F_{crit} from the F table using the df's.
   B. Compare $F_{obtained}$ to F_{crit} and make your decision:

   Reject the null hypothesis if $F_{obtained} > F_{crit}$
   Accept the null hypothesis if $F_{obtained} \leq F_{crit}$

REVIEW

Define and expand on the following terms and relationships:

F-test	Sums of squares
Analysis of variance (ANOVA)	Deviation table
Multilevel design	Error variance
Factorial design	Between-group variance
IV effect	Within-group variance

Error	Source table
Sampling error	Mean square
Grand mean	Formula for F
Means of levels	Meaning of F
Differences from the grand mean	F distributions
Deviations from the sample mean	Degrees of freedom (for numerator and denominator)
Additive model	F and t
Total deviation	

EXERCISES

8.1.   Below are the data from Table 8.3 in this chapter:

SAMPLE 1	SAMPLE 2
7	3
5	7
4	6
8	4

   a. Complete a deviation table.
   b. Make a source table.
   c. Compute $F_{obtained}$.
   d. Look up F_{crit} from an F table using df's.
   e. Compare $F_{obtained}$ to F_{crit}. Are the two samples significantly different?

8.2.   Ten college students volunteered for an experiment to determine if drinking alcohol has an effect on reading comprehension. Reading comprehension was measured by the number of mistakes made on questions about an article they just read. Five students were randomly assigned to the experimental group, which was given 3 ounces of rum to drink within a 30-minute period. The other five students were assigned to the control condition that drank no rum. The results were as follows:

NO ALCOHOL	ALCOHOL
3	16
2	14
6	15
5	13
4	17

   a. Complete a deviation table.
   b. Make a source table.
   c. Compute $F_{obtained}$.
   d. Look up F_{crit} from an F table using df's. Compare $F_{obtained}$ to F_{crit}.
   e. Is there evidence at the 0.05 significance level that the group that drank the alcohol differs in its reading comprehension than the group that did not have the alcohol?

8.3.   Use these data to do a complete ANOVA:

   Sample 1:   3, 2, 6, 5, 4   Sample 2:   16, 14, 15, 13, 17

8.4.   We want to know if motorists in red vehicles receive more traffic citations than motorists in white vehicles. The data are given in citations per year.

RED	WHITE
1	0
2	0
1	2
3	1
4	0

   a. Construct a means table.
   b. Construct a deviation table.
   c. Construct a source table.
   d. Calculate $F_{obtained}$ versus F_{crit} from the F table. Is it significant?
   e. Is there a significant difference between the two groups?
   f. In Chapter 7, you used this exact same data on which to perform a t-test. What was the t-test result, and is your obtained F the same as t^2?

8.5.   Two researchers wanted to know if two of Chicago Transit's busiest elevated train routes, the Red and the Brown, differed from each other with respect to being on schedule. The two researchers began at 6 a.m. on a Monday morning and took 12 readings of two lines. Data are in the form of number of minutes deviation, early or late, according to schedule.
   a. Make a deviation table.
   b. Make a source table.
   c. Compute $F_{obtained}$ and determine if it is significant by comparing it to the F_{crit} obtained from the F table.
   d. Do you feel this is the best setup, to compare one line to the other? Should we just compare each route to its schedule?

DATA	INDEPENDENT VARIABLE A (TRAIN LINE)	
	RED	BROWN
	1) 1	13) 1
	2) 1	14) 3.5
	3) 3	15) 1.5
	4) 4	16) 3
	5) 0.5	17) 2
	6) 5	18) 1
	7) 3	19) 2
	8) 1.5	20) 2.5
	9) 2.5	21) 3
	10) 4	22) 2.5
	11) 7	23) 1
	12) 3.5	24) 1
	Mean 3	2
	Grand mean 2.5	

8.6.   Using what you have learned doing the preceding problems and the data that follows, compute an ANOVA, complete with source table and a short verbal description of your findings. You ran this problem in Chapter 7, except you performed a t-test on it. Does $t^2 = F$ in this case?

   In this problem, a maker of wood protectants wants to know if there is a difference in the amount of time lumber will last once it is treated with one of two products. Product X and Product Y are applied to several pieces of lumber and placed into a special weather aging environment, which ages the wood several years in several days. We have five pieces of lumber treated with each product. Data is given in amount of years before the wood is destroyed by the elements.

DATA: TYPE OF PRODUCT

X	Y
1) 27	6) 33
2) 25	7) 35
3) 27	8) 35
4) 26	9) 33
5) 25	10) 34

8.7.   Revisiting previous data from Chapter 2 problems, Professional Weight Loss Centers is trying to decide which of two different types of weight loss programs will cause clients to lose the most weight, a high carbohydrate or a high protein diet. Pounds lost are cumulative total over an 8-week period.

DATA: TYPE OF DIET

HC	HP
1) 13	11) 19
2) 10	12) 7
3) 13	13) 11
4) 15	14) 9
5) 9	15) 7
6) 10	16) 6
7) 5	17) 3
8) 15	18) 1
9) 10	19) 3
10) 10	20) 4

a.   Construct a means table for this data.
b.   Compute an ANOVA for this data, with a source table.
c.   Compare $F_{obtained}$ and F_{crit} and determine if a significant difference exists between the two groups.

ANSWERS

8.1.   a.

	TOTAL			IV (BETWEEN)			ERROR (WITHIN)		
1. TOTAL DEV	2. TOTAL DEV	3. TOTAL SQUARE	4. IV DEV	5. IV DEV	6. IV SQUARE	7. ERROR DEV	8. ERROR DEV	9. ERROR SQUARE
1. 7 2 5.5	1.5	2.25	6 2 5.5	0.5	0.25	7 2 6	1	1
2. 5 2 5.5	20.5	0.25	6 2 5.5	0.5	0.25	5 2 6	21	1
3. 4 2 5.5	21.5	2.25	6 2 5.5	0.5	0.25	4 2 6	22	4
4. 8 2 5.5	2.5	6.25	6 2 5.5	0.5	0.25	8 2 6	2	4
Mean A 5 6								
5. 3 2 5.5	22.5	6.25	5 2 5.5	20.5	0.25	3 2 5	22	4
6. 7 2 5.5	1.5	2.25	5 2 5.5	20.5	0.25	7 2 5	2	4
7. 6 2 5.5	0.5	0.25	5 2 5.5	20.5	0.25	6 2 5	1	1
8. 4 2 5.5	21.5	2.25	5 2 5.5	20.5	0.25	4 2 5	21	1
Mean B 5 5								
Grand Mean 5 5.5								
Sums of squares		22			2			20

b.

SOURCE	SUMS OF SQUARES (SS)	df	MS	$F_{obtained}$
IV/between	2	$2 - 1 = 1$	2	
Error/within	20	$8 - 2 = 6$	3.3	$F = 2/3.3 = 0.60$
Total	22	7		

c. $F_{obtained} = 0.60$

d. $F_{crit} = 5.99$

e. $F_{obtained} < F_{crit}$; therefore, accept null. The two samples are not significantly different.

8.3. $df_{num} = 1$, $df_{den} = 8$, $F = 302.5/2.5 = 121.00$

8.5.   a.

DEVIATION TABLE:

	TOTAL			IV (BETWEEN)			ERROR (WITHIN)		
	TOTAL DEV	TOTAL DEV	TOTAL SQUARE	IV DEV	IV DEV	IV SQUARE	ERROR DEV	ERROR DEV	ERROR SQUARE
				LEVEL A1					
1)	$1 - 2.5$	-1.5	2.25	$3 - 2.5$	0.5	0.25	$3 - 3.00$	-2	4
2)	$1 - 2.5$	-1.5	2.25	$3 - 2.5$	0.5	0.25	$1 - 3.00$	-2	4
3)	$3 - 2.5$	0.5	0.25	$3 - 2.5$	0.5	0.25	$3 - 3.00$	0	0
4)	$4 - 2.5$	1.5	2.25	$3 - 2.5$	0.5	0.25	$4 - 3.00$	1	1
5)	$5 - 2.5$	-2	4	$3 - 2.5$	0.5	0.25	$0.5 - 3.00$	-2.5	6.25
6)	$5 - 2.5$	2.5	6.25	$3 - 2.5$	0.5	0.25	$5 - 3.00$	2	4
7)	$3 - 2.5$	0.5	0.25	$3 - 2.5$	0.5	0.25	$3 - 3.00$	0	0
8)	$1.5 - 2.5$	-1	1	$3 - 2.5$	0.5	0.25	$1.5 - 3.00$	-1.5	2.25
9)	$2.5 - 2.5$	0	0	$3 - 2.5$	0.5	0.25	$2.5 - 3.00$	-0.5	0.25
10)	$4 - 2.5$	1.5	2.25	$3 - 2.5$	0.5	0.25	$4 - 3.00$	1	1
11)	$7 - 2.5$	4.5	20.25	$3 - 2.5$	0.5	0.25	$7 - 3.00$	4	16
12)	$3.5 - 2.5$	1	1	$3 - 2.5$	0.5	0.25	$3.5 - 3.00$	0.5	0.25
				LEVEL A2					
1)	$1 - 2.5$	-1.5	2.25	$2.00 - 2.5$	-0.5	0.25	$1 - 2.00$	-1	1
2)	$3.5 - 2.5$	1	1	$2.00 - 2.5$	-0.5	0.25	$3.5 - 2.00$	1.5	2.25
3)	$1.5 - 2.5$	-1	1	$2.00 - 2.5$	-0.5	0.25	$1.5 - 2.00$	-0.5	0.25
4)	$3 - 2.5$	0.5	0.25	$2.00 - 2.5$	-0.5	0.25	$3 - 2.00$	1	1
5)	$2.0 - 2.5$	-0.5	0.25	$2.00 - 2.5$	-0.5	0.25	$2 - 2.00$	0	0
6)	$1.0 - 2.5$	-1.5	2.25	$2.00 - 2.5$	-0.5	0.25	$1 - 2.00$	-1	1
7)	$2.0 - 2.5$	-0.5	0.25	$2.00 - 2.5$	-0.5	0.25	$2 - 2.00$	0	0
8)	$2.5 - 2.25$	0	0	$2.00 - 2.5$	-0.5	0.25	$2.5 - 2.00$	0.5	0.25
9)	$3 - 2.5$	0.5	0.25	$2.00 - 2.5$	-0.5	0.25	$3 - 2.00$	1	1
10)	$2.5 - 2.5$	0	0	$2.00 - 2.5$	-0.5	0.25	$2.5 - 2.00$	0.5	0.25
11)	$1.0 - 2.5$	-1.5	2.25	$2.00 - 2.5$	-0.5	0.25	$1 - 2.00$	-1	1
12)	$1.0 - 2.5$	-1.5	2.25	$2.00 - 2.5$	-0.5	0.25	$1 - 2.00$	-1	1
SS	Total		54		Between	6		Error	48
					Check	$54 = 48 + 6$			

b.

SOURCE	SS	df	MS	F	F_{crit}
IV_A	6	1	6	2.75	4.3
Error	48	22	2.1818		
Total	54	23			

c. There is no significant difference between the means of the two train lines, $F(1, 22) = 2.75$, n.s.

d. It would be better to compare each line to its own on-time schedule and figure the deviation from there.

8.7. a.

	DATA: TYPE OF DIET	
	HC	HP
	1) 13	11) 19
	2) 10	12) 7
	3) 13	13) 11
	4) 15	14) 9
	5) 9	15) 7
	6) 10	16) 6
	7) 5	17) 3
	8) 15	18) 1
	9) 10	19) 3
	10) <u>10</u>	20) <u>4</u>
	11	7
	Grand mean	9

b.

SOURCE	SS	dF	MS	$F_{obtained}$	F_{crit}
Type of diet	80.00	1	80.00	4.42	(1, 18) = 4.41
Error	326.00	18	18.11		
Total	406.00	19			

c. The mean number of pounds lost between the two treatment groups is significantly different, $F(1, 18) = 4.4$.

Chapter 9

USING MORE THAN TWO GROUPS

Now it is time for the elegance of analysis of variance (ANOVA) to pay off. We will apply ANOVA to a more powerful type of design—experiments with more than two levels of the independent variable. Happily, we can use the same formulas you learned in the previous chapter. We will do so in a step-by-step manner.

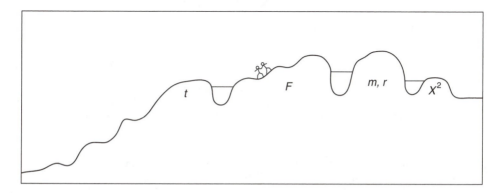

THE EXAMPLE EXPERIMENT

We will use the one-factor version of the experiment on learning introduced in the previous chapter. Recall that there were three study conditions: Just Read, Read and Underline, and Read and Outline. These three conditions are the three *levels* of the independent variable "study method." There is one independent variable. As before, we will be focusing on between-participant designs, meaning that each group of participants receives a different treatment.

The example data set is shown in Table 9.1. There are three participants in each of three groups (or levels). Calculate the grand mean, for use later. (Check your work.[1])

We will now go through the ANOVA for this type of design. Remember that ANOVA requires three main steps:

---
1. **Find sums of squares.** These are provided by the deviation table. Each score's total deviation is divided into total, IV effect, and error; these deviations are squared and summed.
2. **Create source table.** This allows you to compare the IV effect and the error in the F ratio.
3. **Compare.** Obtained F is compared to the critical F.

Do you remember how the three deviations for step 1 are defined? These definitions are central to ANOVA:

---

[1]Grand mean = $(12 + 19 + 20)/3 = 17$.

TABLE 9.1.   Example Data Set

	INDEPENDENT VARIABLE A (STUDY METHOD)	
A_1 JUST READ	A_2 READ AND UNDERLINE	A_3 READ AND OUTLINE
1) 10	4) 17	7) 22
2) 8	5) 22	8) 20
3) 18	6) 18	9) 18
Means = 12	19	20
Grand mean =		

Definitions of the Deviations

Total $= \bar{X}_i - \bar{X}_G$
IV effect $= \bar{X}_A - \bar{X}_G$
Error $= \bar{X}_i - \bar{X}_A$

The main new twist is that you apply the formula for calculating the IV effect to each level. The formula is the same; you simply subtract the mean for a given level from the grand mean. But you do it for each level. Thus, for level 1 it will be:

$$\bar{X}_{A_1} - \bar{X}_G = 12 - 17$$

What will the IV effect be for level 3? Try it right now and check your work.[2]

To reinforce the idea, go back to the preceding box and make notes about the formula for the IV effect. Remember that it applies to each level. The present example has three levels, but other experiments could have four, five, or even ten levels and the same formula would apply.

If you feel adventuresome, complete the calculation of F on your own now. If not, use the step-by-step instructions provided. The completed analysis follows.

DOING THE MULTILEVEL ANALYSIS OF VARIANCE

The data for our learning experiment are reprinted in Table 9.2, along with the grand mean. Use Tables 9.3 and 9.4 to do the ANOVA. After finishing, check your work against the completed tables (Tables 9.5 and 9.6).

TABLE 9.2.

	INDEPENDENT VARIABLE A (STUDY METHOD)	
A_1 J R	A_2 R & U	A_3 R & O
1) 10	4) 17	7) 22
2) 8	5) 22	8) 20
3) 18	6) 18	9) 18
Means = 12	19	20
Grand mean = 17		

[2] $20 - 17 = 3$.

TABLE 9.3. Deviation Table to Be Completed

	TOTAL			IV (BETWEEN)			ERROR (WITHIN)		
	1. TOTAL DEV	2. TOTAL DEV	3. TOTAL SQUARE	4. IV DEV	5. IV DEV	6. IV SQUARE	7. ERROR DEV	8. ERROR DEV	9. ERR. SQUARE
					Sample One (A$_1$)				
1.									
2.									
3.									
					Sample Two (A$_2$)				
4.									
5.									
6.									
					Sample Three (A$_3$)				
7.									
8.									
9.									
Sums of squares	____			____			____		

1. Sums of squares from the deviation table.   Calculate deviations for total, IV, and error.

    A. Make a deviation table with 10 columns. Make enough rows for all of your participants. (For convenience, Table 9.3 is provided, but learn to make your own!)

B–C. Using scores and appropriate means, construct the three deviations for each participant.

D–E. Calculate deviations (enter in columns 2, 5, and 8), square the deviations (enter in columns 3, 6, and 9), and sum the squares. Check that total = IV + error.

2. Source table.   The source table is similar to that of Chapter 8, except for small additions to the formulas for degrees of freedom. The source table interrelates the sources of variance. Complete Table 9.4. In the formulas, we will symbolize the number of levels of A as a, and the formula for degrees of freedom in the denominator will be $df_{numerator} = a - 1$.

    A. Enter the sums.

    B. Enter the df's, using the following formulas:

Degrees of Freedom Formulas

$df_{numerator} = a - 1$, where a is the number of levels in IV$_A$.
$df_{denominator} = N - a$, where N is the total number of scores (and a number of levels of A).
$df_{total} = N - 1$, where again N is the total number of scores.

TABLE 9.4. Source Table

SOURCE	SUMS OF SQUARE (SS)	df	MS	$F_{obtained}$
IV/between				
Error/within				
Total (for checking)				

C–D. In each row, divide SS by df to get mean squares (MS).
E. Divide MS_{IV} by MS_{error} to obtain F.

3. Compare to F_{crit}

A. Get F_{crit} from the F table using the df's.
B. Compare $F_{obtained}$ to F_{crit} and make your decision.

Reject the null hypothesis if $F_{obtained} > F_{crit}$
Accept the null hypothesis if $F_{obtained} \leq F_{crit}$

COMPLETED TABLES

1. Sums of squares from deviation table

TABLE 9.5. Completed Deviation Table

	TOTAL			IV (BETWEEN)			ERROR (WITHIN)		
	1. TOTAL DEV	2. TOTAL DEV	3. TOTAL SQUARE	4. IV DEV	5. IV DEV	6. IV SQUARE	7. ERROR DEV	8. ERROR DEV	9. ERR. SQUARE
				SAMPLE ONE (A1)					
1. $10 - 17$	−7		49	$12 - 17$	−5	25	$10 - 12$	−2	4
2. $8 - 17$	−9		81	$12 - 17$	−5	25	$8 - 12$	−4	16
3. $18 - 17$	1		1	$12 - 17$	−5	25	$18 - 12$	6	36
				SAMPLE ONE (A2)					
4. $17 - 17$	0		0	$19 - 17$	2	4	$17 - 19$	−2	4
5. $22 - 17$	5		25	$19 - 17$	2	4	$22 - 19$	3	9
6. $18 - 17$	1		1	$19 - 17$	2	4	$18 - 19$	−1	1
				SAMPLE ONE (A3)					
7. $22 - 17$	5		25	$20 - 17$	3	9	$22 - 20$	2	4
8. $20 - 17$	3		9	$20 - 17$	3	9	$20 - 20$	0	0
9. $18 - 17$	1		1	$20 - 17$	3	9	$18 - 20$	−2	4
Sums of squares			192			114			78

2. Source table

TABLE 9.6. Completed Source Table

SOURCE	SUMS OF SQUARE (SS)	df	MS	$F_{obtained}$
IV/between	114	2	57	4.3846
Error/within	78	6	13	
Total (for checking)	192	8		

3. Comparison to F_{crit}.   The critical value in the F table is 5.14, with 2 and 6 df. Because $4.38 < 5.14$ (i.e., $F_{obtained} < F_{crit}$), the null hypothesis is not rejected. The difference appears to be due to chance.

INTERPRETATION OF *F* IN THE MULTILEVEL CASE

What would it have meant if we had rejected the null hypothesis in an experiment like the previous one? This is a critical issue because of an important complication that arises with multilevel designs—multiple types of differences could occur:

> When there are more than two levels (or groups) in a design, a significant *F*-value means that there is a difference *somewhere* in the experiment; there may not be differences everywhere, however.

To see this, consider several possible outcomes for our experiment on study method, as listed in Table 9.7.

TABLE 9.7. Three Possible Outcomes of the Study Method Experiment

	LEVEL 1 JUST READ	LEVEL 2 READ AND UNDERLINE	LEVEL 3 READ AND OUTLINE
Case 1	5	20	20
Case 2	5	5	20
Case 3	5	15	30

Case 1 is similar to the data you have been studying; in this case levels 2 and 3 both appear to be better than level 1, but there is no difference between 2 and 3. In case 2, there is no difference between 1 and 2, but there is a difference between those two and level 3. In case 3, differences occur between each level.

If ANOVA were carried out, there could be a significant *F* in each case. But the *F* merely tells us there is a significant difference *somewhere*. To pinpoint the difference, we would have to do follow-up tests of some type.

FOLLOW-UP TESTS

There are two classes of follow-up tests. One class of test should be used only when you have clear hypotheses about possible outcomes of an experiment before the experiment is conducted. These tests are planned ahead of time (*a priori*) and are called *planned comparisons*. The other class of test is designed for when you do *not* have clear hypotheses before the experiment is conducted. They allow you to pinpoint the difference after the fact, in a post-hoc manner.

A Priori Hypotheses: Planned Comparisons

If you have posited clear hypotheses *before* the experiment is conducted, you can plan **planned comparisons.** These are comparisons between groups that are meaningful given your hypotheses. Consider the following set of hypotheses. If generated before the study method experiment was conducted, they would justify certain planned comparisons:

- *H1:* Doing something extra (underlining or outlining) leads to better learning than just reading. This would justify a comparison between the "just read" condition and the other two groups. The comparison would indicate whether underlining and outlining, considered together (averaged together), are better than just reading.

• *H2:* Outlining will be better than underlining. This would justify a comparison between "read and underline" and "read and outline," which would indicate whether one was better than the other.

ANOVA can be tailored to make these comparisons. In general, you simply conduct an ANOVA on a subset of the data. For example, you could compare two conditions within a three-level design by conducting an ANOVA on only those two conditions. Simply omit the data for the third level and analyze the experiment as a two-level design. When your comparison involves combinations of groups (as in H1), you would "weight" the groups in a logical manner. For example, in H1 "just read" would get a weight of 2 and the two other levels weights of 1 to balance the comparison. Such comparisons are discussed in advanced statistics books.

AFTER THE EXPERIMENT: POST-HOC TESTS GIVEN A SIGNIFICANT *F*

Often, researchers are not ready to plan comparisons before an experiment is conducted. In this case, follow-up analyses should be conducted with an appropriate **post-hoc test.** Post-hoc tests correct for the critical reality that you are deciding what to do after the results are in. Post-hoc tests can be very useful. However, post-hoc testing can also be like betting after the race has finished, because you can choose exactly which comparison you will make after looking at the results. Naturally, if you wait until the results are in, you have a better chance of being correct. (That's why you bet before the event in a gambling situation!)

To protect themselves, researchers typically conduct post-hoc tests only if the overall *F* was significant, indicating that there was a difference somewhere. This helps to avoid the problem of data fishing—the increased likelihood of appearing to be correct when you bet after the experiment. We discuss this pitfall next and then discuss how post-hoc tests correct for the problem. Then you will learn a simple post-hoc test.

THE PITFALLS OF DATA FISHING

Let's say you conduct an experiment with five levels of the independent variable. (For example, you add two study conditions to our learning experiment, such as "read, outline, and underline," and "read, outline, underline, and use mnemonic devices.") You do the experiment and after the experiment you decide which groups to compare. It is natural to simply look around for what might be a significant difference. This is **data fishing.** The problem is that large differences can arise by chance. In fact, the probability that a significant difference will arise by chance in *one F*-test is 5% (the 0.05 probability of a type one error). However, with 5 conditions, there are 10 pairs that you could compare (1 and 2, 2 and 3, 2 and 4, etc.). That means that the probability that a significant difference will arise by chance in 1 of your 10 possible comparisons approaches 50%. You need to correct for this, and that is what post-hoc tests do. In essence, post-hoc tests have an increased level of stringency that reduces Type I errors. One post-hoc test is covered here, and additional post-hoc tests are described in advanced statistics texts. The important point to remember is this:

> Every time you conduct another post-hoc statistical test, the overall probability of making a Type I error increases.

As noted, researchers can avoid this by limiting post-hoc testing to experiments that produce a significant overall *F,* and by using statistics designed for post-hoc testing.

A POST-HOC TEST: THE SCHEFFÉ TEST

The Scheffé test provides a good example for beginners because it is simple, its meaning is clear, and it is easy to compute. The test allows you to make any comparison you would like within an experiment. The "penalty" for this is that the test is very stringent—it is difficult to obtain a significant difference with this test.

The Scheffé test requires only that you calculate a new, larger critical value of F from the normal F_{crit}. We will call this F_S:

$$F_S = (a - 1) \times F_{crit}$$

where $(a + 1)$ is the degrees of freedom in the numerator ($df_{numerator}$) and the F_{crit} uses $df_{numerator}$ and df_{error}.

For example, in our learning experiment, F_{crit} was 5.14. With 2 df,

$$F_S = 2 \times 5.14 = 10.28$$

In a post-hoc comparison, the $F_{obtained}$ must be larger than this value to be significant.

As you can see, the F_S is larger than the original F_{crit}, meaning that it will be more difficult to obtain a significant difference. This larger value corrects for what is called the *familywise error rate*—the probability of making a Type I error at least once when you make multiple comparisons.

In fact, the Scheffé test is one of the more stringent tests available. In many cases, a less stringent test may be appropriate. Advanced texts discuss a number of possibilities as well as criteria for chosing the most appropriate one.

COMPUTATIONAL SUMMARY: MULTILEVEL ANOVA FOR BETWEEN-PARTICIPANT DESIGNS

Note: The instructions are the same as in Chapter 8!

1. Get sums of squares from the deviation table:
   A. Make a deviation table. Include enough rows for the participants, the sample means, and the grand mean. Include 10 columns. The first column, marked 0, should have room for the participant numbers and the original scores (X's).
   B. Calculate means for each sample and the grand mean and enter in column 0.
   C. Using the means, form the deviations in columns 1, 4, and 7, and put the results in columns 2, 5, and 8.
   D. Square the deviations and enter into columns 3, 6, and 9.
   E. Sum the deviations in columns 3, 6, and 9 to get sums of squares. Check that

   $$\text{Total} = \text{IV} + \text{error}$$

2. Summarize in source table:
   A. Make a source table and enter the sums.
   B. Calculate the df's and enter them.
   C. In each row, divide SS by df to get mean squares (MS).
   D. Divide MS_{IV} by MS_{error} to obtain F.
3. Compare to F_{crit}:
   A. Get F_{crit} from the F table using the df's.
   B. Compare $F_{obtained}$ to F_{crit} and make your decision:

   $$\text{Reject the null hypothesis if } F_{obtained} > F_{crit}$$
   $$\text{Accept the null hypothesis if } F_{obtained} \leq F_{crit}$$

REVIEW

Define and explain these terms and concepts:
  Formulas for and meaning of the three deviations

  Three steps in conducting ANOVA

  Interpretation of multilevel F

  Planned comparisons

  A priori tests

  Post-hoc tests

  Data fishing

EXERCISES

9.1.   The city's safety council has been observing activity on the three main highways during the morning and evening rush hours to determine if the roads differ on safety. The number of reported accidents on each road for five different days is shown here:

ROAD I	ROAD II	ROAD III
5	4	6
5	5	7
3	5	7
3	5	7
2	6	8

a. Make a deviation table.
b. Make a source table.
c. Compute $F_{obtained}$.
d. Look up F_{crit} from an F table using df's. Compare $F_{obtained}$ to F_{crit}.
e. Is there evidence that there is a difference in the mean number of reported accidents per highway?

9.2.   You are an educational consultant for a large learning center that helps students to improve their scores on achievement tests such as the GMAT, GRE, and MCAT. You want to know which way of learning helps students do the best on the test in the most efficient manner. You have three options: the AAS method, the CP method, or the SEP method. You test five subjects with the GRE on each method.

AAS METHOD	CP METHOD	SEP METHOD
1100	1200	1350
1000	1150	1400
950	1100	1450
1050	1250	1500
950	1200	1300

a. Make a deviation table.
b. Make a source table.
c. Compute $F_{obtained}$.

    d. Is this significant based on the F_{crit} value?

    e. Is there evidence that one method is superior to the others?

    f. Based on your results, would it be wise to do a post-hoc comparison of your different methods?

    g. Outline which groups you would compare post hoc in this study.

9.3. A big seafood processing company called Fish of the Sea wants to know which color of package people prefer for their processed crab treats. They surveyed 15 people on their preference on a scale from 1 to 10 for color for the crab treat product.

DARK BLUE	ROYAL BLUE	DARK GREEN
9	2	6
10	1	7
8	2	8
10	3	7
8	2	7

    a. Make a deviation table.

    b. Make a source table.

    c. Compute $F_{obtained}$.

    d. Is this significant based on the F_{crit} value?

    e. Is there evidence that one color is preferred more than the others?

    f. Based on your results, would it be wise to do a post-hoc comparison of your different methods?

9.4. A citrus farmer wants to know what type of fertilizer helps his orange trees maximize fruit production, Alice Groves fertilizer, JAM Company fertilizer, or DDD fertilizer. He separates his grove into 15 sections, randomly placed throughout his land, and measures his fruit yield from each section in millions of oranges.

    a. Make a deviation table.

    b. Make a source table.

    c. Compute $F_{obtained}$.

    d. Is this significant based on F_{crit} value?

    e. Is there evidence that one fertilizer yields more than others?

    f. Based on your results, would it be wise to do a post-hoc comparison of your different methods?

DATA: FERTILIZER		
AGF	JAM	DDD
1) 1.5	6) 2	11) 3
2) 2.5	7) 3	12) 4
3) 1.5	8) 2.5	13) 4
4) 2.5	9) 2	14) 3
5) 2	10) 2	15) 3.5

9.5. At the Strawberry Festival, officials wish to have a strawberry shortcake eating contest. They want to know if contestants eat strawberries faster when they have Camarosa strawberries, Sweet Charlies, or Mystery strawberries. You are the on-site statistician. How fast can you give the officials their answer? Data is in number of bowls eaten.

CAMAROSA	SWEET CHARLIES	MYSTERY
9	5	5
8	5	5
11	4	4
8	5	3
7	5	3

a. Make a deviation table.
b. Make a source table.
c. Compute $F_{obtained}$.
d. Look up F_{crit} from an F table using df's. Compare $F_{obtained}$ to F_{crit}.
e. Is there evidence that there is a difference in number of bowls of strawberries eaten per type of strawberry?
f. Would it be wise to conduct a post-hoc test on this data?
g. Which groups would we compare if we were to do a post-hoc test of this data?

ANSWERS

9.1. a.

	TOTAL		IV (BETWEEN)			ERROR (WITHIN)		
1. TOTAL DEV	2. TOTAL DEV	3. TOTAL SQUARE	4. IV DEV	5. IV DEV	6. IV SQUARE	7. ERROR DEV	8. ERROR DEV	9. ERROR SQUARE
1. 5 − 5.2	−0.2	0.04	3.6 − 5.2	−1.6	2.56	5 − 3.6	1.4	1.96
2. 5 − 5.2	−0.2	0.04	3.6 − 5.2	−1.6	2.56	5 − 3.6	1.4	1.96
3. 3 − 5.2	−2.2	4.84	3.6 − 5.2	−1.6	2.56	3 − 3.6	−0.6	0.36
4. 3 − 5.2	−2.2	4.84	3.6 − 5.2	−1.6	2.56	3 − 3.6	−0.6	0.36
5. 2 − 5.2	−3.2	10.24	3.6 − 5.2	−1.6	2.56	2 − 3.6	−1.6	22.56
Mean road I = 3.6								
6. 4 − 5.2	−1.2	1.44	5 − 5.2	−0.2	0.04	4 − 5	−1	1
7. 5 − 5.2	−0.2	0.04	5 − 5.2	−0.2	0.04	5 − 5	0	0
8. 5 − 5.2	−0.2	0.04	5 − 5.2	−0.2	0.04	5 − 5	0	0
9. 5 − 5.2	−0.2	0.04	5 − 5.2	−0.2	0.04	5 − 5	0	0
10. 6 − 5.2	0.8	0.64	5 − 5.2	−0.2	0.04	6 − 5	1	1
Mean road II = 5								
11. 6 − 5.2	0.8	0.64	7 − 5.2	1.8	3.24	6 − 7	−1	1
12. 7 − 5.2	1.8	3.24	7 − 5.2	1.8	3.24	7 − 7	0	0
13. 7 − 5.2	1.8	3.24	7 − 5.2	1.8	3.24	7 − 7	0	0
14. 7 − 5.2	1.8	3.24	7 − 5.2	1.8	3.24	7 − 7	0	0
15. 8 − 5.2	2.8	7.84	7 − 5.2	1.8	3.24	8 − 7	1	1
Mean road III = 7								
Grand mean = 5.2								
Sums of squares		40.4			29.2			11.2

b.

SOURCE	SUMS OF SQUARES (SS)	df	MS	$F_{obtained}$
IV/between	29.2	3−1 = 2	14.6	
Error/within	11.2	15−3 = 12	.93	F = 14.6/.93 = 15.6
Total	40.4	14		

c. $F_{obtained}$ = 15.6
d. F_{crit} = 3.88
e. $F_{obtained} > F_{crit}$; therefore, reject null. The roads do differ on the number of accidents reported.

9.3.   a.

DATA: COLOR OF PACKAGE		
DB	RB	DG
1) 9	6) 2	11) 6
2) 10	7) 1	12) 7
3) 8	8) 2	13) 8
4) 10	9) 3	14) 7
5) 8	10) 2	15) 7
9	2	7
Grand mean = 6		

DEVIATION TABLE:

	TOTAL			IV (BETWEEN) LEVEL			ERROR (WITHIN)	
TOTAL DEV	TOTAL DEV	TOTAL SQUARE	IV DEV	IV DEV	IV SQUARE	ERROR DEV	ERROR DEV	ERROR SQUARE
LEVEL DB								
1) 9 − 6.00	3	9	9 − 6.00	3	9	9 − 9.00	0	0
2) 10 − 6.00	4	16	9 − 6.00	3	9	10 − 9.00	1	1
3) 8 − 6.00	2	4	9 − 6.00	3	9	8 − 9.00	−1	1
4) 10 − 6.00	4	16	9 − 6.00	3	9	10 − 9.00	1	1
5) 8 − 6.00	2	4	9 − 6.00	3	9	8 − 9.00	−1	1
LEVEL RB								
6) 2 − 6.00	−4	16	2 − 6.00	−4	16	2 − 2.00	0	0
7) 1 − 6.00	−5	25	2 − 6.00	−4	16	1 − 2.00	−1	1
8) 2 − 6.00	−4	16	2 − 6.00	−4	16	2 − 2.00	0	0
9) 3 − 6.00	−3	9	2 − 6.00	−4	16	3 − 2.00	1	1
10) 2 − 6.00	−4	16	2 − 6.00	−4	16	2 − 2.00	0	0
LEVEL DG								
11) 6 − 6.00	0	0	7 − 6.00	1	1	6 − 7.00	−1	1
12) 7 − 6.00	1	1	7 − 6.00	1	1	7 − 7.00	0	0
13) 8 − 6.00	2	4	7 − 6.00	1	1	8 − 7.00	1	1
14) 7 − 6.00	1	1	7 − 6.00	1	1	7 − 7.00	0	0
15) 7 − 6.00	1	1	7 − 6.00	1	1	7 − 7.00	0	0
Sums of squares		138			130			8
Check							138	

b.–c.

SOURCE TABLE:					
SOURCE	SS	df	MS	$F_{obtained}$	F_{crit} = 3.88
IV/between	130	2	65	97.5*	
Error/within	8	12	0.6	667	
Total	138	14			

d. $F(2,12) = 97.5^*$. Yes it is significant.

e. Yes, there is a significant difference between the mean preference score of colors.

f. Yes, we could do a post-hoc test for a more specific result.

9.5.   a.

DATA: STRAWBERRY TYPE		
CAM	SC	MYS
1) 9	6) 5	11) 5
2) 8	7) 5	12) 5
3) 11	8) 4	13) 4
4) 8	9) 5	14) 3
5) 7	10) <u>5.8</u>	15) <u>3</u>
<u>8.6</u>	4.8	4
Grand mean = 5.8		

DEVIATION TABLE:

TOTAL			IV (BETWEEN)			ERROR (WITHIN)		
TOTAL DEV	TOTAL DEV	TOTAL SQUARE	IV DEV	IV DEV	IV SQUARE	ERROR DEV	ERROR DEV	ERROR SQUARE
			LEVEL CAM					
1) 9 − 5.8	3.2	10.24	8.6 − 5.8	2.8	7.84	9 − 8.6	0.4	0.16
2) 8 − 5.8	2.2	4.84	8.6 − 5.8	2.8	7.84	8 − 8.6	−0.6	0.36
3) 11 − 5.8	5.2	27.04	8.6 − 5.8	2.8	7.84	11 − 8.6	2.4	5.76
4) 8 − 5.8	2.2	4.84	8.6 − 5.8	2.8	7.84	8 − 8.6	−0.6	0.36
5) 7 − 5.8	1.2	1.44	8.6 − 5.8	2.8	7.84	7 − 8.6	−1.6	2.56
			LEVEL SC					
6) 5 − 5.8	−0.8	0.64	4.8 − 5.8	−1	1	5 − 4.8	0.2	0.04
7) 5 − 5.8	−0.8	0.64	4.8 − 5.8	−1	1	5 − 4.8	0.2	0.04
8) 4 − 5.8	−1.8	3.24	4.8 − 5.8	−1	1	4 − 4.8	−0.8	0.64
9) 5 − 5.8	−0.8	0.64	4.8 − 5.8	−1	1	5 − 4.8	0.2	0.04
10) 5 − 5.8	−0.8	0.64	4.8 − 5.8	−1	1	5 − 4.8	0.2	0.04
			LEVEL MYS					
11) 5 − 5.8	−0.8	0.64	4 − 5.8	−1.8	3.24	5 − 4.00	1	1
12) 5 − 5.8	−0.8	0.64	4 − 5.8	−1.8	3.24	5 − 4.00	1	1
13) 4 − 5.8	−1.8	3.24	4 − 5.8	−1.8	3.24	4 − 4.00	0	0
14) 3 − 5.8	−2.8	7.84	4 − 5.8	−1.8	3.24	3 − 4.00	−1	1
15) 3 − 5.8	−2.8	7.84	4 − 5.8	−1.8	3.24	3 − 4.00	−1	1
Sums of		74.4			60.4			14
Check	74.4							

b.–c.–d.

SOURCE TABLE:					
SOURCE	SS	df	MS	$F_{obtained}$	F_{crit} = 3.88
IV/between	60.4	2	30.2	25.9*	
Error/within	14	12	1.17		
Total	74.4	14			

e. There is a significant difference between number of strawberries eaten depending on type of strawberry. $F(2,12) = 25.886*$.

f. F is significant; therefore, we can proceed with a post-hoc test to obtain a more definitive answer. However, from the means, it looks as if the Camarosa are the favored type.

g. We would compare the three types of strawberries using a t-test such as Tukey's least significant difference test to calculate the difference between groups, which would be significant.

Chapter 10

USING MORE THAN ONE INDEPENDENT VARIABLE

So far, we have been analyzing only one variable at a time. However, behavior is almost always multiply determined. For example, love rarely occurs for a single factor; people are complex and love (like other behaviors) involves complex combinations of factors. Life is multifaceted, and that's what makes it interesting. For these same reasons, it is important and interesting to conduct experiments with multiple factors. How can we analyze multifaceted behavior with statistics? How can we examine the unique effects of combinations of factors? Multifactor ANOVA is the key.

The same principles of ANOVA will be applied, but to designs with two or more independent variables. Each level of one independent variable is combined with ("crossed with") each level of the other independent variable(s). Such designs are called **factorial designs,** as you may recall. These designs have important advantages. In particular, you can obtain interaction effects, which capture unique combined effects.

Factorial designs provide a lot of information within a compact package. For example, rather than providing only one possible IV effect as in previous designs, factorial designs provide three or more effects. In fact, simply describing and understanding the design is a considerable challenge. Our emphasis will be on describing and understanding. For the most part, you should now know the basic principles of ANOVA that we will use.

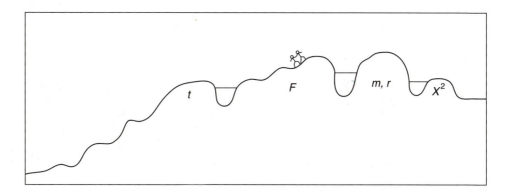

Our goal is to first learn to describe multifactor experiments, and then to begin to understand the analysis. We will begin with the many pieces, and then look at the whole process to get perspective. The actual computation of the ANOVA is quite straightforward—it follows the principles you have learned. However, factorial designs involve a lot of information, resulting in an analysis with many numbers. Therefore, computation will not be emphasized. Once you understand the analysis, you can leave efficient computation to the computer.

🏃 CONCEPT CHAIN:

AN EXAMPLE DESIGN

Let's say that our study method experiment from earlier chapters revealed that underlining and outlining both help, compared to just reading. In our next experiment, we decide to examine how underlining and outlining work with different subject areas. We choose history and math. We use a factorial design to examine underlining and outlining *in combination* with history and math.

We will continue to use a between-participant design, because this type is easiest. Remember that *between-participant* means each group of participants is treated in a different way (receives a different condition).

To start, we will talk only about the design—what are the treatment conditions and what information can we get from them? We won't think about participant scores yet.

Our factorial design combines two levels of study method ("underlining" and "outlining") with two levels of the second independent variable, subject area ("history" and "math"). This is a 2×2 factorial design (two levels of each variable), which is the simplest possible factorial. We will focus on the 2×2.

What is in the 2×2 design? You will find information at three levels. Let's go over the information now. An example with participant scores will follow.

MOST BASIC LEVEL: CELLS

The most basic level of a design is the individual treatment conditions. These are the treatments received by particular groups of participants. They are also called **cells** in a factorial design.

> In a factorial design, the **cells** are obtained by combining the variables.

We need a way to designate (name and describe) the cells. Letters and numbers will be used, as was done in previous chapter.

> We will use A_1 and A_2 to designate the two levels of A, and B_1 and B_2 for the two levels of variable B.
>
> When combined, we get conditions such as A_1B_1.

Combining two levels of one variable with two levels of the other variable gives us four combinations, which can be described in a 2×2 table such as Table 10.1. The head-

TABLE 10.1. Cells of a Factorial Design to be Completed

	Factor A: Study Method	
	A_1B_1 Underline History	A_2B_1 . . .
Factor B: Subject Area	A_1 . . .	

ings for the columns (Factor A) and rows (Factor B) begin to describe the design. The first cell (the treatment condition), in the upper left of the 2×2 box, is the combination of Underlining and History. It is designated cell A_1B_1. The group of participants in that cell use underlining with the subject of history. Write the other three combinations in the table below, starting with the hints provided. Remember that a different group of participants will receive each treatment. (The answers appear in Table 10.2.)

THERE ARE FOUR CELL MEANS

From the four cells, we get four cell means—one for each cell. Cell means tell us what happened within a particular cell (or treatment condition).

THE ENTIRE DESIGN

We will now talk about the design as a whole for a moment. The entire design is shown in Table 10.2. For now, check your notations in Table 10.1 against those in Table 10.2. The additional notations are the other levels of information, which we now turn to.

NEXT LEVEL: MAIN EFFECTS AND FOUR MAIN EFFECT MEANS

We need means that tell us what happened within each level of each independent variable. Main effect means tell us what happened with one variable, while ignoring the other variable. For example, what happened with the participants who used "underline," regardless of subject area? To answer this we look at the mean of *all* A1 participants—the mean of participants in A_1B_1 and A_1B_2. This is a main effect mean. This mean is designated by "A_1, Underline in general" in Table 10.2.

There are four main effect means—two for A (A_1 and A_2) and two for B (B_1 and B_2). They are shown in the margins of Table 10.2 in the right column and the bottom.

HIGHEST LEVEL: ONE GRAND MEAN

Last, there is one **grand mean,** which is the mean of all participants in the experiment. It does not tell us much, but we use it in calculating deviations. There are several ways

TABLE 10.2. Completed Illustration of a Factorial Design, with Added Notations

	Factor A: Study Method		
	A_1B_1 Underline History	A_2B_1 Outline History	B_1 History in general
Factor B: Subject Area	A_1B_2 Underline Math	A_2B_2 Outline Math	B_2 Math in general
	A_1 Underline in General	A_2 Outline in General	Grand Mean

to calculate it. For example, we could take the mean of all main effect means for one variable (e.g., variable A, or variable B).

Summary: Three Types of Means

Cell means tell us what happened within one treatment condition.
Main effect means tell us what happened within a level of an IV. Comparing main effect means tells us about the *overall* effect of a variable.
Grand mean is the mean of all data and is useful in calculating deviations.

DONE!   ⅄

THE EXAMPLE MADE CONCRETE WITH NUMBERS

Now we will fill in our abstract design with participant scores. We will use these scores to calculate means and talk about what the means mean. We have two participants in each of our four cells, for a total of eight participants. Their data are shown in Figure 10.1, within the boxes. Learn to think about the factorial design by calculating the means (all nine of them!). You will calculate:

1. *Four cell means.* Put these below the box for the cell (immediately below the participants' data).
2. *Four main effect means.* These go in the margins, where it says "Main Effect Means—."
3. *Grand mean.*

After calculating, compare your results to the answers given in Figure 10.2. Then do some interpretation, discussed below.

INTERPRETING THE MAIN EFFECTS

We can look at means to make an initial interpretation of the effects in the experiment. Let's take a minute to do one level of interpretation—main effects. For example, we

FIGURE 10.1.   A factorial design and hypothetical data.

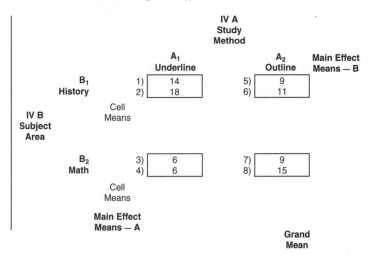

compare the main effect means for A_1 and A_2 to learn about "the main effect of IV A." What was the (main) effect of A in the experiment? Not much! There is no difference between 11 and 11.

The main effect means for B (B_1 versus B_2) tell us about the main effects for B. What do you think about B? There is more going on with the B main effect means—13 versus 9. There may be an effect here. To see if it is a real IV effect or an effect attributable to chance, we would conduct the ANOVA.

THE COMPLETED TABLE

Does your work look like Figure 10.2? If so, you are ready to move on.

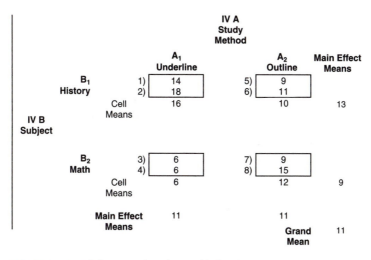

FIGURE 10.2.   All the means have been added in this figure.

Exercise

Time to stretch (your understanding). Think of a new 2×2 factorial experiment with factors that interest you. Describe the experiment and label the means you would calculate.

Make statistics meaningful!

CONCEPTUALIZATION:

THREE IV EFFECTS IN THE 2 × 2 FACTORIAL

As noted, the designs of the previous chapters had only one IV effect. Our factorial design, however, provides three different effects. Each of these effects provides unique information.

These effects are now defined. The means of Figure 10.2 are copied in Figure 10.3 and used as examples. As we started to do earlier, we will use means to talk about possible effects. This is a sensible thing to do, especially while learning about factorial design. Experienced researchers also look at means. Of course, we would follow up with ANOVA to get the definitive answer about whether the effects are real or not.

One additional note: The three effects are independent of each other; whether or not one effect occurred has no bearing on the other effects.

Main Effect of IV A

This is the overall effect of A, regardless of B. This effect is conveyed by the main effect means for A. In our example, those means are 11 and 11, so there was no main effect of A. Study method made no *overall* difference in this experiment.

Main Effect of IV B

This is the overall effect of B, regardless of A. This effect is conveyed by its main effect means (for B). The means in the example were 13 and 9, which implies that there could be a main effect of B. (We need to do the statistical test to know.) Subject area might have made an *overall* difference.

Interaction of A and B

This last effect is likely to be new to you. Yet, it is the most complex and the most interesting when it occurs. An interaction means that the effect of one variable (e.g., A) dif-

FIGURE 10.3. The data repeated for your convenience.

			IV A			
			A_1 Underline		**A_2 Outline**	**Main Effect Means**
IV B	**B_1 History**	1)	14	5)	9	
		2)	18	6)	11	
	Cell Means		16		10	13
	B_2 Math	3)	6	7)	9	
		4)	6	8)	15	
	Cell Means		6		12	9
	Main Effect Means		11		11	
					Grand Mean	11

fered, depending on the level of the other variable (e.g., B). There is in fact an interaction in our data (surprise!). Can you find it?

Because of its multidimensional nature, you can see the interaction in multiple ways. I will begin by asking if the effect of study method (IV A) is the same at both levels of IV B—that is, is the effect of study method the same for history and math, or different? Check and read on.

The answer is that the effect is quite different. Outlining is good for history and bad for math, whereas underlining is a little better for math than for history. (At least in our hypothetical study.) We could also see this by looking at IV B's effect at the two levels of IV A: Is the effect of subject area the same with underlining and outlining? The answer is no.

This is an example of an interaction. The effect of one variable differed, depending on the other variable. A step-by-step method for detecting interactions is presented later. However, there is also a convenient visual method that you can use with graphs. Let's start with a graph of our data (Figure 10.4). This 2 × 2 graph features two lines, one for each level of IV A. The angle of the lines indicates the effects of the bottom variable, IV B, on that level of IV A. The fact that the tilt is different for the two lines indicates there is (or could be) an interaction in the data. That is, the differing tilts indicate that IV B had different effects, depending on the level of IV A. When the line-tilts are parallel, in contrast, there is no interaction. Thus,

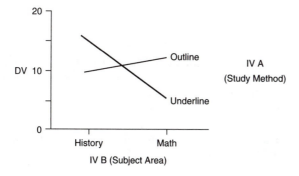

FIGURE 10.4. The 2 × 2 graph of the results from our study method experiment.

In a graph, parallel lines mean *no* interaction; nonparallel lines mean interaction.

As noted, the concept of interaction is very important because it is a unique kind of effect that psychologists can uncover. It is one of the secrets underlying our complex world. We will return to this idea.

DONE! 𝑋

WHERE WE ARE GOING

You have now been introduced to factorial design and the three IV effects that a 2×2 design provides. We now begin to cover the actual computation of a 2×2 ANOVA. However, as noted, it is complex. To simplify it, we will focus on the deviations that go into the deviation table to produce sums of squares. The deviations are rather elegant, and they fit together in the deviation formula, which is a useful concept that you should understand and memorize. Then we will take the five sums of squares at the bottom of the deviation table and complete the ANOVA.

🧍 **CONCEPTUALIZATION:**

FIVE SUMS OF SQUARES IN THE FACTORIAL DESIGN

The actual deviation table is shown in Table 10.3. several pages ahead. Refer to it and follow the deviations as we discuss them. I recommend xeroxing it, to make looking at it easy.

The ANOVA for a 2×2 factorial requires five sums of squares. The ANOVA provides three separate F values—one F for each of three effects. The top of the F-value fractions are determined by the corresponding three deviations (IV A, IV B, and A $\times$ B interaction). The "Total" deviation is used only for checking, and the "Error" deviation is your familiar friend, error. Error is at the right of the deviation table, and we will begin with it.

ERROR DEVIATIONS

Remember that the error is the deviation of an individual score from the rest of the participants in the condition (or cell). In the present ANOVA, it is the deviation of an individual score from the *cell mean,* or

$$\text{Error} = X_i - \bar{X}_{AB}$$

where the mean is the participant's AB cell mean. For example, the first participant's error in Table 10.3 would be 14–16.

TOTAL

Now let's move to the left side of Table 10.3. "Total" is the total deviation in a score. As before, it is the deviation of an individual score from the grand mean,

$$\text{Total} = X_i - \bar{X}_G$$

IV A EFFECT

This is the deviation of the participant's level of A from the grand mean:

$$\text{IV A effect} = \bar{X}_A - \bar{X}_G$$

Remember to use the mean for A that is appropriate for the participant. The first participant's IV A effect would be 11–11. The same would be true for all four participants receiving A1. For the other participants, the mean of A2 would be used.

TABLE 10.3. Two-Way ANOVA Deviation Table Illustrated

	TOTAL			IVA (BETWEEN)			IVB (BETWEEN)			A × B INTERACTION			ERROR (WITHIN)		
	TOTAL DEV	TOTAL DEV	TOTAL SQUARE	IVA DEV	IVA DEV	IVA SQUARE	IVB DEV	IVB DEV	IVB SQUARE	A × B DEV	A × B DEV	A × B SQUARE	ERROR DEV	ERROR DEV	ERROR SQUARE
CELL A1B1															
1)	14 − 11	3	9	11 − 11	0	0	13 − 11	2	4	16 − 11 − 13 + 11	3	9	14 − 16	−2	4
2)	18 − 11	7	49	11 − 11	0	0	13 − 11	2	4	16 − 11 − 13 + 11	3	9	18 − 16	2	4
CELL A1B2															
3)	6 − 11	−5	25	11 − 11	0	0	9 − 11	−2	4	6 − 11 − 9 + 11	−3	9	6 − 6	0	0
4)	6 − 11	−5	25	11 − 11	0	0	9 − 11	−2	4	6 − 11 − 9 + 11	−3	9	6 − 6	0	0
CELL A2B1															
5)	9 − 11	−2	4	11 − 11	0	0	13 − 11	2	4	10 − 11 − 13 + 11	−3	9	9 − 10	−1	1
6)	11 − 11	0	0	11 − 11	0	0	13 − 11	2	4	10 − 11 − 13 + 11	−3	9	11 − 10	1	1
CELL A2B2															
7)	9 − 11	−2	4	11 − 11	0	0	9 − 11	−2	4	12 − 11 − 9 + 11	3	9	9 − 12	−3	9
8)	15 − 11	4	16	11 − 11	0	0	9 − 11	−2	4	12 − 11 − 9 + 11	3	9	15 − 12	3	9
Sums of squares			132			0			32			72			28
Check			132 = 0 + 32 + 72 + 28												

IV B Effect

This is the deviation of the participant's level of B from the grand mean:

IV B effect = $\bar{X}_B - \bar{X}_G$

Remember to use the mean for B that is appropriate for the participant. The first participant's IV B effect would be $13 - 11$. The same would be true for all four participants receiving B1.

Interaction of A × B

Interaction is often referred to as "A × B," which is read as "A by B." This is because it is the combination of A and B that is crucial:

Interaction is a unique effect of a combination of variables (e.g., a unique effect of a combination of A and B).

It occurs when (by earlier definition) the effect of one variable depends on the level of another variable.

This can be seen by briefly considering some examples of interactions. In our study method experiment, the crucial thing was not the IVs themselves (not the main effects), but the combination of one IV with the other—the combination of study method and subject area. Another dangerous interaction involves combinations of prescription drugs. Today, one of the leading causes of hospital admissions is drug interaction. When people take two different drugs, the drugs may combine to have a unique and very dangerous effect. Although the side effects of either one taken alone may be small, the combination can be deadly.

Thus, interaction is an effect that is above and beyond that of the independent variables alone. This reality is central to the calculation of interaction. Write the idea down now, in your own words.

Interaction

In calculating the "above and beyond effect," we start with an AB combination—the a cell mean. However, this cell mean contains more than the unique effect. The cell mean contains three things: (1) the unique, combined effect, (2) the (main) effect of IV A, and (3) the (main) effect of IV B. We need to remove the main effects to see interaction.

Calculating the A × B interaction. We will describe this interaction several times because it is rather complex. We start with a cell mean, which contains both the unique effect and the main effects. Then we subtract the main effects. Also, for balance (because we subtract two means), we need to add one mean, which is the grand mean. That is,

Interaction = Cell mean   (contains three effects)
             minus Main effect of A   (subtract one mean)
               minus Main effect of B   (subtract another)
                   plus Grand mean   (add for balance)
         = Unique effect of combination   (leftover: Interaction!)

Thus, we determine what is unique in the combination by subtracting everything else (subtracting the two main effects), and then adding something neutral (the grand mean) for balance. This formula leaves us with what is unique to the AB combination—the interaction effect. In symbols, this is:

$$\text{Interaction} = \bar{X}_{AB} - X_A - \bar{X}_B + \bar{X}_G = \text{Unique effect of combination}$$

It is time for an example. For the first participant in our study, the calculation of the deviation for interaction is,

$$\text{Interaction} = 16 - 11 - 13 + 11 = 3 = \text{Unique effect of that combination}$$

Using other participant scores, calculate some more interaction deviations. Check your answers against Table 10.3 (the interaction calculations are in the appropriate columns).

Remember that after the deviations are calculated, they are squared and then summed. We then put the sums of squares into the source table.

DONE! 人

PUTTING IT TOGETHER: THE ENTIRE DEVIATION FORMULA

We can now put all the pieces into a single elegant formula, in which the total deviation is broken down into the other four deviations. The formula is given first in words, then in symbols. To study it, write it down again in words, and then in symbols, connecting the verbal formula to the symbolic one. Then apply it to individual scores taken from the cells of our example experiment (see Figure 10.5). Remember to use the correct means for each score. For example, if the score is from cell A2B2, use the means of A2 and B2 for main effects and the mean of A2B2 at the beginning of the interaction deviation.

$$\text{Total} = (\text{Main effect of A}) + (\text{Main effect of B}) + (\text{Interaction}) + (\text{Error})$$
$$x_i - \bar{X}_G = (\bar{X}_A - \bar{X}_G) + (\bar{X}_B - \bar{X}_G) + (\bar{X}_{AB} - \bar{X}_A - \bar{X}_B + \bar{X}_G) + (x_i - \bar{X}_{AB})$$

Word formula:

Symbol formula:

Apply the formula to some individual scores (i.e., write down each of the five deviations) on a separate sheet.

Further consolidate this by writing the formula (symbols and words) from memory on a separate sheet.

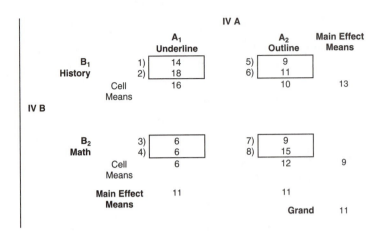

FIGURE 10.5.   The data once more, for your convenience.

TIME OUT FOR A REVIEW

At this point, let me review where we are. You should have learned to think about a factorial design and each of its aspects, including the three effects it provides and the five deviations. You should memorize the deviation formula. Write it down regularly and think about what each deviation means. The deviation formula is a major part of the factorial ANOVA process and understanding it will lead to an understanding of its meaning.

The deviation table is constructed from the deviation formula, and the table provides the five essential sums of squares. I won't require you to make an entire deviation table, but your professor might, and you are invited to do so on your own (use Table 10.3 as a guide). We now cover the rest of the ANOVA.

🏃 **STEP-BY-STEP PROCEDURE:**

DOING THE ANOVA

Follow the usual steps:

1. Get sums of squares from the deviation table.
2. Use the source table to interrelate the variances.
3. Make comparisons between obtained and critical F's.

Next the sums of squares from the bottom of Table 10.3 are determined and then steps 2 and 3 of the factorial ANOVA are covered.

THE SUMS OF SQUARES

Table 10.4 provides the sums of squares that you get from the full deviation table in our example experiment. Use them to complete our ANOVA.

TABLE 10.4.   The Top and Bottom Lines from the Deviation Table

	TOTAL SQUARES	IVA SQUARES	IVB SQUARES	AXB SQUARES	ERROR SQUARES
Sums of squares	132	0	32	72	28

SOURCE TABLE FOR A 2 × 2 FACTORIAL DESIGN

The source table for a factorial design works the same way as previous source tables, with the exception that you now have three rows for the three effects. Within each of these rows, you will calculate and MS and *F* for one of the effects.

Use the sums of squares from our example to complete Table 10.5. You might be able to complete the table using the logic in your head, rather than the steps listed in the accompanying box. Using either method, complete the table. The completed source table is given in Table 10.6.

TABLE 10.5.   Source Table

SOURCE	SUMS OF SQUARE (SS)	df	MS	$F_{obtained}$
IV A effect				
IV B effect		1		
A × B effect		1		
Error/within		4		
Total (for checking)		7		

Steps for Completing Factorial Source Table

A. Enter the sums of squares.
B. Enter df's. (The formulas are given later, so most of the df's are completed for you.)
C–D. Within each row, divide SS by df to get mean squares (MS).
E. Within the three effect rows, divide MS for the effect by MS_{error} to obtain the *F* values.

COMPARE THE OBTAINED AND CRITICAL *F*'S

For each of your obtained *F*'s in Table 10.5, you would compare it to the appropriate critical values from the *F* table. Use the appropriate df's and look at Table 8.9 in Chapter 8. The appropriate value of F_{crit} for each of the three effects has 1 and 4 degrees of freedom, and is 7.71. What effects are there? Compare the obtained *F*'s and check your work.[1]

DONE!

---

[1] The only significant effect was the A × B interaction. The *F*'s for the other two effects were smaller than the critical *F*.

TABLE 10.6.   Completed Source Table

SOURCE	SUMS OF SQUARE (SS)	df	MS	$F_{obtained}$
IV A	0	1	0	0
IV B	32	1	32	4.57
A × B	72	1	72	10.29
Error/within	28	4	7	
Total (for checking)	132	7		

DEGREES OF FREEDOM

In this ANOVA, you need four different degrees of freedom, as well as the total for checking. They are listed here.

Degrees of Freedom for a Factorial Design with Two Variables

$df_A = a - 1$, where a is the number of levels in A.

$df_B = b - 1$, where b is the number of levels in B.

$df_{A \times B} = (a - 1)(b - 1)$.

$df_{error} = N - ab$, where N is the total number of scores.

$df_{total} = N - 1$.

INTERPRETING 2 × 2 GRAPHS

Calculating a factorial ANOVA is complex (as you now know!). Be sure to take time to consolidate the material and rest. You have been climbing high! Once you are rested, let's take a minute to look around. I want to show you how to look at 2 × 2 graphs. We won't worry about statistical significance. Our problem is telling whether or not any of the three effects might be present, which we can do visually.

We need to ask three questions: Is there a main effect of A? Of B? An interaction? We must do these one at a time because each effect is independent of the others. This process is illustrated in the graphs of Figure 10.6. We first look at IV A, in panel A. What we need are the main effect means for A—the means for each level of A. We get those in the graph by going to the middle of the lines, marked by short line and an "m." This

FIGURE 10.6.   The 2 × 2 graph of the results from our study method experiment.

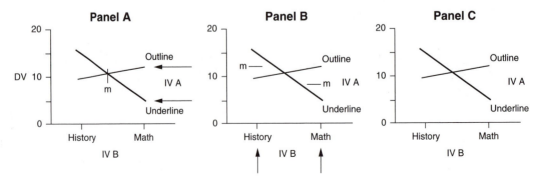

is the same place for the two levels of A, so you see only one line/m. There is no main effect of A. There would be a possible main effect if there were a difference (if one line/m was higher in the graph than the other—higher on the Y axis, or the dependent variable).

Next we look at IV B, in panel B. We need the main effect means for B—the means for each level of B. We get those by going to the middle of the data points, again marked by line/m's (two in this case). Because one line/m is higher, there may be an effect of IV B. (However, our ANOVA told us this could be due to chance.) In summary, we have used the main effect middle method:

Main Effect Middle Method

Find main effects by going to middles.

Last, we ask if there is an interaction (see Figure 10.6, panel C). Are the lines illustrating the data parallel? In this case, they are not and there is an interaction. We can also check for intersection using one of two step-by-step methods, a row method or a column method, as shown next.

Step-by-Step Methods for Checking for the A × B Interaction

Method 1: Row Method

1. Calculate the differences between the pair of cell means within each row and write them down (i.e., $A_1B_1 - A_2B_1$ and $A_1B_2 - A_2B_2$).
2. If these differences are different in size, there may be an interaction.

Method 2: Column Method

1. Calculate the differences between the pair of cell means within each column and write them down (i.e., $A_1B_1 - A_1B_2$ and $A_2B_1 - A_2B_2$).
2. If these differences are different in size, there may be an interaction.

As an exercise, apply both methods to our data and check your numbers.[2]

Let's consolidate the process. Apply what you've learned to interpret the graphs shown in Figure 10.7. Make notes to help your memory and then check your work.[3]

FIGURE 10.7.   A new 2 × 2 for you to complete.

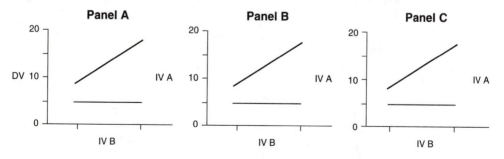

[2] The row method gives differences of +6 and −6; there may well be an interaction.
[3] The column method gives differences of +10 and −2; again, there may be an interaction. Both IVs and the interaction have main effects.

REVIEW

Define the following terms:
Factorial design
Cells
Main effect means
Grand mean
Interaction
What are the three effects in a 2×2 design?
What is an interaction?
How can you tell if an interaction is present?
Write the entire deviation formula and name the five deviations.
Provide a complete source table.

EXERCISES

10.1. The results for a 2×2 experiment are shown here:

a. Calculate all of the means.
b. Write the full deviations for several participants.
c. Using the following sums of squares (from the complete deviation table),
   do the ANOVA (source table and comparisons of F values).

TOTAL	IVA	IVB	A $\times$ B	ERROR
174	18	98	50	8

10.2. An I/O psychologist wants to know which display will work best for commercial airline pilots. He also wants to know if there's a difference in preference for the two displays between pilots with 2 years or more of experience with commercial airliners and those with less than 2 years of experience. The pilots were asked to rate their display from 1 to 10, with 10 being best and 1 being worst for ease of readability.

a. Calculate the cell means for each condition. Also calculate the main effect mean for each level of each IV, and calculate the grand mean.
b. Following the example in Problem 10.1, write the deviations for participants 1, 7, 10, and 12.
c. Using the following sums of squares, do the ANOVA (source table and comparisons of F values):

TOTAL	DISPLAY	EXPERIENCE	$D \times E$	ERROR
432	12	27	12	18

10.3. You work for a cologne company that manufactures cologne for both men and women. However, sales have been slack and the vice president of sales wants you to figure out what the problem is. You run a series of consumer tests and find that neither sex likes the color of the box. You come up with two preferred colors from your study and you wish to know if there is a difference between which box color males prefer and which females prefer. You ask 16 consumers how likely they would be to buy the cologne based on the color of the box on a scale from 1 to 5, with 5 being most likely and 1 being least likely.

Color of Box

		Red		Light Blue	
	Male	1)	5	9)	2
		2)	4	10)	3
		3)	3	11)	2
		4)	4	12)	3
Gender					
	Female	5)	1	13)	5
		6)	1	14)	3
		7)	1	15)	3
		8)	3	16)	3

a. Calculate the cell means for each condition. Also calculate the main effect mean for each level of each IV, and calculate the grand mean.
b. Following the example in Problem 10.1, write the deviations for all participants.
c. Using the following sums of squares, do the ANOVA (source table and comparisons of F values):

TOTAL	COLOR	GENDER	$C \times G$	ERROR
23.75	0.25	2.25	12.25	9.00

10.4. You work for an advertising firm that has a vegetable grower as a client. Your client wants to know if placing the carrots in a yellow bag versus a blue bag will help sell carrots. The client also wants to know if there is a gender preference since studies show that most grocery shopping is done by women and they want to target that audience. Twelve participants fill out a form indicating their package preference on a scale of 1 to 7, with 1 being least preferred and 7 being most preferred.

Gender

		Male		Female	
	Yellow	1)	3	7)	7
		2)	2	8)	7
Package		3)	1	9)	7
Color					
	Blue	4)	7	10)	3
		5)	6	11)	2
		6)	5	12)	1

a. Calculate the cell means for each condition. Also calculate the main effect mean for each level of each IV, and calculate the grand mean.
b. Following the example in Problem 10.1, write the deviations for all participants.
c. Using the following sums of squares, do the ANOVA (source table and comparisons of F values):

TOTAL	GENDER	COLOR	G × C	ERROR
68.25	0.75	0.75	60.75	6.00

d. What would you tell your client about what color to make the carrot packages? Do you see a main effect of color or gender here? Is there a significant interaction?

10.5. You are a teacher and you want to know if there is a difference in scoring on a reading comprehension test for students whose first language is either Spanish or English (although both groups speak and read English equally well according to a prior achievement test). You also want to know if time of day has an effect. You test 8 children on a comprehension scale of 1 to 100.

		Time of Day			
		Morning		Afternoon	
	Spanish	1)	99	5)	65
		2)	81	6)	75
First Language					
	English	3)	62	7)	90
		4)	78	8)	100

a. Calculate the cell means for each condition. Also calculate the main effect mean for each level of each IV, and calculate the grand mean.
b. Following the example in Problem 10.1, write the deviations for all participants.
c. Using the following sums of squares, do the ANOVA (source table and comparisons of F values):

TOTAL	TIME OF DAY	FIRST LANGUAGE	TD × FL	ERROR
1427.50	12.50	12.50	1012.50	390.0

d. Should you test different groups at different times of the day? Is there is significant interaction here?

ANSWERS

10.1. a.

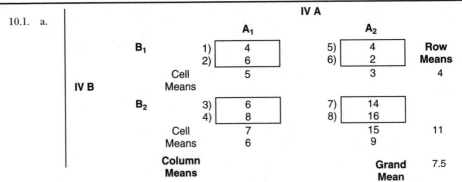

DEVIATION TABLE FOR PROBLEM 10.1:

b.

	TOTAL			IVA (BETWEEN)			IVB (BETWEEN)			A × B INTERACTION			ERROR (WITHIN)		
	TOTAL DEV	TOTAL DEV	TOTAL SQUARE	IVA DEV	IVA DEV	IVA SQUARE	IVB DEV	IVB DEV	IVB SQUARE	A × B DEV	A × B DEV	A × B SQUARE	ERROR DEV	ERROR DEV	ERROR SQUARE
							CELL A1B1								
1)	4 − 7.5	−3.5	12.3	6 − 7.5	−1.5	2.25	4 − 7.5	−3.5	12.25	5 − 6 − 4 + 7.5	2.5	6.25	4 − 5	−1	1
2)	6 − 7.5	−1.5	2.25	6 − 7.5	−1.5	2.25	4 − 7.5	−3.5	12.25	5 − 6 − 4 + 7.5	2.5	6.25	6 − 5	1	1
							CELL A1B2								
3)	6 − 7.5	−1.5	2.25	6 − 7.5	−1.5	2.25	11 − 7.5	3.5	12.25	7 − 6 − 11 + 7.5	−2.5	6.25	6 − 7	−1	1
4)	8 − 7.5	0.5	0.25	6 − 7.5	−1.5	2.25	11 − 7.5	3.5	12.25	7 − 6 − 11 + 7.5	−2.5	6.25	8 − 7	1	1
							CELL A2B1								
5)	4 − 7.5	−3.5	12.3	9 − 7.5	1.5	2.25	4 − 7.5	−3.5	12.25	3 − 9 − 4 + 7.5	−2.5	6.25	4 − 3	1	1
6)	2 − 7.5	−5.5	30.3	9 − 7.5	1.5	2.25	4 − 7.5	−3.5	12.25	3 − 9 − 4 + 7.5	−2.5	6.25	2 − 3	−1	1
							CELL A2B2								
7)	14 − 7.5	6.5	42.3	9 − 7.5	1.5	2.25	11 − 7.5	3.5	12.25	15 − 9 − 11 + 7.5	2.5	6.25	14 − 25	−1	1
8)	16 − 7.5	8.5	72.3	9 − 7.5	1.5	2.25	11 − 7.5	3.5	12.25	15 − 9 − 11 + 7.5	2.5	6.25	16 − 15	1	1
Sums of squares			174			18			98			50			8
Check			174 = 18 + 98 + 50 + 8												

c. Source table:

SOURCE	SS	df	MS	$F_{obtained}$	$F_{crit} = 7.71$
IV A	18	1	18	9	
IV B	98	1	98	49	
A × B	50	1	50	25	
Error	8		4	2	
Total	174	7			

Each effect is a significant difference because the obtained values (9, 49, and 25) are larger than the critical value of 7.71.

10.3. a.

Color of box

			Red		Light Blue	Row means
		1)	5	9)	2	Row means
	Male	2)	4	10)	3	
		3)	3	11)	2	
		4)	4	12)	3	

Gender

Cell mean = 4   Cell mean = 2.5   Mean = 3.25

		5)	1	13)	5	
	Female	6)	1	14)	3	
		7)	1	15)	3	
		8)	3	16)	3	

Cell mean = 1.5   Cell mean = 3.5   Mean = 2.5

Column means = 2.75   3

Grand mean = 2.88

b. Check deviation table for Problem 10.1.

c. Source table:

SOURCE	SS	df	MS	$F_{obtained}$	F_{crit}
Color	0.25	1	0.25	0.33, n.s.	(1, 12) = 4.75
Gender	2.25	1	2.25	3.00, n.s.	(1, 12) = 4.75
Display × Experience	12.25	1	12.25	16.33*	(1, 12) = 4.75
Error	9	12	0.75		
Total	23.75	15			

10.5. a.

Time of Day

			Morning		Afternoon	Row means
	Spanish	1)	99	5)	65	Row means
		2)	81	6)	75	

First Language

Cell mean = 90   Cell mean = 70   80

| | English | 3) | 62 | 7) | 90 | |
| | | 4) | 78 | 8) | 100 | |

Cell mean = 70   Cell mean = 95   82.50

Column means = 80   = 82.50

Grand mean = 81.25

b. Check deviation table for Problem 10.1.

c. Source table:

SOURCE	SS	df	MS	$F_{obtained}$	F_{crit}
Time of day	12.50	1	12.50	0.128, n.s.	(1, 4) = 7.71
First language	12.50	1	12.50	0.128, n.s.	(1, 4) = 7.71
TD × FL	1012.50	1	1012.50	10.385*	(1, 4) = 7.71
Error	390.00	4	97.50		
Total	1427.50	7			

I would test the Spanish group in the morning; however, the English group does not seem to perform differently between the two times of day. There is also no significant difference between the English and Spanish group comprehension test scores either. There is a significant interaction here, $F(1,4) = 10.385^*$.

Chapter 11

RELATIONS BETWEEN VARIABLES:
LINEAR REGRESSION AND CORRELATION

So far, we have studied methods for deciding whether an IV caused differences between treatment conditions. Now we consider new ways of looking at data—methods that are not restricted to experiments. The methods analyze the more general concept of *relations* between variables. Is one variable related to other ones? Which combination of variables best predicts another variable? The methods are often applied to research in which all of the variables are measured (dependent variables, as opposed to manipulated independent variables).

These methods are important for a variety of reasons. First, they are useful in exploratory research, when one is not sure which variables are important. For example, recent medical research has examined a myriad of variables related to diet, exercise, and health, and has found some to be more important than others. The primary statistical methods have been correlation and regression. These methods are also useful for studying complex real-world situations that involve many variables, and for studying variables that cannot be manipulated ethically, such as effects of real-life stress or environmental hazards.

We focus here on the simplest types of relations, although more complex relations are mentioned. The two main statistics you will learn are the slope, m, measured by regression, and the correlation, r. These two statistics are complementary, as you will see.

We begin by reexamining our original helping data.

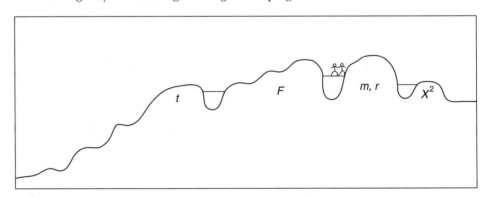

ILLUSTRATING RELATIONS BETWEEN VARIABLES: GRAPHS OF MEANS

Let's begin with the graph of the means from our helping experiment that you first saw in Chapter 3, now shown as Figure 11.1. As a reminder, the independent variable is plotted along the X axis (the horizontal axis). It has two levels: the control condition, which is now assigned a value of 1, and the experimental (good mood) condition, now assigned a value of 2.

As you now know, both central tendency and variability are crucial properties of data. Variability corresponds to error, and in the figure variability is shown by the *error*

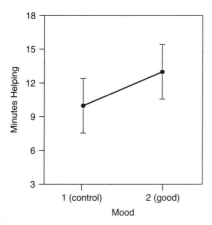

FIGURE 11.1. A graph of the means from our helping experiment, with bars indicating the standard deviations.

bars above and below the data points. The error bars show the size of the standard deviation (SD); the length in each direction from the data point (up or down) corresponds to one SD.

For present purposes, the most important thing about Figure 11.1 is that it illustrates the general relation between mood and helping. The figure indicates that helping changes as a function of mood—as mood increases, helping increases. The two variables, mood and helping, *covary*—as one changes, the other changes in a systematic manner.

ILLUSTRATING RELATIONS FOR ALL SCORES: THE SCATTERPLOT

We now move beyond means to instead graph individual data points for each participant. We do this with a **scatterplot.** A scatterplot provides a more detailed illustration of the relation between two variables because it contains each data point in a study, for example, each participant's score. The original helping data for each participant are graphed as a scatterplot in Figure 11.2. Let's discuss the scatterplot.

In a scatterplot, the data points are positioned according to their *X* and *Y* coordinates. *Coordinates* are simply the values along the dimensions (the horizontal and vertical axes). The *X* coordinates are the levels of mood, which are either 1 (for the control condition) or 2 (for the good mood experimental condition). As you can see, half of the data points have an *X* value of 1 and half have a 2. That is because we controlled mood in the experiment. The *Y* coordinates are the amount of time spent helping (in minutes). Scores along this (dependent) variable vary because of error. In fact, the amount of scatter up and down corresponds to the amount of error.

> A **scatterplot** consists of individual data points; each data point represents a pair of values, one on the *X* axis and one on the *Y* axis.

In summary, each data point is the relation between mood condition and helping for one participant. When the data points are viewed together, you can begin to see the

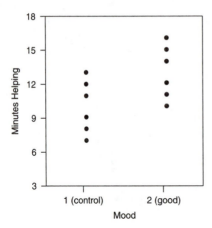

FIGURE 11.2.   A scatterplot of our familiar helping data. Each point is one participant's data.

relationship for an entire experiment. We will be focusing on these larger relationships. Also, remember that we can see error in a scatterplot.

REGRESSION EXAMPLE

Now it is time to cover new statistical ground. Imagine that instead of manipulating mood, we simply measured the mood of our participants. We asked each participant to rate his or her mood on a scale from 0 (worst possible) to 8 (best possible). Assume that previous research has established that the intervals on this scale are approximately equal, so the scale approximates an interval scale.

Thus, mood becomes another measured variable. Then we gave each participant an opportunity to help. We have only one group of participants because everyone was treated the same way. For each participant, we have two pieces of data: rated mood and the amount of time spent helping. A hypothetical set of data is shown in Table 11.1. No-

TABLE 11.1.   Rated Mood and Amount of Time Helping (in Minutes) for Each of 12 Hypothetical Participants

	RATED MOOD	TIME HELPING
1.	2	8
2.	2	9
3.	5	12
4.	1	7
5.	4	13
6.	4	11
7.	4	10
8.	7	16
9.	5	12
10.	5	14
11.	4	11
12.	5	15

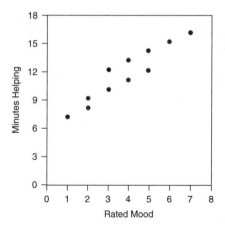

FIGURE 11.3. Minutes helping as a function of rated mood, in a scatterplot.

tice that the rated mood varies continuously between 0 and 8, instead of having only two levels. This allows for richer relations between the two variables, and the scatterplot becomes more meaningful.

The relations are graphed in the scatterplot shown in Figure 11.3. In this figure, rated mood is on the X axis and minutes helping on the Y axis (as previously). What happens as rated mood increases? Look at the figure and decide. The relations will be discussed.

Look more at the main relation indicated by the data in Figure 11.3. Can you provide a single description of the relation? Try using one very simple geometric or mathematical concept that covers most of the data. Draw it in Figure 11.3, or jot down your thoughts before going on. Keep the relation very simple and use a pencil if unsure.

Possible Relations in Figure 11.3

If you suggested a straight *line* for describing the relation, then good. If not, try to imagine how a straight line would fit the data. Draw one in, straight through the middle of the data. As before, the relation is that as mood increases, helping increases. This relationship is linear, because it is well described by a straight line. Regression goes beyond the idea that one variable covaries with another, to describe the relation in terms of lines.

Linear regression describes a relation between variables, in terms of the *slope* of a straight line.

Lines have several important properties. In linear regression, the most important property is that lines have a **slope**—the slant of the line. The slope answers the question "How much does one variable change as the other variable changes by one unit?" In our example slope tells us "how much helping increases with each one-unit increase in mood." As you will see, helping increases by 1.48 minutes with each increment in mood. We discuss slopes in more detail shortly.

CORRELATION: THE STRENGTH OF A RELATION

Now use a line to describe a second set of data, presented in Figure 11.4. Draw a line that fits the data. Ask yourself, "Is the linear relation as strong as in Figure 11.3?"

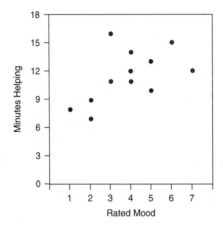

FIGURE 11.4.   Minutes helping as a function of rated mood, in a scatterplot (second data set).

Which relation is stronger and why?

The correct answer is that the relation in Figure 11.4 is not as strong. A straight line does not come as close to the data points in Figure 11.4 as it does in Figure 11.3. The differences between the line and the data points are deviations. They correspond to (guess what?) error. As in our previous statistics, this kind of error is caused by nuisance variables.

Thus, when there is more error, the relation is weaker. How do you measure the *strength* of a relation? Regression does not work well for measuring strength of relations. Instead, the related concept of correlation is used. **Correlation**—the statistic *r*—measures the strength of a relation after putting the two variables on a common (standard) scale of *z* scores, or standard units. Correlation measures how close the data points come to the line that relates them. The closer the data points, the stronger the relation.

Regression, in contrast, leaves the two variables in their actual units rather than standard units. This feature makes the slopes meaningful, because you can relate a given amount of mood to a number in minutes of helping, for example.

In practice, correlation and regression are complementary and are often used together. We now provide more detail for each statistic. We begin with regression, which describes relations.

N **CONCEPT CHAIN:**

REGRESSION LINES

In describing relations, remember that our two variables are referred to as the X variable and the Y variable. Our present example involves relations between rated mood (X) and minutes helped (Y). The data from Figure 11.3 are shown in Figure 11.5, with the regression line superimposed. The regression line summarizes the relation between X and Y, in a manner somewhat analogous to the way a mean summarizes a sample of scores. Like a mean, the regression line is idealized, and may or may not correspond to individual data points. A regression line indicates a central tendency that "moves with" the value of X. In Figure 11.5, the central tendency increases with X. Note that only some of the actual data points fall directly on the regression line. In other data sets, none of the actual data points will fall on the regression line. Nevertheless, the regression line provides a good summary of the data if the relation is linear.

The values of Y along the regression line are designated $\hat{Y}$. They have this designation because they are not the same as the actual Y values (the actual data points). The $\hat{Y}$-values are defined by the regression line that describes the data. Let's look at the regression line in Figure 11.5:

$$\hat{Y} = 1.485X + 5.807$$

Like all lines, the regression line has two properties, the first of which, slope, is of most importance in regression.

FIGURE 11.5. Minutes helping as a function of rated mood, in a scatterplot with the regression line superimposed and the regression equation provided at the bottom.

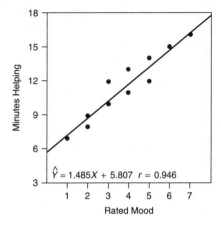

$\hat{Y} = 1.485X + 5.807$ $r = 0.946$

SLOPE: THE REGRESSION COEFFICIENT

This property specifies how much Y changes as X changes by one unit. In our example, the question is "How much does helping increase with each one-unit increase in mood?" The answer to this question is the *slope* of the line. In Figure 11.5, the slope is positive and its value is 1.485. This means that as mood increases by one rated point, the minutes of helping increases by 1.485 on the average. In Figure 11.6, shown later (with the same data as Figure 11.4), the slope is somewhat less (0.861), meaning that helping increases by 0.86 minutes on average with each one-unit increase in mood. The slope is also called the **regression coefficient.**

> The **slope** (regression coefficient) tells us how much Y changes with each unit change in X.
> The larger the slope value, the greater the change in Y with units of X.
> Slopes can be positive or negative:
>   If variable X and Y go up together, the slope is positive.
>   If variable X goes up while Y goes down, the slope is negative.

INTERCEPT

The second property of regression lines is meaningful in some cases. It concerns the predicted value of Y when X has a value of zero. For example, in our case one could ask "How much helping occurs when a person has the worst possible mood (rating of 0)?"

> The **intercept** of a line is the value of $\hat{Y}$ When X is zero (where $\hat{Y}$ intercepts the X axis of zero).

The intercept can be seen in Figure 11.5 by looking at the value of Y when X is zero (the very left-hand edge of the graph). That is, when the mood is zero, what is the value of Y? Figure this out and check your work.[1] Mathematically, this is the starting point of the line.

The value of "zero" may or may not make sense in a particular study. In our study, there is a zero level on the mood scale ("worst possible mood"). However, one could debate whether a mood of zero is really meaningful or not. We won't debate that point here. In other cases, zero might be a meaningful level. For example, we could measure how people did on an exam and how much time they studied. Zero study time is a meaningful concept (although not a very smart one). Even if all students studied for positive amounts of time, we could use regression to predict how well (how poor) performance is at the zero intercept (see below).

In addition to the properties of slope and intercept, *error* is an important concept in regression (and in correlation).

ERROR

As noted earlier, **error** is the deviation of actual data points from the idealized regression line. The regression line is like a group mean that changes systematically with X. Each point on the line (each $\hat{Y}$) is the mean value of Y at that level of X. When actual data points differ from this prediction, it is error.

---

[1] A visual estimate would be 6 or a little less. A simple mathematical method will be provided shortly.

There is relatively little error in Figure 11.5, because the data points are close to the line. Figure 11.6, however, illustrates a case with more error—the second data set, first seen in Figure 11.4. Two of the deviations are indicated by brackets. Draw brackets to illustrate more of the deviations.

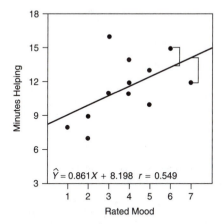

FIGURE 11.6.   Data with more error: minutes helping as a function of rated mood, in a scatterplot with the regression line superimposed and the regression equation provided at the bottom. Two examples of error are indicated by brackets at upper right.

As in experiments, error is caused by nuisance variables. This may include factors like time of data, errors of measurement, and other factors that can influence behavior. In the case of helping, all of the factors that could contribute to error in an experiment could contribute to error in regression and in correlation. Error is measured most directly in correlation; in fact, error is the opposite of correlation in that correlations become weaker as error increases. We will return to this shortly.

DONE!   𝟀

𝟀   **CONCEPTUALIZATION:**

USING REGRESSION FOR PREDICTION

Once a good description of a relation has been obtained with regression, it can be used for **prediction.** That is, we can predict values of the Y variable ($\hat{Y}$'s) given values on the X variable. When we do this, the X variable is often called the *predictor variable* or even the *independent variable*. The Y variable is called the *predicted variable* because Y's are being predicted from X's.

For example, let's say that someone rated his or her mood as 6. Looking at Figure 11.7, how long do you think the person would help? Try to figure out the $\hat{Y}$ value. Then predict $\hat{Y}$ for an X value of 3. Try this and then read on.

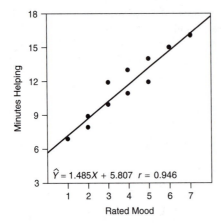

FIGURE 11.7. Minutes helping as a function of rated mood, in a scatterplot with the Regression Line superimposed and the Regression Equation provided at bottom.

You can answer the first question by finding the value of 6 on the X axis. Then, as illustrated in Figure 11.8 go straight up to the regression line. Mark this point, and then go straight leftward to the Y axis (see Figure 11.8). The value you get is the prediction, $\hat{Y}$. The value should be 15 minutes or a bit less. When doing this, be sure to use the regression line for your prediction rather than the data points.

When the mood is 3, the prediction is about 9.5 minutes of helping. This process is also illustrated by the arrows in Figure 11.8.

For greater precision, this prediction process can be done easily with mathematics, using the regression equation, as discussed next.

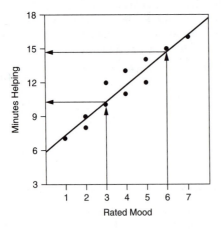

FIGURE 11.8. Lines have been added to Figure 11.7 to illustrate prediction.

REGRESSION EQUATION

The two main properties of lines, the slope and the intercept, are "parameters" in the **regression equation.** They are often designated by m and b, respectively. These parameters are fairly easy to calculate from your data, and the step-by-step method for doing so is presented at the end of this chapter.

The regression equation gives the predicted value *x* as a function of a particular *x:*

$$\hat{Y} = mX + b$$

where *m* is the slope (regression coefficient) and *b* is the *Y* intercept.

As a simple exercise, calculate two values of $\hat{Y}$ for a new regression line, in which *m* = 1 and *b* = 5. Do this by plugging in the values for *m*, *X*, and *b* into the right side of the equation and then calculating the result. First, calculate *Y* when *X* is 2. Second, calculate *Y* when *X* is 7. Check your work.[2]

DONE!   ⅄

SUMMARY EXAMPLE

Let's put these ideas together in the context of a meaningful example. Let's say that you are interested in the relation between money and love. Does money buy you love? In statistical terms, is love related to money? To determine this, imagine that you used couples, and decided to focus on money spent by males and love experienced by females. For each couple, you used a measure of how much money the male spent on dates and gifts per week on average, and a measure of how much love was felt by the female (ranging from 1 is a little to 5 is lots of love). To keep the problem simple, you used only four couples. (You remember that larger numbers would provide better estimates, but you wanted to keep the example simple for learning purposes.)

The data are shown in Table 11.2. Follow these steps to learn about regression:

1. Make a scatterplot, with money along the *X* axis and love along the *Y* axis. In making the graphs, show the entire ranges of the variables ($0–$50 on *X*, and 1–5 on *Y*).

2. Try to draw the best regression line, using your intuitive number sense.

TABLE 11.2.   Money Spent by Males and Love Experienced by Females

COUPLE	X (MONEY SPENT)	Y (LOVE EXPERIENCED)
1.	$50	5
2.	5	1
3.	20	3
4.	4	4
5.	30	2

Now answer these questions:

1. How well does the line describe the data? If its strength was measured (by correlation), how strong would it be?

---

[2] Solutions: $y = 1 \times 2 + 5 = 2 + 5 = 7$ and $y = 1 \times 7 + 5 = 7 + 5 = 12$.

2. The slope m turns out to be 0.044 dollars/love unit, and the intercept b is 2.048. What does each of these values mean? How much love is predicted when $X = \$40$? Draw the regression line over your data.

After finishing, check your work.[3]

LETTING THE COMPUTER "FIT" YOUR REGRESSION LINE

Regression equations are usually calculated from a set of data by a computer program. The program determines which line will "fit" the data best—that is, produce the smallest error deviations. Because lines are defined by the slope (m) and the intercept (b), the program looks for the best-fitting combination of parameters m and b. The program provides you with the slope and intercept values, and you can predict other Y values by using the parameters and plugging X values into the regression equation, as in the previous exercises.

Note that the terms m and b are not always used by the computer program. Because these are both parameters, the parameters are sometimes called beta, or β. β_0 may be used for the intercept and β_1 for the slope. As noted, the slope is the regression coefficient, and it is also called the beta-weight. All of these are terms for how much Y changes for each unit change in X.

🏃 **CONCEPTUALIZATION:**

MEASURING THE STRENGTH OF A RELATION: CORRELATION

Correlation complements regression by measuring the *strength* of a relation. How closely is an X variable related to a Y variable? In terms of regression, the strength of a correlation is how little error there is in the predictions (how little the Y's differ from the Y's). Thus, when error deviations between the idealized line and the data points are smaller, the correlation is stronger. When error deviations are larger, the trail becomes "bumpy" and the correlation is weaker.

Correlation provides a value, r, that ranges between -1 and $+1$. When r is zero, there is no relation. When r is close to $+1$ or -1, the relation is very strong. The sign of the correlation tells you whether the relation (line) is positive (goes up) or negative (goes down). A strong or high correlation means that the data are fit by a line with little error, as in Figure 11.5, where the r is $+0.95$. Look at Figure 11.5. As the relation weakens, error increases, meaning larger deviations from the line. Larger deviations can be seen in Figure 11.6, where the r is 0.55. However, an r is 0.55 is still a strong relation in most areas of psychology. In general, a relation is viewed as weak when r becomes less than about 0.25.

Correlation values are symbolized as *r:*

    $r = 1$ indicates a strong *positive* relation (Y goes up as X goes up).
    $r = 0$ indicates no relation.
    $r = -1$ indicates a strong *negative* relation (Y goes down as X goes up).

---

[3] (1) The line describes the data fairly well. There is a moderate relation between money and love. (Although there is error, the correlation value turns out to be moderately strong.) (2) The slope of 0.044 means that for ever dollar spent, love increases by 44/1000 of a unit. The intercept of 2.048 suggests that if zero dollars were spent, the love experienced would be just over 2. The prediction for $40 work of love is 3.8 ($= 0.044 \times 40 + 2.048$).

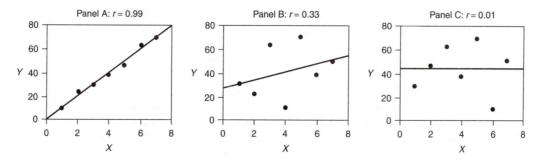

FIGURE 11.9. Three examples of correlations, ranging from strong (A) to moderate (B) to near-zero (C).

More examples of correlations are shown in Figure 11.9, with values of r at the top. The lines are best-fitting regression lines. Panel A shows a very strong positive relation. Panel B shows a moderate positive relation ($r = 0.33$). The correlation of 0.33 is reasonable in psychology—for example, the correlation between personality and behavior is often about 0.30. Panel C shows no relation ($r = 0.01$). Interestingly, a regression line can be calculated for the data in panel C, and it is shown. When there is no relation, the best prediction of Y is the mean of Y. The nearly flat line in panel C is at the mean of Y.

DONE!   𝓧

𝓧   **CONCEPTUALIZATION:**

z SCORES AND CORRELATION

The strength of a correlation is calculated by directly relating variation in variable X to variation in variable Y. Because the number scales used to measure X and Y often have different ranges, we must standardize the data on each scale—that is, we need to equalize the variances. For example, money ranged from 4 to 50, whereas love ranged from 1 to 5. To relate the variation on these two scales, we standardize them using **z scores,** or standard scores. Recall that a standard normal distribution can be divided into segments with widths of one standard deviation, or standard unit, or z score. These units are useful because they apply to any normal distribution, and provide a way to standardize it (see Figure 11.10, and Chapter 4 for review).

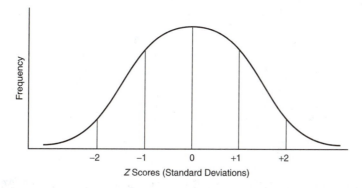

FIGURE 11.10. A frequency distribution with z scores.

After calculating the mean and the population standard deviation of a data set, the z score is calculated as follows. For each score, X_i,

$$z \text{ score} = \frac{(X_i - \bar{X})}{\text{SD}}$$

Note that the SD is the population standard deviation, calculated using N (rather then the N-1 used with samples). You will get to use z scores in the next section.

We will calculate correlation using the **z-score correlation formula.** The z-score formula is elegant, meaningful, and simple. How do you like that? We will apply the formula to three data sets that are possible outcomes of the money and love study discussed earlier. One outcome is familiar and two are new.

z SCORE CORRELATION FORMULA

Table 11.3 shows the three data sets, with most of the z scores calculated. There are two at the bottom of data sets B and C for you to calculate. The means and standard deviations are provided at the bottom of the data sets. Also, note that the mean of the z scores in a set of data is always zero, and that the standard deviation of z scores, is always 1. You can use this fact for checking your work. After calculating the z scores, check your work.[4]

TABLE 11.3.   Three Money/Love Data Sets to Work With

A)

	MONEY	LOVE	Z_X	Z_Y	$Z_X \times Z_Y$
1	50	5	1.648	1.414	2.330
2	5	1	−0.982	−1.414	1.388
3	20	3	−0.105	0.000	0.000
4	4	4	−1.040	0.707	−0.735
5	30	2	0.479	−0.707	−0.339
Mean	21.800	3.000	0.000	0.000	r=0.529
SD	17.116	1.414	1.118	1.118	

B)

	MONEY	LOVE	Z_X	Z_Y	$Z_X \times Z_Y$
1	50	4	1.648	0.707	1.165
2	5	1	−0.982	−1.414	1.388
3	20	3	−0.105	0.000	0.000
4	4	2	−1.040	−0.707	0.735
5	30	5	?	?	?
Mean	21.800	3.000	0.000	0.000	r = ?
SD	17.116	1.414	1.118	1.118	

---

[4] Data set B, pair 5, $z_x = 0.479$, $z_y = 1.414$; data set C, pair 5, $z_x = 0.479$, $z_y = -0.707$.

C)

	MONEY	LOVE	Z_X	Z_Y	$Z_X \times Z_Y$
1	50	1	1.648	−1.414	−2.330
2	5	5	−0.982	1.414	−1.388
3	20	3	−0.105	0.000	0.000
4	4	4	−1.040	0.707	−0.735
5	30	2	?	?	?
Mean	21.800	3.000	0.000	0.000	r = ?
SD	17.116	1.414	1.118	1.118	

Once we have z scores, the correlation is easy to calculate. The main calculation is of **cross-products.** Cross-products are obtained by multiplying the z_x and z_y in each pair. They are essential to relations between numbers, because they reveal whether or not X and Y covary.

Cross-Products

A cross-product is $z_x \times z_y$.
The value is positive when both x and y are positive or both are negative.
The value is negative when one is positive and the other negative.

Notice that in data set A in Table 11.3, the cross-products tend to be positive, indicating that Y goes up as X does. This is even more pronounced in data set B. In contrast, in data set C the cross-products are generally negative, indicating the as Y goes up, X goes down.

The cross-products are the essence of correlation, because correlation is the mean of the cross-products. Thus, when the cross-products are large and positive, the correlation will be high and positive; when the cross-products are both positive and negative, the correlation will tend to be small; and when they are large and negative, the correlation will be high and negative.

Correlation is the **mean of the cross-products:**

$$r = \frac{\sum_{i=1}^{N} (z_{x_i} \times z_{y_i})}{N}$$

Thus, the last steps of correlation are to sum the cross-products and then divide by N (the number of pairs) to get the mean. The correlation will range between −1 to +1. I've calculated the r for the first data set, leaving you the other two data sets to do. Look at each data set first and think about the relation. How strong is it? Look at the cross-products. What do they say? After calculating the r's, check your work.[5]

The z-score method illustrates the meaning of correlation. Correlation measures the strength of the relation between two variables, by standardizing the two variables on

---

[5] Data set B, pair 5, $z_X \times z_Y = 0.678$; $r = 0.793$; data set C, pair 5, $z_X \times z_Y = -0.339$, $r = -0.959$.

the same scale (z scores) and using cross-products. Correlation is the mean of the cross-products. There is also a computational method for correlation. It can be easier to use with large sets of numbers, but it is neither elegant nor meaningful. It is provided at the end of this chapter.

DONE!   ⅄

⅄   **CONCEPTUALIZATION:**

CORRELATION, REGRESSION, AND VARIANCE: THE COEFFICIENT OF DETERMINATION

Remember ANOVA? It involved three types of variance: total variation, variation due to the independent variable (IV), and error variation. Typically, researchers are most interested in variation due to the IV; error variation is error. Add the IV variance and error variance and you get the total variation. There is a direct analogy between these three sources of variation and concepts in correlation and regression. Specifically, if you square the correlation value r, you get R^2, which is analogous to the variation due to the IV. That is, R^2 indicates how much of the variation in the Y value is explained or predicted by the X variable. R^2 is known as the **coefficient of determination.**

R^2, the Coefficient of Determination

The proportion of variation in Y that is explained or predicted by X, or the proportion of variation in Y that is described by the regression line.

We are dealing with proportions here, and proportions add to 1. Thus, if you subtract R^2 from 1, the remaining proportion is error:

$1 - R^2 =$ Error

As in ANOVA,

Total variation = Variation due to X + Error

or

$1 = R^2 +$ Error

However, the meaning of error is slightly more deep in regression and correlation. In an experiment, error is almost always the uninteresting part of the variation; error is the effect of the nuisance variables, which the researcher is not interested in. In regression and correlation, the focus is on relations between variables and the importance of relations. Error includes the effects of all of the other, unmeasured variables on the variable of interest. Therefore, a small correlation value (error is large and R^2 is small) suggests that the influence of the measured variable is small and there are other variables that have large influences on the behavior. In fact, R^2 is a good index of the potential importance of a variable.

> ### R^2 as an Index of Potential Importance
> When R^2 approaches 1, the X variable is highly related to the Y variable. As R^2 approaches 0, the X variable is unrelated to the Y variable.

Look back at Figures 11.5 and 11.6. In Figure 11.5, there is a very strong relation. The R^2 is 0.895, indicating that the relation between X and Y explains almost all of the variation in Y. We can also express this in percentages; the percentage of variance accounted for is 89.5. Other variables account for only 10.5% of the behavior of Y. Such strong relations are rather rare in the behavioral sciences, however. The relation between personality variables and behavior, for example, is generally similar to the relation shown in Figure 11.9, panel B. Look at that relation. The R^2 is 0.109 (0.33^2), meaning that the X variable explains only 10.9% of the variance in Y. The many other influences on behavior, including error, explain the remaining 89.1% of the variance.

DONE! 人

TESTING THE SIGNIFICANCE OF REGRESSION AND CORRELATION VALUES

Regression provides slope values (m or b) and correlation provides r values. However, like any statistics, these values are estimates, and estimates are likely to contain error because of error variation. Given a slope value (say, $m = 1.485$), we should ask how much this value is likely to deviate from the (unknown) population value. Given an r value, we can ask if it is significantly different from zero. Is an r of .15 likely to be caused by chance alone (null hypothesis) or does it appear to be a real effect?

1. **The standard error of slope values in regression (SE_m).** This tells us how much a slope value is likely to vary, on the average. It is calculated from the definition of error provided earlier ($1 - R^2$) and the SD of Y:

$$SE_m = SD_y \times (1 - R^2)$$

2. **To test the significance of an r value.** Significance tell us if an r is unlikely to be due to chance (researcher's hypothesis). A two-tailed (nondirectional) test is assumed. The process is quite simple:
    a. Calculate degrees of freedom, using $N - 2$, where N is the number of pairs.
    b. Using df, look up the critical value of r in Table 11.4. If the obtained r is greater than this value, it is significant. (Use the absolute value of r.)

Note that the critical values of r decrease greatly as sample size (measured by degrees of freedom) increases. This is because, as you know, larger samples provide better estimates.

TABLE 11.4.   Critical Values of *r* in a Two-Tailed (Nondirectional) Test, for $p < 0.05$

df	CRITICAL r (0.05%)	df	CRITICAL r (0.05%)
1	0.9969	16	0.4683
2	0.9500	17	0.4555
3	0.8783	18	0.4438
4	0.8114	19	0.4329
5	0.7545	20	0.4227
6	0.7067	25	0.3809
7	0.6664	30	0.3494
8	0.6319	35	0.3246
9	0.6021	40	0.3044
10	0.5760	45	0.2875
11	0.5529	50	0.2732
12	0.5324	60	0.2500
13	0.5139	70	0.2319
14	0.4973	80	0.2172
15	0.4821	90	0.2050
		100	0.1946

TWO LIMITATIONS OF LINEAR REGRESSION AND CORRELATION

Linear regression and correlation have two main limitations. These limitations are helpful in learning the concepts.

ONLY LINEAR RELATIONS ARE MEASURED

> Linear regression and correlation are designed for relations that are linear in nature.

Linear relations form a straight line when graphed, as can be seen in panels A and B of Figure 11.11. Panel A shows a positive relation and B shows a negative relation. Other relations, however, are not linear, as shown in panel C. Linear regression will not measure them.

Some nonlinear relations can be measured with other types of regression. The relation shown in panel C can be measured with *curvilinear regression* (see an advanced statistics text). The basic idea is that the data are fit by a curve or some other simple mathematical function rather than by the formula for a straight line. Because the particular type of relation shown in panel C is seen fairly often in behavioral sciences, let's focus on that example.

Panel C of Figure 11.11 depicts the classic relation between arousal and performance, which is termed an *inverted-U* function. The relation is obtained when performance is measured as a function of arousal. When arousal is very low (the left side of the function in panel C), performance is low—e.g., the person may be sleepy. As arousal increases (middle of the function), performance increases up to some optimal point. As arousal becomes very high (right side of the function), performance decreases—the person is overwrought or "wired."

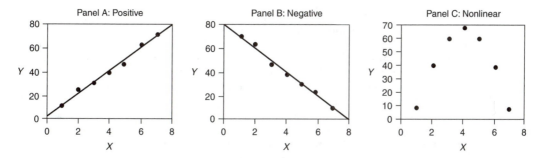

FIGURE 11.11. Three examples of relations in regression. Panels A and B are good linear relations, with regression equations as follows: (A) $y = 9.679x + 1.429$; (B) $y = -9.679x + 78.857$. Panel C is a nonlinear relation that should not be analyzed with linear regression. (Curvilinear regression could be used.

Because of the possibility of nonlinear relations, one should always check the data using a scatterplot and the "eyeball method." That is, look at your scatterplot whenever doing correlation or regression.

A RELATION DOES NOT IMPLY CAUSALITY

> The fact that a relation exists does *not* indicate that *X* causes *Y*.

When relations are obtained with regression or correlation, the relations may or may not be causal in nature. Even if the relation is strong, it may be noncausal. Consider the possible relation between the goodness of people's suntans and their GPA. If we measured students' suntans and their GPAs, what is likely to happen to the GPAs as suntans became better and better? Most likely, there would be a negative relation—as the goodness of a student's suntan goes up, GPA goes down. Does this mean that suntans *cause* low GPAs?

Suntans probably do not cause low GPAs. Instead, there may be some other cause. Any guesses?

On the other hand, several decades ago health researchers began to notice a relation between smoking and lung cancer. When this relation was first measured, it was a positive relation that could be measured with regression or correlation. It was not clear, however, if the relation was causal or not. Considerable further research has been conducted since then and it has established that the relation is causal.

These examples illustrate that relations may or may not be causal in nature. Determining whether or not a relation is causal requires further research. Further research could involve experimentation. In addition, some correlational methods to be described could be used.

A major problem in inferring causality from a relation is that there might be a third variable that is the real cause. This problem has an intuitive name.

THE THIRD VARIABLE PROBLEM

When a strong relation is observed, can we infer the one variable caused the other? The answer is a loud "No!" A major problem with such a conclusion is the **third variable problem**—there might be a third variable that causes variation in the two measured variables. Because the same third variable influences both of the measured variables, it appears that there is a relation between the measured variables. The third variable influences correlation and regression in a manner analogous to the influence of confounds on *t*-tests and *F*-tests. Like confounds, third variables that are related to *X* and *Y* influence the top of the statistical ratio, increasing correlation and regression values.

As an example of the third variable problem, let's return to our finding of a relation between the goodness of people's suntans and their GPAs. Did you think of a third variable that might be the real determinant of GPA (and suntan)? If not, do so now.

Perhaps a more likely cause is study time. This third variable could cause differences in each of the other two variables. Decreases in study time could decrease GPA. And, perhaps because spending little time studying means students have less to do, a decrease in study time could cause an increase in tanning time and increase the goodness of a suntan. (This is sometimes a problem at my school.)

In addition, other potential variables could be considered, such as goodness of previous schooling, interest in the subjects, and aptitude for the subjects. All of these variables should be considered as possible causes of the relation between suntan and GPA. Such possibilities mean that the finding of a relation does not necessary mean much; further research should be used to examine the variety of possible explanations of the relation. Conducting an experiment with the relevant factors is one method for testing causality. In addition, one can use advanced methods that involve correlation and regression. Two useful methods are described shortly.

REGRESSION AND CORRELATION VERSUS *t*-TESTS AND ANOVA

At this point, it is useful to discuss the differences between experimental analyses (ANOVA and *t*-test) and correlational analyses (regression and correlation). Either type of analysis can be applied to a set of data. Furthermore, all of these approaches are closely related mathematically. IVs and predictor variables influence the top of the statistical ratios (as do confounds and related third variables), whereas error influences the bottoms of the ratios. Some computer programs calculate the ANOVA (and *t*-test) as a special case of general regression. So, what is the difference between the approaches?

The crucial difference is not in the mathematics, but in the design decisions and interpretations that a researcher makes—the thinking process. Perhaps the most crucial issues concern the variables: Is one or more variables actively controlled by the experimenter? Is one or more IVs manipulated or are all variables measured?

Use the logic of the ANOVA/*t*-test when independent variables are controlled by the researcher. Causal interpretations are permitted in this case.
Use the logic of regression/correlation when the variables are measured by the researcher. Causal interpretations should be made with great caution.

For example, when mood is manipulated by the researcher (e.g., by providing free gifts), experimental analyses such as *t*-test and ANOVA are most appropriate. We can conclude the manipulation *caused* observed effects in the dependent variable, if the effects are significant. In contrast, when mood is measured in the participants along with helping, correlational analyses are more appropriate. Causal interpretations can be made only after further research.

Because you are being introduced to statistics, you should focus your thinking on these two types of situations. In fact, summarize the difference here:

> Summarize the differences:

Now I can tell you that there are cases that occupy the fuzzy boundary between these two situations. For example, when a researcher uses an independent variable based on attributes of the participants (e.g., gender, or personality traits), the variable is preexisting. Statistical methods such as ANOVA can be used to analyze its effects, but cautions such as the third variable problem should be heeded. Also, statisticians sometimes use regression analyses to analyze an experiment because it provides certain technical advantages. (The mathematics of regression are more general than ANOVA mathematics. You can learn more about this in an advanced statistics course.)

The general point is that the decisions a researcher makes about the methods and purpose of a study determine the statistical logic that is appropriate. People learn to choose the correct statistic through extensive study, which may involve asking the help of experts. The purpose of this text is to get you started on the learning process by providing a solid foundation.

ADVANCED METHODS OF CORRELATION AND REGRESSION

Advanced methods can provide information relevant to causality with correlational data. The methods allow us to look at possible relations between many variables simultaneously, and determine which of many possible relations are potentially important or unimportant. As an example, we will consider one simplified problem—our problem of the determinants of GPA.

CORRELATION MATRICES

Given data for a set of measured variables, a **correlation matrix** provides the correlation values (r's) between all possible pairs of variables. For example, if there are 10 variables, a correlation matrix would show the r value for every pair of variables. We could then look at which relations are strongest (and potentially most important). Let's look at Table 11.5, which is a hypothetical correlation matrix for six variables—GPA and five possible determinants of GPA. The variables are written across the top (designating columns) *and* along the left side (designating rows). The correlations are printed where pairs of variables meet. For example, if you look at the GPA row, you find the correlation with suntan in the Suntan column ($r = -0.35$; as Suntan gets better GPA goes down).

Note the blanks along the diagonal. The blanks are where one variable meets itself—the correlation of a variable with itself is always 1.0. You can also see that the cor-

TABLE 11.5.   Hypothetical Correlation Matrix between Six Variables

	GPA	SUNTAN	INTEREST	STUDYTIME	MATHAPT.	VERBALAPT.
GPA	—	−0.35	0.35	0.55	0.20	0.30
Suntan	−0.35	—	−0.40	−0.50	−0.15	−0.10
Interest	0.35	−0.40	—	0.60	0.35	0.40
StudyTime	0.55	−0.50	0.60	—	0.15	0.25
MathApt.	0.20	−0.15	0.35	0.15	—	0.18
VerbalApt.	0.30	−0.10	0.40	0.25	0.18	—

relations above the diagonal are the same as below the diagonal, because every variable meets every other variable twice in the matrix.

Let's focus on the relations with GPA. You can find how the other variables correlate with GPA by looking across the GPA row. Do so, and decide which ones appear most important. Discussion follows.

The strongest relation with GPA is StudyTime ($r = 0.55$), suggesting that StudyTime may be the primary determinant of GPA. Other variables have a weaker but still considerable positive relation (e.g., interest and aptitudes) and may also contribute to GPA. Suntan is nagatively related, and appears to hurt GPA. If you look at the Suntan row and find where StudyTime meets Suntan, you can see that there is a strong negative relation between the two. Suntan appears to reduce Study-Time. How do we explain that?

In summary, a correlation matrix indicates which relations are potentially most important. In the present case, StudyTime is the most important relation involving GPA and may be a cause of increasing GPA. Study Time should be studied in further research. Several other variables are also positively related and may cause some increase in GPA; they may also be worthy of further study. Suntan is negatively related to GPA, but this may occur because it is related (negatively) to a variable (StudyTime) that is strongly related to GPA.

MULTIPLE REGRESSION

Multiple regression allows us to go further in analyzing the relations in a set of data. It can provide slope values for several variables simultaneously, along with an intercept value. In addition, it has the important feature of allowing you to examine interactions between variables, as factorial ANOVA does.

Once you have slope values for several variables and the intercept, you can make predictions based on the set of variables. This is critical because many decisions (e.g., college admissions) should be based on a combination of factors. Multiple regression provides a prediction formula that is an extension of the linear formula you learned earlier. The formula is extended by providing slope values (*b*'s) for each variable. You can also compare the *b*'s to each other, to see which is most important.

Multiple regression also provides information relevant to causality. The thinking is this: Given two or more variables that are related to a third, dependent variable, what happens if we *remove* the effects of one variable? For example, we have seen that StudyTime and Suntan are both related to GPA. If we removed the effects of StudyTime on GPA, would there be any unique effects of Suntan or other variables left?

Technically, "removing the effects of a variable" is termed *factoring out* or *parcelling out* the variable. There are two possible effects of factoring out a variable. Let's say we factor out the effects of StudyTime on GPA.

One possible effect is that once an important variable has been removed, other variables no longer have an effect. For example, the correlation for Suntan and GPA could become 0 when the effects of StudyTime have been factored out. This would suggest that the negative effect Suntan appeared to have (the *r* in the correlation matrix) occurred only because Suntan was related to StudyTime, which was the crucial, causal determinant of differences in GPA. It may be that people who studied less also tended to have better suntans, but than suntan had no direct effect on GPA. (If students could find a way to work on their Suntan without reducing StudyTime, there might be no negative effects of suntan—at least none on GPA.)

Another possibility is that once an important variable has been removed, other variables still have an effect of their own. For example, after factoring out the effects of StudyTime, the aptitudes (Math and Verbal) might still have a small effect—let's say the *r*'s are reduced to 0.15 and 0.20, respectively. These are called *partial correlations*. Their significance could be tested. If significant, the partial correlations would mean that the aptitudes have a small but unique contribution to determining GPA that does not overlap with the effects of StudyTime.

The purpose of these last two sections has been to introduce you to some useful advanced methods that involve correlation and regression. These methods begin to provide information about causality, because they can be used to rule out possible causes. These methods, like all of the methods covered in the book, are worthy of advanced study.

REFERENCE: CALCULATING REGRESSION AND CORRELATION VALUES

You can use a calculator (or even pencil and paper) to calculate the regression parameters m and b. There's also a computation formula for r that may be useful if you are working with many numbers. These calculations use cross-products, which are the values of $X \times Y$ for each pair of scores, and which are designated XY. The formulas are given below and instructions for using them follow.

THE REGRESSION FORMULA FOR THE SLOPE m

$$m = SS_{XY}/SS_{XX}$$

THE REGRESSION FORMULA FOR THE INTERCEPT b

$$b = \bar{Y} - m \times \bar{X}$$

THE CORRELATION FORMULA

$$r = \frac{N(\Sigma XY) - (\Sigma X)(\Sigma Y)}{\sqrt{[N(\Sigma X^2) - (\Sigma X)^2][N(\Sigma Y^2) - (\Sigma Y)^2]}}$$

and in a more mnemonic form:

$$r = \frac{(N \times \text{Sum}XY) - (\text{Sum}X \times \text{Sum}Y)}{\sqrt{((N \times \text{Sum}X^2) - (\text{Sum}X)^2)((N \times \text{Sum}Y^2) - (\text{Sum}Y)^2)}}$$

For our example, we will use a simple set of six pairs of scores on variables X and Y. See the raw data given in Table 11.6. Each pair of scores is for one participant. Try calculating the r using the step-by-step methods and then check your work against the answers that follow.

TABLE 11.6.   Raw Data

	X SCORE	Y SCORE
Participant 1	3	14
Participant 2	1	16
Participant 3	4	23
Participant 4	4	37
Participant 5	8	25
Participant 6	6	41

STEP-BY-STEP METHOD FOR REGRESSION AND CORRELATION VALUES

1. Construct a correlation table with five columns and enough rows for each pair of scores and the sums. N is the number of pairs. See the example in Table 11.7.
2. From each X and Y, calculate their product (for the XY column), the square of X, and the square of Y. Then sum each column. Notice the notations used in the Sums row; they are used in the correlation formula.
3. For m, sum the XY column, then divide by sum of XY (X^2) column.
4. For b, calculate mean of Y's and subtract ($m \times$ mean of X's).
5. For r, use the eight-step calculation method described next, or use your own method.

EIGHT-STEP CALCULATION OF CORRELATION FORMULA

1. Multiply $N \times$ SumXY and enter_____(1).
2. Multiply Sum$X \times$ Sum$Y$ and enter_____(2).
3. Subtract (1) minus (2) and enter_____(3).
4. a. Multiply $N \times$ SumX^2_____(4a)
   b. Square Sum$X$_____(4b)
   c. Subtract (4a) minus (4b)_____(4c).
5. a. Multiply $N \times$ SumY^2_____(5a)
   b. Square Sum Y_____(5b)
   c. Subtract (5a) minus (5b)_____(5c).
6. Multiply (4c) by (5c) and enter_____(6).

TABLE 11.7.   Correlation Table

	X SCORE	Y SCORE	XY	X^2	Y^2
Participant 1	3	14	42	9	196
Participant 2	1	16			
Participant 3	4	23			
Participant 4	4	37			
Participant 5	8	25			
Participant 6	6	41			
$N = 6$ Sums:					
	Sum$X$	Sum$Y$	SumXY	SumX^2	SumX^2

TABLE 11.8.   Completed Correlation Table

	X SCORE	Y SCORE	XY	X^2	Y^2
Participant 1	3	14	42	9	196
Participant 2	1	16	16	1	256
Participant 3	4	23	92	16	529
Participant 4	4	37	148	16	1369
Participant 5	8	25	200	64	625
Participant 6	6	41	246	36	1681
$N = 6$	Sums: 26	156	744	142	4656
	Sum$X$	Sum$Y$	SumXY	SumX^2	SumX^2

7. Take square root of (6) and enter_____(7).
8. Divide (3)/(7) and you have $r =$_____.

COMPLETED STEP-BY-STEP METHOD FOR CALCULATING CORRELATION

1. Construct a correlation table with five columns and enough rows for each pair of scores and the sums. N is the number of pairs. See the example in Table 11.8.
2. From each X and Y, calculate their product (for the XY column), the square of X, and the square of Y. Then sum each column. Notice the notations used in the Sums row; they are used in the correlation formula.
3. $m = 744/142 = 5.239$
4. $b = (156/6) - (m \times 26/6) = (26) - (5.239 \times 4.33) = 3.315$
5. Work the correlation formula by using the step-by-step calculation method, or use your own method. The eight-step formula is shown below.

EIGHT-STEP CALCULATION OF CORRELATION FORMULA

1. Multiply $N \times$ SumXY and enter ___4464___ (1).
2. Multiply Sum$X \times$ Sum$Y$ and enter ___4056___ (2).
3. Subtract (1) minus (2) and enter ___408___ (3).
4. a. Multiply $N \times$ SumX^2 ___852___ (4a)
    b. Square Sum$X$ ___676___ (4b)
    c. Subtract (4a) minus (4b) ___176___ (4c).
5. a. Multiply $N \times$ SumY^2 ___27936___ (5a)
    b. Square Sum$Y$ ___24336___ (5b)
    c. Subtract (5a) minus (5b) ___3600___ (5c).
6. Multiply (4c) by (5c) and enter ___633600___ (6).
7. Take square root of (6) and enter ___795.98995___ (7).
8. Divide (3)/(7) and you have $r =$ ___0.513___.

REVIEW

Define and explain the following terms and phrases:

Scatterplot

Linear regression

Slope (m)

Correlation

Regression coefficient

Intercept (*b*)

Error

Prediction

Regression equation:

$y\text{-hat} = mX + b$

Correlation value (*r*)

z score

z-score correlation formula

Cross-product

Coefficient of determination (R^2)

Two Limitations of Regression Correlation

Third variable problem

Correlation matrix

Multiple regression

EXERCISES

11.1. The intercept is 10 and the slope is 2. What value of *Y* is predicted if
   a. $X = 4$?
   b. $X = 8$?

11.2. Find the correlation of *X* and *Y*:

	X SCORE	Y SCORE
Participant 1	11	2
Participant 2	33	5
Participant 3	64	9
Participant 4	99	6
Participant 5	34	7
Participant 6	14	6

11.3. The intercept of a line is 14 and the slope is 5. What value of *Y* would we get if
   a. $a = 1$
   b. $a = 13$
   c. $a = 2$
   d. $a = 18$

11.4. The equation for a line is $Y = 2X - 5$. If $Y = 11$, what does *X* equal?

11.5. The equation for another line is $Y = 4X + 15$. If $X = 10$, what does *Y* equal?

11.6. A health psychologist wants to know if there is a relationship between years of smoking and age at death and if we can come up with a formula to tell people how long they will live based on how many years they have smoked.

The data on 10 smokers (either currently at the time of death or having smoked for a significant number of years and then quit before their death) is presented below:

X YEARS OF SMOKING	Y AGE AT DEATH
1. 40	55
2. 25	45
3. 50	75
4. 30	90
5. 18	78
6. 15	81
7. 55	72
8. 13	79
9. 53	65
10. 44	62

a. Draw up a chart like the one found in Table 11.8 and use the step-by-step method to figure the correlational relationship here.

b. What is the regression formula for this data?

c. Do you see any confounds or problems with this data? What other factors could be working here?

11.7. A pediatrician wants to know the actual correlation between how much parents smoke and the number of respiratory illnesses that befall her patients in a year. She takes a sample of 10 patients from her files. The raw data follows:

X (NUMBER OF CIGARETTES SMOKED PER DAY AROUND CHILD/DAY)	Y (NUMBER OF INFECTIONS PER YEAR)
20.00	2.00
25.00	5.00
35.00	10.00
45.00	10.00
49.00	5.00
35.00	7.00
22.00	9.00
20.00	4.00
25.00	5.00
60.0	12.00

a. Draw up a chart like the one found in Table 11.8 and use the step-by-step method to figure the correlational relationship here.

b. What is the regression formula for this data?

c. Do you see any confounds or problems with this data? What other factors could be working here?

11.8. Mothers Against Drunk Driving (MADD) has done a 17-year study, starting in 1982, claiming that a cumulative total of more than 14,000 lives have been saved by minimum drinking age laws. Since 1982, all states in the United States have changed their drinking age from 18 to 21, with many changing over in the mid-1980s.

YEAR	LIVES SAVED	ACTUAL YEAR
1	578	1982
2	609	1983
3	709	1984
4	701	1985
5	840	1986
6	1071	1987
7	1148	1988
8	1093	1989
9	1033	1990
10	941	1991
11	795	1992
12	816	1993
13	848	1994
14	851	1995
15	846	1996
16	846	1997
17	861	1998

a. Draw up a chart like the one found in Table 11.8 and use the step-by-step method to figure the correlational relationship here.
b. What is the regression formula for this data?
c. You are MADD's statistician and you are called before Congress to give your opinion on whether the minimum drinking age should be returned to 18 since drunk driving fatalities are down less than they were in the mid-1980s. Do you think that these laws are working to curtail drunk driving fatalities? What could be a confound here?

11.9. An admissions officer at a state university with a large minority outreach program, wishes to print enticing information as to the relationship between years of education and annual income. The levels of education are defined as follows: high school graduate = 12; college = 13–16; graduate or professional school = 17–20; internship or post-doctoral educa-tion = 21+.

LEVEL OF EDUCATION	INCOME (IN THOUSANDS PER YEAR)
12	$18
13	$15
17	$22
22	$63
20	$55
11	$12
18	$105
14	$27

a. Draw up a chart like the one found in Table 11.8 and use the step-by-step method to figure the correlational relationship here.
b. What is the regression formula for this data?
c. What might be some problems with this data? Specifically, what might be the problem with the administrator drawing data only from his office?

ANSWERS

11.1.   a. $2 \times 4 + 10 = 18$
       b. $2 \times 8 + 10 = 26$
11.3.   a. 19;   b. 79;   c. 24;   d. 104
11.5.   55
11.7.   a. Chart:

X	Y	XY	X^2	Y^2
20	2	40	400	4
25	5	125	625	25
35	10	350	1225	100
45	10	450	2025	100
49	5	245	2401	25
35	7	245	1225	49
22	9	198	484	81
20	4	80	400	16
25	5	125	625	25
60	12	720	3600	144
Sum = 336	69	2578	13010	569

    $r = 0.649$

    b. Regression formula: Number of infections per year $= 0.151 \times$ (Number of cigarettes smoked around child/day) $+ 1.83$.

    c. Yes, there are problems. Did the child's mother smoke during pregnancy? Was mother exposed to second-hand smoke during pregnancy. Which parent smoked around child? Does child has some congenital problem that predisposes him or her to respiratory infections?

11.9.   a. Chart:

X	Y	XY	X	Y
12	18	216	144	324
13	15	195	169	225
17	22	374	289	484
22	63	1386	484	3969
20	55	1100	400	3025
11	12	132	121	144
18	105	1890	324	11025
14	27	378	196	729
Sum = 127	317	5671	2127	19925

    $r = 0.71*$

    b. Regression formula: Income $= 5.76 \times$ (Years of education) $+ -51.81$.

    c. This particular sample may not be representative of the U. S. population in general. We do not have information on race, gender, family of origin or socioeconomic status. This admissions officer should conduct more careful reasearch with larger samples if he wants his results to be valid!

Chapter 12

ANALYZING CATEGORICAL DATA

The statistics we have studied are designed for analyzing ratio or interval scales, in which the items on the scale differ from each other quantitatively—that is, they are larger or smaller along some type of measurement scale. As noted in the discussion of measurement scales (way back in Chapter 1), statistics used with such data are **parametric statistics.** Not all data are ratio or interval, however. Sometimes responses are more categorical in nature. For example, we might measure political alliance (e.g., Republican, Democrat, Independent) or classify children's behavior on a playground (e.g., cooperative play, independent play, aggression, inactivity). Such data are categorical, or *nominal* in nature. *Nominal* means that the possible value are not related to the others in any quantitative way—they are labels, names, or categories. To analyze such data, we must use **nonparametric statistics,** which do not involve continuous values.

Nominal data are often represented as frequencies in each category; for example, the frequency of people having each political alliance or the frequency of each playground behavior. We can analyze such data, looking for interesting differences, with a simple procedure called **chi-square** (pronounced "ki-square," where "ki" rhymes with "pie"). Chi-square provides a new use of the null hypothesis. In this chapter, we focus on the most basic case, in which the null hypothesis is based on chance.

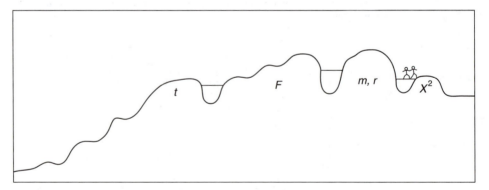

🚶 **CONCEPTUALIZATION:**

THE BASIC IDEA OF CHI-SQUARE (χ^2)

We will begin with a simple example. Imagine that we are testing a coin for fairness. We flip the coin 100 times and record the frequency of each of the two possible outcomes. We want to know if this is a fair coin. Our first step is to create a table with a cell for each outcome, and to enter the obtained frequencies in the appropriate cells. We need to leave room in the cells of the table for some calculations. Thus, we generate a table with two cells for data, like that shown in Table 12.1. We call the data we have obtained the **obtained frequencies.** Chi-square contrasts obtained frequencies with **expected frequencies.**

> **Obtained frequencies** are the obtained data. They are contrasted with expected frequencies.
> **Expected frequencies** are frequencies that would be expected based on a hypothesis that provide expectations, such as the null hypothesis.

TABLE 12.1.   Obtained Frequencies of Heads and Tails

Heads	70
Tails	30

In our example, the most logical hypothesis is the null hypothesis, which is that chance alone determines the coin flips. What frequencies would you expect if chance alone worked (if the coin was fair)? Generate the best expectation and enter it in Table 12.1, below the corresponding obtained frequencies. Enclose your expected frequencies in parentheses, to set them off from the obtained frequencies.

The table should look like Table 12.2. The expected frequencies are based on the idea that if chance alone determines the outcomes, the most likely outcome would be that each outcome occurs half of the time.

Chi-square focuses on the differences between the expected frequencies and the obtained frequencies. This is done by applying the chi-square calculation to each cell.

Chi-Square Calculation

$$\frac{(\text{Observed} - \text{Expected})^2}{\text{Expected}}$$

This calculation takes the difference between the expected and observed frequency in each cell, squares it, and "normalizes" it by dividing by the expected frequencies.

In the first cell, the calculation is $(70 - 50)^2/50 = 8$. Write this to the right of Table 12.2. Do the calculation for the second square. Then, below your table, add up the calculations to get your chi-square value. After finishing, compare your work to the completed table, Table 12.3.

TABLE 12.2.   Observed and Expected Frequencies

Heads	70 (50)
Tails	30 (50)

TABLE 12.3.   Completed Chi-Square Table

Heads	70 (50) $(70 - 50)^2/50 = 8$
Tails	30 (50) $(30 - 50)^2/50 = 8$

Chi-square obtained = 8 + 8 = 16

The next step is to determine if the chi-square value is significantly different from what would be expected if chance alone were working. As with other tests, this is done by comparing the obtained value to the critical value. In this case, you will need a table of critical chi-square values, which you will learn about. In the present case, the critical value is 3.84. Because the obtained value is greater than the critical value, we can reject the null hypothesis. We can conclude that this coin's behavior was not governed by pure chance. We shouldn't use this coin for gambling (at least not with our friends!).

The steps for chi-square are summarized in the box. To practice, let's say that another coin was flipped 50 times; 30 times it came up heads and 20 times tails. Construct the table and carry out the analysis using the step-by-step method. The answer follows.

Step-by-Step Method for Chi-Square

1. Set up the *observed* frequencies (your obtained data) in a table. Each category is a *cell*.
2. For each cell, determine the *expected* frequency—the frequency that would be most likely to occur if chance alone determined it.
3. For each cell, do this calculation: $\dfrac{(\text{Observed} - \text{Expected})^2}{\text{Expected}}$.
4. Add these normalized differences to get the chi-square value.

You should obtain a chi-square value of 2 for the coin-flipping experiment. The next section introduces the table of critical values for chi-square, so you can test your obtained value.

DONE!

TESTING THE SIGNIFICANCE OF A CHI-SQUARE VALUE

Use your knowledge of significance testing to test the significance of the obtained chi-square of 2.0. Is this likely to be real or can we attribute it to chance? The df's are explained here and the table of critical values is provided (Table 12.4).

In looking up the critical value, you use one value for the degrees of freedom. The value for degrees of freedom depends on the number of categories in the data and the number of variables. With one variable, as in our example, the number of categories is designated by *a* and df is given by *a*-1. Check significance and then check

TABLE 12.4. Critical Values of Chi-Square with 5% Region of Rejection

df	$\chi^2_{0.05}$	df	$\chi^2_{0.05}$
1	3.84	21	32.67
2	5.99	22	33.92
3	7.81	23	35.17
4	9.49	24	36.42
5	11.07	25	37.65
6	12.59	26	38.89
7	14.07	27	40.11
8	15.51	28	41.34
9	16.92	29	42.56
10	18.31	30	43.77
11	19.68	40	55.76
12	21.03	50	67.50
13	22.36	60	79.08
14	23.68	70	90.53
15	25.00	80	101.88
16	26.30	90	113.14
17	27.59	100	124.34
18	28.87	120	146.57
19	30.14		
20	31.41		

your work.[1] If you can do this with confidence, good. If not, write down the steps and thinking in your own words.

EXPECTED FREQUENCIES WITH MORE THAN TWO CATEGORIES

When there are more than two categories and the expected frequencies are based on chance, the following formula can be used to determine them:

$$E = N/a$$

where E is the expected frequency, N is the total frequency, and a is the number of categories.

CONCEPTUALIZATION:

EXTENDING THE BASIC IDEA TO CONTINGENCIES

Chi-square can get more complex and more interesting. We can apply it to cases with two or more variables, and to the issue of whether the variables exhibit a contingency or independence. Independence means they are unrelated, whereas contingency involves a relation between the two variables.

---

[1] With $(a - 1) = (2 - 1) = 1$ df, the critical value is 3.84, which is more than the obtained value of 2.0. Therefore, the null hypothesis is reasonable (we cannot reject it).

> **Independence** means that the frequencies in one variable do *not* depend on the level of another variable. This is analogous to the idea that there is *no* interaction between two variables.
> **Contingency** means that the frequencies in one variable depend on the level of another variable. This is analogous to the idea of an interaction between the variables, in which the effects of one variable depend on the level of another variable.

When there is more than one variable, use the second formula in the following box. In that formula, b is the number of categories in the second variable.

> ### Degrees of Freedom for Chi-Square
>
> $df = (a - 1)$ if there is only one variable in your table
> $df = (a - 1) \times (b - 1)$ if there are two variables in your table.
> For these equations, a and b are the number of categories of your first and second variable, respectively.

For example, let's consider the question of whether people like their mates to have the same or different color of hair. If there is a contingency, the hair preference should depend on the participants' hair color—e.g., preferences for light or dark hair should depend on whether the participant has light or dark hair. Independence, in contrast, would mean that light-haired people had the same preferences as dark-haired people. We can view this issue in a **contingency table,** in which the distribution of frequencies is contingent on another variable.

CONTINGENCY TABLES

A contingency table typically has two variables—one row variable and one column variable. In our hair-color example, we will look at a hypothetical distribution of hair preferences as a function of participant's hair color. Assume that a sample of 50 people with light hair and 50 with dark hair was asked which type of hair they preferred their mates to have. Their preferences are shown in a 2×2 contingency table (Table 12.5).

If you sum the frequencies in the two rows of Table 12.5, you can see that there is a difference in overall frequency of preferring light or dark hair. Dark hair is preferred somewhat more overall (64 versus 35 times). This fact needs to be taken into account when we calculate the expected frequencies. To calculate expected frequencies, use the following steps. Apply them in Table 12.5. Once you have your four expected frequencies, apply the chi-square calculation and sum the results to get the obtained chi-square

TABLE 12.5.   Chi-Square Contingency Table

		PARTICIPANT'S HAIR COLOR		
		Light	Dark	
HAIR PREFERENCE	Light	20	15	row 1
	Dark	30	35	row 2
		column 1	column 2	total

value. Then test your obtained value against the appropriate critical value. Check you work by looking at the completed table (Table 12.6).

Steps for Analyzing a Chi-Square Contingency Table

1. Calculate *row* frequencies for the dependent variable (hair preference) by summing across. Write them by "row 1" or "row 2." Calculate the *total* frequency by summing the row frequencies. Enter them by "total" in Table 12.5.
2. Calculate the relative frequencies (rf) by dividing the row frequencies by the total frequency: rf = row frequency/total frequency; write rf in aproriate row.
3. Calculate column frequencies for the independent variable (participant hair color).
4. To get the expected frequencies in each cell, multiply the appropriate column frequency by the rf: E = column frequency $\times$ rf. Write in parentheses in cell.
5. Apply the chi-square calculation, $(O - E)^2/E$, to each cell and sum them to obtain the chi-square value.

The value obtained in Table 12.6 is less than the critical value of 3.84. The degrees of freedom, using the formula for two variables, are $(2 - 1) \times (2 - 1) = 1$. This means that these preferences could have occurred by chance—there is no reliable difference in the preferences of light- and dark-haired people, and hair preference is independent of one's hair color.

DONE! 𝑋

THIS IS CHI-SQUARE

We have covered the basic idea of chi-square. However, note that you can apply chi-square in a number of interesting ways, including to designs with additional categories or variables. The only requirement is that you must be able to specify the expected frequencies based on a clear hypothesis.

TABLE 12.6. Completed Chi-Square Contingency Table

		PARTICIPANT'S HAIR COLOR		
	Light	20 (E = 0.35 × 50 = 17.5) (20 − 17.5)²/17.5 = 0.357	15 (E = 0.35 × 50 = 17.5) (15 − 17.5)²/17.5 = 0.357	row 1 35 rf = 35/100 = 0.35
HAIR PREFERENCE	Dark	30 (E = 0.65 × 50 = 32.5) (30 − 32.5)²/32.5 = 0.192	35 (E = 0.65×50 = 32.5) (35 − 32.5)²/32.5 = 0.192	row 2 65 rf = 65/100 = 0.65
		column 1 50	column 2 50	total 100

Chi-square = 0.357 + 0.357 + 0.192 + 0.192 = 1.099

The relative frequencies (rf's) are calculated below the row frequencies, and used to calculate the expected frequencies in each cell.

The expected frequencies need not be based on the null hypothesis of chance alone being the determinant. You can generate expected frequencies based on any clear idea. For example, your expected frequencies could be based on the clear (but rather silly) notion that a coin will turn up "heads" 63.936662% of the time on the average. You could collect data with the coin and use chi-square to see if obtained frequencies differ from the expected frequency of 63.936662% heads. Most likely, your expected frequencies will be a fraction, but that is OK as long as they honor the hypothesis.

Another use of chi-square is to test a mathematical model. The model can be used to generate expected frequencies, and chi-square can be used to compare these frequencies to obtained frequencies. In this case, a theorist usually hopes that the expected frequencies will be similar to (i.e., not statistically different from) the obtained frequencies. Of course, a good researcher will do this carefully, and consider factors like sample size and error. These factors influence the power of a chi-square test, as they do for other tests.

As this topic implies, statistics is not a set of fixed, rigid tools. Rather, it is a complex set of methods with underlying principles. Although the basic principles are widely agreed on, there is room for argument and controversy concerning the more complex issues. There are, in fact, journals devoted to such issues. More constructively, the principles of statistics can be used by innovative researchers to create new statistics, to ask new questions, and to solve new problems. It does take considerable study to become skillful with statistics, but the possible uses of statistics are limited only by your creativity and effort.

REVIEW

Define the following terms:

Parametric statistics	Obtained frequencies
Nonparametric statistics	Expected frequencies
Nominal data	Contingency tables
Chi-square	

EXERCISES

12.1. McCloskey wanted to see if physics training helped people to correctly solve a simple but tricky question about motion. He asked a fairly simple physics question of physics and nonphysics majors. He recorded how many answered it correctly and how many incorrectly. The table is shown here; calculate the chi-square and determine if it is significant. Did training help? There is one degree of freedom in these data, so the critical value of chi-square is 3.84.

TYPE OF MAJOR		
	Physics	Nonphysics
Correct	26	8	row 1
Incorrect	14	32	row 2
	column 1	column 2	total

TYPE OF ANSWER (rows: Correct, Incorrect)

12.2. In a fictitious study, happy or sad people were asked whether they preferred a yellow or purple room. Does mood have a significant effect on color preference? (Again, the critical value is 3.84.)

MOOD		
	Happy	Sad
Yellow	22	8	row 1
Purple	10	18	row 2
	column 1	column 2	total

COLOR PREFERENCE (rows: Yellow, Purple)

12.3. Isen *et al.*'s (1976) original helping[2] data, introduced in Chapter 1, are reproduced again here. Calculate the frequencies of helping and nonhelping subjects in each group. Construct the contingency table and calculate chi-square.

	Control Group		Experimental Group
1.	Did not	1.	Helped
2.	Did not	2.	Helped
3.	Did not	3.	Helped
4.	Did not	4.	Helped
5.	Helped	5.	Did not
6.	Did not	6.	Helped
7.	Did not	7.	Helped
8.	Did not	8.	Helped
9.	Did not	9.	Helped
10.	Did not	10.	Helped
11.	Did not	11.	Did not
		12.	Helped

12.4. A school psychologist is going over placement forms and records and is wondering if the test used to place students according to ability is appropriate and if those students are now properly placed in their respective programs. The top row is students with good abilities and the bottom row is students with poor abilities according to the placement test.

[2] Isen, A. M., Clark., M., & Schwartz, M. F. (1976). Duration of the effect of good mood on helping: "Footprints on the sands of time." *Journal of Personality & Social Psychology, 34*, 385-393.

PROPER PLACEMENT?		
	Yes	No

PLACEMENT TEST ABILITY		Yes	No
	High	27	15
	Low	8	50

a. Calculate the expected values and row frequencies for this data.

b. Calculate chi-square and degrees of freedom and determine if the result is significant.

12.5. A psychologist wants to know how categorically high or low stress levels affect problem-solving ability. One hundred participants were studied. The top row is high stress level and the bottom row is low stress level.

PROBLEM-SOLVING ABILITY		
	High	Low

STRESS LEVEL		High	Low
	High	25	35
	Low	25	15

a. Calculate the expected values and row frequencies for this data.

b. Calculate chi-square and degrees of freedom and determine if the result is significant.

12.6. An educational consultant wants to know if math ability and reading ability are contingent on each other.

READING ABILITY		
	High	Low

MATH ABILITY		High	Low
	High	25	35
	Low	25	15

a. Calculate the expected values and row frequencies for this data.

b. Calculate chi-square and degrees of freedom and determine if the result is significant.

12.7. An eating disorders clinic wants to know if a certain video helps or harms in deprogramming clients' body image distortions. The clinic wants to know if people have internalized less or more after viewing or listening to the videotape. This is a follow-up of a previous study wherein the researcher believed that viewing causes more internalization than listening to the narrative of the video. The previous research gave mixed results, which the current research is attempting to parse out. Here is the raw data for 20 subjects:

	LISTEN	VIEW
	More	More
	More	More
	Less	More
	Less	More
INTERNALIZATION:	Less	More
	Less	More
	Less	Less
	More	More
	Less	More
	Less	Less

a. Construct a contigency table from this data.
b. Fill in all expected values and rf's and chi-square values for this table.
c. Calculate the expected values and row frequencies for this data.
d. Calculate chi-square and degrees of freedom and determine if the result is significant.

ANSWERS

12.1.

26	8	34
17	17	0.425
4.765	4.765	
14	32	46
23	23	0.575
3.522	3.522	
40	40	80
	Chi-sq. =	16.57

12.3.

	Control	Exper.	
Yes I will!	1	10	11
	5.261	5.739	0.478
	3.451	3.163	
No	10	2	12
	5.739	6.261	0.522
	3.163	2.9	
	11	12	23
		Chi-sq. =	12.68

12.5.
a. EV = 30; 30; 20; 20; rf = 0.60 (high); 0.40 (low)
b. Chi-square = 0.83 + 0.83 + 1.00 + 1.00 = 4.33; chi-square critical = 3.84; df = 1; this is significant.

12.7.

a.–b.

Type of Video Experience

Level of Internalization	Listening	Viewing	
More	3 (5.5) chi= 1.14	8 (5.5) chi= 1.14	11 rf =0.55
Less	7 (4.5) chi= 1.39	2 (4.5) chi= 1.39	9 rf=0.45

c. EV = 5.5; 5.5; 4.5; 4.5; rf = 0.55 (more internalized); 0.45 (less internalized)
d. Chi-square = 1.14 + 1.14 + 1.39 + 1.39 = 5.06; critical chi-square = 3.84, df = 1; it is significant.

Chapter 13

PERSPECTIVE: LOOKING BACK AT YOUR JOURNEY

You are near the end of your journey! You met some major challenges! Additional study will be in order before your exam, but you should be able to see your car in the trail parking lot. Before leaving the lot, however, we should talk a bit about the sights you've seen. We should briefly look back at the statistics and distinguish them from each other. Looking back at your trail can help you understand each statistic and help you determine which one to use when a statistical problem arises. Research on experts indicates that they know not only individual ideas, but similarities and differences between related ideas. You are in an excellent position to begin learning these relationships.

We will begin with our now-familiar helping experiment. Then we will consider how the study might be expanded for some of the more advanced statistics you have learned. An important goal of this section is to help you choose a statistic when a new research problem arises. The problems at the end of this chapter will help you integrate the material.

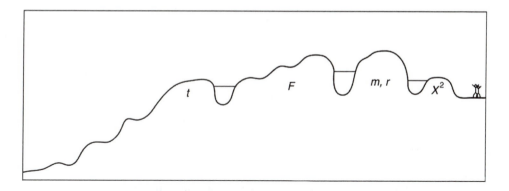

DESCRIPTIVE STATISTICS

Let's look again at our helping data. The amounts of time spent helping by each participant are shown once more in Table 13.1 and plotted in Figure 13.1 as a scatterplot. In a scatterplot, each data point is positioned according to its X and Y values (see Chapter 11). The Y value in our example is time helping and the X value is determined by the mood conditions (good mood or control).

Consider the data in each sample. How could you describe each sample to another person in a concise way? What are the two main types of descriptive statistics?

The main descriptive statistics provide information about central tendency and variability. The mean is used most often for central tendency (the median is good if there are outliers, however). Standard deviation is used most often for describing variability, and it corresponds to the average amount of deviation of individual scores from the mean.

TABLE 13.1.   Amount of Time in Minutes that Each of 12 Hypothetical Participants Helped Another Person

CONTROL GROUP	EXPERIMENTAL GROUP
1. 8	7. 10
2. 9	8. 16
3. 12	9. 12
4. 7	10. 14
5. 13	11. 11
6. 11	12. 15

Central tendency and variability are also important for inferences about populations. Most inferential statistics are based on a comparison between effects (measured by differences in central tendency, for example) and error (measured by standard deviation, for example). Let's review the statistics you've seen.

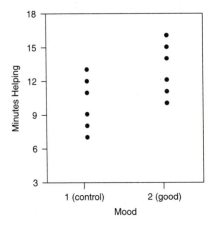

FIGURE 13.1.   A scatterplot of our familiar helping data. Each point represents one participant's data.

t-TEST: ARE THESE TWO SAMPLES THE SAME OR DIFFERENT?

The *t*-test is suited for experiments with two conditions, such as our familiar experiment. In such an experiment, the independent variable (IV) has two levels, produced by manipulating the IV. The test assesses whether the two levels (two samples in a between-participants design) are likely to be from the same population (meaning there is no IV effect) or from different populations (meaning there is an IV effect). The *t*-test compares the IV effect (the difference between the two means) to the standard error of the difference (obtained from the standard deviations of the two samples).

ANOVA: ONE-FACTOR AND MULTIFACTOR

ANOVA produces the *F* statistic. ANOVA can also be applied to experiments with two conditions, such as our helping experiment, but it can do more as well. One-factor ANOVA can be applied to experiments with one variable and more than two levels. For example, if we manipulated mood in four ways and also had a control condition, that would be a total of five levels of the IV mood. A one-factor ANOVA would provide one *F* value that would tell us if there was a difference anywhere among the five conditions. If there was a significant *F* value, we could use follow-up tests to pinpoint where the difference occurs.

A further crucial advantage of ANOVA is that it can be applied to experiments with more than one IV. This is the multifactor ANOVA. For example, let's say that we decided to do our helping experiment on Mondays and Saturdays, because we wanted to look at the relation between mood and helping as a function of day. We could have two mood conditions (good mood, control) and two days of the week, and randomly assign participants to conditions. Our ANOVA would produce three *F* values, one for each of the two main effects (mood and day) and one for the interaction. What would it mean if there was an interaction? Write your answer down and check your work.[1]

In all of the ANOVAs, the *F* values compare the IV effect (measured as variation due to the IV) to error variation. This corresponds to the comparison between IV effect and standard error in the *t*-test.

REGRESSION AND CORRELATION: RELATIONS BETWEEN VARIABLES

We could apply regression and correlation to our original helping data. However, these statistics are most suited for looking at relations between more continuous variables. In addition, regression and correlation are often applied to studies in which all variables are measured, with no actively manipulated IV. We could change our study by measuring mood rather than manipulating it, for example. Chapter 11 described a new helping study in which each participant rated mood on a scale from 0 to 8. The relation between rated mood and helping was analyzed. Correlation would tell us about the strength of the relation. Again, correlation compares an "effect" to error. In this case, the effect is the change in helping that corresponds directly to changes in the X variable mood. All other variation is error. Linear regression would tell us more about the relation between mood and helping, by providing a line with a slope and intercept that describes that relation. The slope is most important because it tells us how much change in *Y* (helping) to expect for each unit of change in *X* (mood).

The regression and correlation approach is designed for measured variables that may or may not have a causal relationship. Conclusions about causality can be made only with great caution and further data. The data may come from more detailed analyses or further research, including experiments with actively manipulated IVs.

RELATIONS BETWEEN STATISTICS

Interestingly, regression can be used to provide *t* values and all of the *F* values of an ANOVA. The mathematics of regression "contain" the *t*-test and *F*-test as special cases. And the *F*-test contains the *t*-test as a simple case. You can learn more about these math-

---

[1] An interaction means that the effects of one variable depend on the level of the other variable. For example, the effect of mood might vary depending on the day of the week. If there was no interaction, it would mean that the effect of mood was the same on Mondays and Saturdays in our example.

ematical relations in a more advanced course. For the initial learning of statistics, it helps to think about the statistics as two sets of tools designed for different research situations.

The crucial difference is whether there is an actively manipulated IV or not. The *t*-test and *F*-test are best suited for experiments in which independent variables are actively manipulated and we can make the inference that the IV caused differences in the dependent variable. Regression and correlation are best suited for research with two or more measured (dependent) variables. Regression and correlation are useful for examining many possible relations between the variables, but causal conclusions should be made with great caution and only after further detailed analysis, and perhaps after additional research that may include experimentally manipulated IVs.

CHI-SQUARE FOR CATEGORIES

Most of our statistics are suited for dependent variables that are parametric in nature. However, with nominal variables in which the possible values are categories (e.g., colors such as red, blue, brown), other, nonparametric statistics are appropriate. We examined one nonparametric statistic, Chi-Square. Chi-square compares frequencies of categories and can be used to determine if the frequencies differ from what would be expected by chance. For example, in the very first helping study we discussed, by Isen, Clark, and Schwarz (1976),[2] the possible responses were to "help" or "not help." Chi-square can be used to see if the frequencies in the good mood and control conditions differed from what would be expected by chance (i.e., an even distribution of frequencies), and you could do this analysis in Problem 12.3 of Chapter 12. Chi-square can also be used to see if the frequencies differ from what would be expected by any other clear hypothesis.

HAVE WE MISSED SOMETHING?

We've covered methods for analyzing ratio or interval data (e.g., *t*-test, ANOVA, regression), and a method for analyzing nominal data (chi-square). Are we missing a type of data?

In fact, we have not discussed *ordinal data,* in which the possible values differ from each other only in order (e.g., order of finishing a race). There simply wasn't enough room in this text for all types of data and ordinal data are fairly infrequent. If you do need to analyze ordinal data, the appropriate test is a nonparametric statistical test. Many nonparametric tests are generally similar to the *t*-test or *F*-test, but they use "weaker mathematical assumptions." You can learn more about them in a more advanced text or from your professor.

THE CREATIVE NATURE OF STATISTICS

One last comment is that statistics is a creative enterprise. For example, there are different ways of applying chi-square, there is an art to planning comparisons or choosing a post-hoc test, and there is an art to designing regression analyses. Indeed, an expert statistician is able to tailor statistics to provide sensitive and powerful tools for analyzing

---

[2] Isen, A. M., Clark, M., & Schwartz, M. F. (1976). Duration of the effect of good mood on helping: "Footprints on the sands of time." *Journal of Personality & Social Psychology, 34,* 385–393.

data and learning about behavior. This involves creative decisions and rewarding feelings when the job is well done.

Also, in coming years you can expect that the expert's understanding of statistics will grow and deepen as they continue to debate the meaning of statistics and consider new ideas. Statistics is a live, changing field. You can contribute to this process. Once again, happy trails!

EXERCISES

These problems are designed to help you review the chapter and integrate the material. For each research scenario described, pick the most appropriate statistic for analyzing the data. What information will the analysis provide? What property of the research scenario is critical for your choice of analysis?

1. Dr. Know is interested in the relation between pre-exam study time and test performance. The student-participants read the course material when it is assigned and then engage in study periods of varying length the night before the exam. Each student is randomly assigned to a study period of 30 minutes, 2 hours, or 4 hours in length. Which type of analysis is appropriate and why?

2. Dr. Knowmore thinks that the effectiveness of study periods depends on the topic that is studied. Therefore, Dr. Knowmore varies the length of the study period, as well as the topic. She uses the three lengths of study period. In addition, half of the student-participants study statistics and half study history.

3. Sally found the research on mood and helping interesting, but she is curious about other variables that may influence helping. She wanted to measure a large number of variables and measure their effects. She used a survey to measure numerous variables, including helping, which she measured by self-report. Which statistical approach is appropriate?

4. Dr. Tom want to compare performance for students using *Student-Friendly Statistics* with performance for students using another text. He randomly assigns the texts to two different groups of students and measures exam performance for each group.

5. Dr. Domestic loves a clean carpet. He wants to see which of his two favorite carpet shampoos are best. He finds 10 carpets and cleans half of each carpet with one of the shampoos. He then has a lab measure the amounts of remaining dirt carefully. His data are ten pairs of numbers, one pair for each carpet. In each pair there is an observation for Shampoo A and one for Shampoo B.

6. Dr. Admissions is interested in which factors predict success in college. He measures everything he can from student applications, and then obtains the final grade point averages.

7. Eric believes that there is an interaction between amount of exercise and the level of fun of the exercise. He conducts a study in which participants have either a large amount of exercise or a small amount, and the exercise is either fun (dancing) or not fun (running). He uses physiological measures to calculate amount of health gained.

8. John studies vacations after students have finished their statistics course. He wonders if longer vacations are more satisfactory. He asks a sample of students the length of their vacation and how well they liked it on a rating scale.

9. Dr. Ultimate does a big study on learning statistics. She has two instructors each teach two sections of statistics—one section with *Student-Friendly Statistics* and one with the old standard text. Students are randomly assigned to one of the four sections. Dr. Ultimate also measures the students' interest in the topic, their attendance, the number of hours they study, and how many exercises they worked out. Finally, she uses as her dependent measure performance an exam given one year after the statistics class is over, because she is interested in long term retention.

ANSWERS

1. In this case, a one factor, multi-level analysis of variance (ANOVA) is necesary because there are three levels of the one independent variable, study time. The ANOVA would tell the researcher if there was a difference anywhere in the study. This type of analysis is appropriate because of two critical properties: There is one independent variable but more than two levels of the variable. If there were only two levels of the variable, then a *t*-test could be used.

3. Sally should use a Correlation/Regression approach. She could measure a great many variables including gender, age, personality characteristics, course load and work load, and previous experiences helping. The strength of the relation between each of these variables and reported helping is measured by correlation. Regression would describe these relations in terms of slope— how much of a change in helping is there for each unit of change in a predictor variable? Is the relation positive or negative? Multiple regression could be used to compare the combined and separate contributions of these variables. It is possible that a combination of variables predicts helping best. For example, some combination of personality characteristics and variables reflecting amount of free time might be most effective. However, because Correlation and Regression involve measured variables rather than actively manipulated independent variables, causal interpretations should be made with great caution (and typically after additional research).

5. This one is a bit tricky. A *t*-test would be appropriate, but not just any *t*-test. This scenario requires a *t*-test for dependent samples, covered briefly at the end of Chapter 7. The critical property is that the pairs of observations are related to each other because they are from the same carpet. There is a dependency between scores. Further, this test requires that carpets be treated like participants. That is, each carpet has produced a pair of scores in the same way that each participant can produce a pair of scores when a within-participant design is used. The *t*-test assesses the differences between the pairs of scores in a sensitive way. The advantage of this method is that differences between carpets are factored out of the analysis. That is, if some carpets were really dirty to begin with, but others were quite clean, the variation between carpets would not enter into the analysis. Only the differences within the pairs of numbers for each carpet would be used. This method is not an advantage when there is no relation between the pairs of numbers; a regular *t*-test for independent samples is more sensitive.

7. Eric needs to use analysis of variance for multiple factors because there is more than one factor in this study and Eric is interested in interaction. There are two independent variables in his study. The analysis will reveal whether each variable has a main effect and whether or not there is an interaction. A possible interaction would be this: With short exercise, non-fun exercise might result in the greater gain, but with long exercise, fun exercise might be better. Thus, the effects of exercise length would depend on the level of fun of the exercise.

9. This is another tricky problem because elements of two approaches should be applied. Stop and use this clue if you can, then read on.

   This is like many complex problems where several statistical approaches can be used. The effects of instructor (which of the two was most effective?) and the effects of textbook (which was best?) can be examined with multi-factor analysis of variance. This analysis separates the effects of instructor and textbook (the two main effects). In addition, analysis of variance examines possible interactions between instructor and textbook. The effects of the remaining variables can be examined with correlation and regression. The strength of relations between the measured variables and exam performance would be measured, and the nature of the relations would be described. In a more advanced statistics course, researchers learn to combine analysis of variance approaches with correlation and regression. Thus, the effects of instructor and textbook, as well as their interaction, could be examined together with the other variables in a large multiple regression analysis, for example. This is one example of the creative nature of statistics and of how statistics can be used to examine complex real-world problems in detail.

COPING WITH MATH AND TEST ANXIETY

Many people with otherwise good skills in math experience high levels of anxiety in statistics classes that interfere with learning and test performance. What people don't realize is that they can learn skills to conquer the anxiety itself. The following tips can be very helpful:

1. Reduce your general anxiety level before you study or during study. Take a walk or short jog before starting, study while listening to relaxing music, or take short study breaks to walk, take a bath, or do a relaxing activity.
2. Develop positive self-talk: "I am capable of this."
3. Do as the Olympic athletes do: Use your imagination to picture yourself in your classroom during a test feeling some anxiety, but able to work through problems.
4. Break large tasks into smaller manageable parts. *Student-Friendly Statistics* is composed of short one- and two-page units.
5. Consider the student counseling services offered at most colleges and universities. You deserve to be able to work up to your potential and not be brought down by anxiety. Most counseling services offer straightforward help in overcoming your fears.

Avoid the following:

1. *Excessive caffeine and other stimulants.* Many people use these during "crunch" times of the semester, but chemically raising your overall arousal level will only make it harder to fight fear.
2. *Comparing yourself to others.* There will always be the person whose notes are perfectly organized or who breezes through class while barely studying. It's easy when you are feeling insecure in certain areas to notice others and compare yourself to them. Don't! Remember that you are capable of this and you are working at your own pace.
3. *Studying with the wrong crowd.* Study groups can be helpful, but emotions can be contagious. If others in your group are making you more anxious, consider studying alone.
4. *Perfectionistic expectations.* Avoid saying to yourself, things like "this semester I won't ever fall behind on the reading." Expect that you will continue to feel some of your fear, whatever it is, but that you are learning to manage it better and that it will affect your performance less and less.
5. *Negative self-labels.* You have a fear. Many people do. You are not stupid or weak or a failure. And you are learning to overcome the fear.

INDEX

Page numbers followed by a *f* indicate figure; those followed by a *t* indicate table.